Praise fo

"Fr. Wade Menezes, a priest ... 1-dred challenging daily meditations that are brief but incisive, on different spiritual themes, aimed at helping men become better men in their walk with the Lord. These reflections, in *Stand Firm, Be Strong*, are a great gift to the Church, reflecting a profound spirituality for men. They can be used for private daily meditation and also as a follow-up to a retreat that has sent them searching for greater depth in their spiritual lives. On day 85, Fr. Menezes reminds his readers that 'holiness is not an isolated task,' and 'we need to encourage one another toward holiness to become great saints.' With the help of these meditations, men can help other men to become great saints!"

— **Bishop Robert J. Baker**, Bishop Emeritus
of the Diocese of Birmingham in Alabama

"The Church needs good men — strong, virtuous, pious, holy men! In his book *Stand Firm, Be Strong*, Fr. Wade Menezes, CPM, offers men a six-month daily devotional grounded in the Word of God and the wisdom of the saints. Each daily entry takes only a few minutes to read, but the impact and good fruit it will bring about in the lives of individual men will be everlasting. I highly recommend this daily devotional!"

— **Fr. Donald Calloway, MIC**, Author, *30 Day Eucharistic Revival:
A Retreat with St. Peter Julian Eymard*

"The devil knows that godly men, especially fathers, are the first principle of life in the family, the culture, and the Church. That is why he and his minions have trained every weapon they possess on men, to a degree we have not seen in two thousand years of Christian history. In *Stand Firm, Be Strong*, Fr. Wade Menezes has given us a tremendous weapon for our spiritual warfare — a must-read for any and every man of God. It presents the challenge, beauty, and hope of the gospel, while presenting all the tools our Blessed Lord has given us as men *to be able to live the gospel*. This is a book you need to buy in bundles. Read it! Love it! Live it! And give your extra copies to all the men you are closest to in your life."

— **Tim Staples**, Senior Apologist, Catholic Answers

"Few people love you so much that they don't pull punches for the sake of your eternal life. Fr. Wade Menezes, CPM, is one such person. His book *Stand Firm, Be Strong* is sobering, loving, and exhortative as he helps men to become saints. Be forewarned: if you read this book and start applying it daily, get ready to be transformed. A real man is a person of virtue, and this book sets you on a journey of lifelong virtue — a two-hundred-day journey not just to virtuous manhood but to manly sainthood. The world needs more holy men who reflect Jesus Christ; this book will help you to become such a man."

— **Marcus B. Peter, Th.D.**, Ave Maria Radio

"The recovery of authentic manhood is an urgent need in the Church and in the world today. Rather than being invented anew, authentic manhood needs to be recovered and freshly lived out. Following and responding to both Scripture and the wisdom of the saints, men can learn and practice the truth of their dignity. This thoughtful and inspiring book by Fr. Wade Menezes, *Stand Firm, Be Strong*, is a trustworthy guide not only for healing our imaginations but, indeed, for helping men become who we are called to be."

— **Leonard J. DeLorenzo, Ph.D.**, McGrath Institute for Church Life, University of Notre Dame

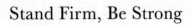
Stand Firm, Be Strong

STAND FIRM, BE STRONG

A Men's Catholic Daily Devotional of Scripture and Saints

by Fr. Wade L.J. Menezes, CPM
Fathers of Mercy

EWTN Publishing, Inc.
Irondale, Alabama

Imprimi Potest: Very Reverend David M. Wilton, CPM,
Superior General, Fathers of Mercy
Nihil Obstat: Colin B. Donovan, S.T.L., *Censor Librorum*
Imprimatur: Most Reverend William F. Medley, D.D.,
Bishop of Owensboro, Kentucky
June 24, 2024, Solemnity of the Nativity of St. John the Baptist

EWTN Publishing, Inc.
5817 Old Leeds Road, Irondale, AL 35210

Distributed by Sophia Institute Press, Box 5284, Manchester, NH 03108.

paperback ISBN 978-1-68278-411-2
ebook ISBN 978-1-68278-412-9

Library of Congress Control Number: 2024944275

2nd printing

For every man,
that each one will cooperate with Almighty God –
Father, Son, and Holy Spirit – to become the man
He wants him to become

Be watchful, stand firm in your faith,
be courageous, be strong.

— 1 Corinthians 16:13

Contents

Introduction

I was inspired to write and compile this book because I wanted to make a contribution to the rather small library of what are *specifically* Catholic *daily* devotionals written *specifically* for men. There are Catholic prayer books for men and Catholic spiritual-warfare manuals. There are also specific devotionals for married men and for dads. But I wanted to write a Catholic daily devotional for males of *all* vocations and states in life: the single man, the married man, the widowed man, the Catholic cleric of any degree (bishop, priest, or deacon) and the consecrated religious man (that is, professed brother or priest in vows). I also wanted to write a daily devotional that didn't feature *only* Scripture quotes or *only* saints' quotes but *both* Scripture *and* saints' quotes that have an important message and teaching quality that could then be coalesced into a daily meditation that focused strongly on some aspect of the spiritual life and Church teaching. I hope I have delivered in this regard and that men — of any faith — will benefit from this book.

It is worth mentioning, too, a few points about the physical properties of the book. I wanted this book to be the size of a standard "reader" (5.5 by 8.5 inches), and not the smaller, squarish size of many daily devotionals or daily readers. The reason for this is that I want the book to be easily grabbed and handled by its reader. I want each man who is faithfully and diligently reading this book as he begins his day to refer to his daily meditation several more times *on that same day*. I want the president and the CEO of a large company to be able to toss this book in his briefcase and an electrician and a trucker to throw it on the front seat of his truck. I want the high school teacher and the university professor to have it on his desk; I want the farmer to have it in the cab of his tractor and the welder to have it on a shelf at his workstation in his shop. I want the consecrated monk in the monastery to have this book inside his chapel choir stall to begin his day with. I want the active diocesan priest to have it readily placed in his church sacristy or on the vestry counter so he can read it each morning before he celebrates Mass and maybe even draw homiletic fodder from it.

Likewise, my hope is that the man reading this book will "mark it up" — that is, that each time he reads it, he will have, say, a red or blue pen or a yellow highlighter with him to write down notes in the margins or to highlight certain portions of the text itself. I want the male reader to make note of things that stand out for him while he's reading the book — maybe certain points regarding Church teaching that he didn't know before or realize the importance of; for example, a specific virtue that he decides now to improve upon in his life, or a specific vice that he becomes determined now to root out.

The book itself is a two-hundred-day *daily* devotional that is written to help "jump-start" a man's spiritual life in what is meant to be a committed six-month journey fed through carefully selected Scripture and saints' quotes with accompanying meditations. It should be noted, too, that while each day's meditation is autonomous and stands on its own subject matter, each day's meditative theme does cross over to align with other days' meditative themes. This is noted at the end of each day's meditation, wherein the reader will see, for example, "See days 67, 82, 83, and 143." While the crossover days listed at the end of each day's meditation do not constitute an exhaustive list, they do serve as guides to further develop the themes or points at hand. Examples of certain themes or points covered in the book include the importance of living a Trinitarian spirituality, the sacraments, the Most Holy Eucharist and the importance of Eucharistic

Adoration, virtue, vice, the reality of sin, sanctifying grace, filial fear versus servile fear, and the importance of fostering devotion to the Blessed Virgin Mary and St. Joseph. Thus, I ask the reader to pay attention to these crossover days' meditations, as I want this book to be not only a daily spiritual manual and meditative tool but also a catechetical guide, so that the man reading it may grow in his knowledge of the spiritual life and Church teaching. This same benefit applies to a *group of men* (for example, a weekly men's parish prayer group), whose members may choose to read the book simultaneously with assigned readings.

Also worth mentioning is the old saying "Behind every great man is a great woman." So it is, then, that I have taken the liberty within this men's Catholic daily devotional to quote from several great female saints of the Church. To name just a few, I've quoted: St. Teresa of Ávila, the Carmelite mystic and reformer; St. Margaret Mary Alacoque, the visionary of the Sacred Heart; St. Faustina Kowalska, the Divine Mercy seer; and St. Teresa Benedicta of the Cross (St. Edith Stein), the Carmelite philosopher and martyr who died at Auschwitz during World War II. There are a few other great and saintly ladies who are quoted as well. These females were stalwart in their faith and passionately in love with Jesus Christ and with His Word. They were also staunch defenders of Holy Mother Church — the Bride of Christ — and her teachings. These women were, in fact, true daughters of the Church and, in a certain sense, spiritual mothers. May their words of wisdom inspire and teach the male reader of this book how to be a true and faithful *son* of the Church.

This book also contains an appendix of selected prayers that I hope my readers will benefit from spiritually. These include some standard and traditional daily prayers such as the Acts of Faith, Hope, Charity, and Contrition. You will also find four popular and important litanies that, hopefully, men will become accustomed to pray weekly on each litany's traditionally assigned day: the Litany of the Holy Eucharist (Thursday), the Litany of the Sacred Heart of Jesus (Friday), the Litany of the Blessed Virgin Mary (Saturday), and the Litany of St. Joseph (Wednesday).

One final point, here, about the book's cover. I have selected Ary Scheffer's (1795–1858) *Temptation of Christ* (1854). An old adage goes, "Don't judge a book by its cover." In this case, however, I hope you will. This is because Scheffer's famous painting was chosen for several reasons.

First of all, the entire scene of the temptation of Christ in Scripture (see Matt. 4:1–11; Mark 1:12–13; Luke 4:1–13) shows forth the basic reality of the daily struggle of man regarding the lust of the flesh, the lust of the eyes, and the pride of life (see 1 John 2:16). In short, if the devil is bold enough to try to tempt the God-Man Himself, then he is likewise bold enough to try to tempt *anyone*. But Christ is our Model, and He shows us how to respond to temptation.

This brings me to my second point as to why I chose Scheffer's painting: it goes very well with the book's title. Indeed, in the artwork, Jesus Christ is shown "standing firm" and "being strong" against Satan and his wiles during His temptation in the desert. I like the fact, too, that Scheffer's Christ looks somewhat calm while rebuking the devil. In other words, Christ Himself is the one *totally in control* of the situation. This is a great reminder for each of us men in our daily lives whenever temptations come. That said, thirdly, the devil still appears somewhat subtle, cunning, and crafty, which is also very realistic (see Gen. 3:1). Simply put, there's a lot of theology in Scheffer's *Temptation of Christ*.

Lastly, while I wish Scheffer would have made Christ's halo a Trinitarian one, with a three-point design, thus showing that He is, indeed, the Second of the Three Divine Persons of the Blessed Trinity, he did not. Scheffer was inspired to paint religious art, but he was not a Catholic (see, for example, his well-known painting *Saints Augustine and Monica* [1854]). Although online images of Scheffer's *Temptation of Christ* are now considered in the public domain, the *original* is still a very famous painting, so to alter the plain halo into a Trinitarian one for the book's cover would have been, I believe, both imprudent and nonartistic.

I wish to close this introduction by providing a quote from St. Augustine that I believe conveys well what I hope this daily devotional will lead its male reader to embrace intellectually and to live joyfully, including what is meant by the words "pray constantly," as 1 Thessalonians 5:17 teaches:

> Our thoughts in this present life should turn on the praise of God, because it is in praising God that we shall rejoice for ever in the life to come; and no one can be ready for the next life unless he trains himself for it now....
>
> ... [S]ee that your praise comes from your whole being; in other words, see that you praise God not with your lips and voices alone, but with your minds, your lives and all your actions.
>
> ... [P]rovided we do not cease to live a good life, we shall always be praising God. You cease to praise God only when you swerve from justice and from what is pleasing to God.[1]

Indeed, may every man in every circumstance of his life — the good, the bad, the joyful, and the sorrowful — seek to praise Almighty God in all things, and may he always "stand firm and be strong" (see 1 Cor. 16:13).

Fr. Wade L. J. Menezes, CPM
Fathers of Mercy

---

[1] *Discourse on the Psalms*, Ps. 148, in *Liturgy of the Hours*, vol. II, 864–865.

Day 1

The Committed Man of God

Be watchful, stand firm in your faith, be courageous, be strong. (1 Cor. 16:13)

Jesus is with you even when you don't feel His presence. He is never so close to you as He is during your spiritual battles. He is always there, close to you, encouraging you to fight your battle courageously. He is there to ward off the enemy's blows so that you may not be hurt. (St. Pio of Pietrelcina [St. Padre Pio])[2]

Psalm 31:24 states, "Be strong, and let your heart take courage." Also, Joshua 1:9 teaches you to "be strong and of good courage; be not frightened, neither be dismayed; for the LORD your God is with you wherever you go." What a task you have as a man: as a provider, protector, and defender of yourself, your loved ones, your faith, your culture, and your society. Commit yourself to Jesus Christ, live your Baptism and Confirmation as never before, and strive for holiness and strength in your vocation and state in life whether you are single, married, or widowed, or a bishop, a diocesan priest, a religious order priest, a deacon, or a professed religious brother. Let nothing deflect you from these goals, and lead others to holiness by your example. Regular reception of the sacraments of Eucharist and Reconciliation — holy Confession — proves indispensable in this regard. Commit yourself to becoming a committed Catholic man of God. (See days 2, 3, 105, 145, 167, and 175.)

[2] Letter to Raffaelina Cerase, August 15, 1914, in Melchiorre and Alessandro da Ripabottoni da Pobladura, eds., *Letters Volume II: Correspondence with the Noblewoman Raffaelina Cerase (1914–1915)*, 2nd ed. (San Giovanni Rotondo: "Padre Pio da Pietrelcina" Editions, 1987), 168.

Day 2

Manhood

Be strong, and show yourself a man, and keep the charge of the Lord your God, walking in his ways and keeping his statutes, his commandments, his ordinances, and his testimonies … that you may prosper in all that you do and wherever you turn. (1 Kings 2:2–3)

Whoever has grown from infancy to manhood and attained to spiritual maturity possesses the mastery over his passions and the purity that makes it possible for him to receive the glory of the [Holy] Spirit. (St. Gregory of Nyssa)[3]

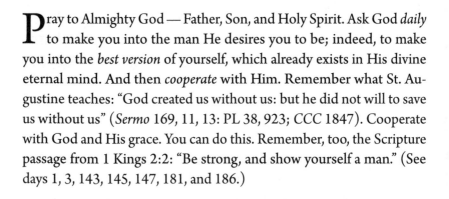

P ray to Almighty God — Father, Son, and Holy Spirit. Ask God *daily* to make you into the man He desires you to be; indeed, to make you into the *best version* of yourself, which already exists in His divine eternal mind. And then *cooperate* with Him. Remember what St. Augustine teaches: "God created us without us: but he did not will to save us without us" (*Sermo* 169, 11, 13: PL 38, 923; *CCC* 1847). Cooperate with God and His grace. You can do this. Remember, too, the Scripture passage from 1 Kings 2:2: "Be strong, and show yourself a man." (See days 1, 3, 143, 145, 147, 181, and 186.)

---

[3] Homily on the Songs of Songs, in *Liturgy of the Hours*, vol. II, 959.

Day 3

Strength and Fortitude

Finally, be strong in the Lord and in the strength of his might. (Eph. 6:10)

In tribulations, turn to God with confidence. You will obtain strength, light, and knowledge. In joys and successes, turn to God with fear and sincerity. You will escape all snares and be free of everything false. (St. John of the Cross)[4]

—————————

Are you a fortitudinous man? Your Baptism and Confirmation call you to be. What, exactly, is the virtue of fortitude? The *Catechism of the Catholic Church* teaches that *"fortitude* is the moral virtue that ensures firmness in difficulties and constancy in the pursuit of the good. It strengthens the resolve to resist temptations and to overcome obstacles in the moral life. The virtue of fortitude enables one to conquer fear, even fear of death, and to face trials and persecutions. It disposes one even to renounce and sacrifice his life in defense of a just cause" (*CCC* 1808). Pursuing the good, the true, and the beautiful will *not* always be easy when you choose to live a life of virtue, but cultivating the virtue of fortitude will surely help you to achieve those goals. Remember this: "The LORD is my strength and my song; he has become my salvation" (Ps. 118:14). (See days 1, 2, 90, 109, 130, 145, 149, and 180.)

---

[4] Fr. Frederick Schroeder, *Every Day Is a Gift* (Totowa, NJ: Catholic Book Publishing, 1984), 183.

Day 4

Having No Duplicity or Guile

Jesus saw Nathanael coming to him, and said of him, "Behold, an Israelite indeed, in whom is no guile!" Nathanael said to him, "How do you know me?" Jesus answered him, "Before Philip called you, when you were under the fig tree, I saw you." Nathanael answered him, "Rabbi, you are the Son of God! You are the King of Israel!" Jesus answered him, "Because I said to you, I saw you under the fig tree, do you believe? You shall see greater things than these." And he said to him, "Truly, truly, I say to you, you will see heaven opened, and the angels of God ascending and descending upon the Son of man." (John 1:47–51)

We must remember how near he [God] is and that no thought of ours, no conversation we hold is hidden from him. It is right, therefore, that we should not turn our backs and flee from God's will....

We must then put away all duplicity. (Pope St. Clement I)[5]

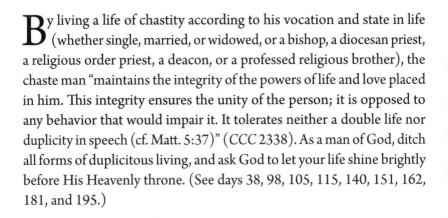

By living a life of chastity according to his vocation and state in life (whether single, married, or widowed, or a bishop, a diocesan priest, a religious order priest, a deacon, or a professed religious brother), the chaste man "maintains the integrity of the powers of life and love placed in him. This integrity ensures the unity of the person; it is opposed to any behavior that would impair it. It tolerates neither a double life nor duplicity in speech (cf. Matt. 5:37)" (CCC 2338). As a man of God, ditch all forms of duplicitous living, and ask God to let your life shine brightly before His Heavenly throne. (See days 38, 98, 105, 115, 140, 151, 162, 181, and 195.)

---

5 *Letter to the Corinthians*, chaps. 21, 23, in *Liturgy of the Hours*, vol. IV, 444–445.

Day 5

Shunning Sin

Let not sin therefore reign in your mortal bodies, to make you obey their passions. Do not yield your members to sin as instruments of wickedness, but yield yourselves to God as men who have been brought from death to life, and your members to God as instruments of righteousness. For sin will have no dominion over you, since you are not under law but under grace. (Rom. 6:12–14)

Avoid evil, cast danger aside....

I earnestly admonish you, therefore, my brothers, to look after your spiritual well-being with judicious concern. Death is certain; life is short and vanishes like smoke. (St. Francis of Paola)[6]

What a gift you, as a Catholic man, have in the Sacrament of Confession. To be able to return to God's sanctifying grace after a mortally sinful fall and to strengthen that grace after a venial fall are great gifts indeed. Don't miss out on the opportunity to receive the Sacrament of Confession faithfully and regularly. In such a challenging culture, monthly Confession is a great spiritual practice; for example, on the first Friday of the month, in honor of the Sacred Heart of Jesus, or on the first Saturday, in honor of the Immaculate Heart of Mary. Regular Confession, coupled with regular, worthy reception of the Eucharist, helps you to pursue a life of virtue, peace, and hope and to work toward eternal life. Always remember what Romans 6:22 reminds you: "Now that you have been set free from sin and have become slaves of God, the return you get is sanctification and its end, eternal life." (See days 17, 92, 94, 116, 127, 134, and 135.)

---

[6] *Epistola a. 1486*: A Galuzzi, *Origini dell'Ordine dei Minimi*, in *Liturgy of the Hours*, vol. II, 1757.

Day 6

Commitment

Commit your work to the LORD, and your plans will be established. (Prov. 16:3)

Love consists of a commitment which limits one's freedom — it is a giving of the self, and to give oneself means just that: to limit one's freedom on behalf of another. (Pope St. John Paul II)[7]

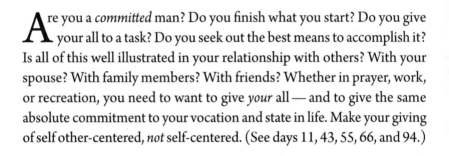

A re you a *committed* man? Do you finish what you start? Do you give your all to a task? Do you seek out the best means to accomplish it? Is all of this well illustrated in your relationship with others? With your spouse? With family members? With friends? Whether in prayer, work, or recreation, you need to want to give *your* all — and to give the same absolute commitment to your vocation and state in life. Make your giving of self other-centered, *not* self-centered. (See days 11, 43, 55, 66, and 94.)

---

[7] Karol Wojtyła, *Love and Responsibility*, trans. J. T. Willetts (San Francisco: Ignatius Press, 1993), 135.

The Person without Christ

If you love me, you will keep my commandments. (John 14:15)

When a house has no master living in it, it becomes dark, vile and contemptible, choked with filth and disgusting refuse. So too is a soul which has lost its master, who once rejoiced there with his angels. This soul is darkened with sin, its desires are degraded, and it knows nothing but shame....

Woe to the soul if the Lord does not walk within it to banish with his voice the spiritual beasts of sin. Woe to the house where no master dwells, to the field where no farmer works, to the pilotless ship, storm-tossed and sinking. Woe to the soul without Christ as its true pilot; drifting in the darkness, buffeted by the waves of passion, storm-tossed at the mercy of evil spirits, its end is destruction. Woe to the soul that does not have Christ to cultivate it with care to produce the good fruit of the Holy Spirit. Left to itself, it is choked with thorns and thistles; instead of fruit it produces only what is fit for burning. Woe to the soul that does not have Christ dwelling in it; deserted and foul with the filth of the [disordered] passions, it becomes a haven for all the vices. (St. Macarius)[8]

You need Jesus Christ in your life. He is your Savior. But many things — such as the practice of vice — can make you forget about Jesus Christ. When you reach that point, life becomes a slippery slope. The Second Vatican Council teaches that "often men, deceived by the Evil One, have become vain in their reasonings and have exchanged the truth of God for a lie, serving the creature rather than the Creator (cf.

---

[8] Homily 28, in *Liturgy of the Hours*, vol. IV, 596.

Rom. 1:21, 25). Or some there are who, living and dying in this world without God, are exposed to final despair" (*Lumen Gentium* 11). Don't fall into this trap of the Evil One. Nothing pleases the devil more than to see you fail in your pursuit of virtue and virtuous living. Return to Jesus Christ, your Savior. (See days 28, 58, 103, 106, and 196.)

Day 8

Fraternity and Brotherhood

But I say to you that every one who is angry with his brother shall be liable to judgment; whoever insults his brother shall be liable to the council, and whoever says, "You fool!" shall be liable to the hell of fire. So if you are offering your gift at the altar, and there remember that your brother has something against you, leave your gift there before the altar and go; first be reconciled to your brother, and then come and offer your gift. (Matt. 5:22–24)

God does not receive the sacrifice of one who lives in conflict; and he orders us to turn back from the altar and first be reconciled with our brother, that God too may be appeased by the prayers of one who is at peace. The greatest offering we can make to God is our peace, harmony among fellow Christians, a people united with the unity of the Father, the Son and the Holy Spirit. (St. Cyprian)[9]

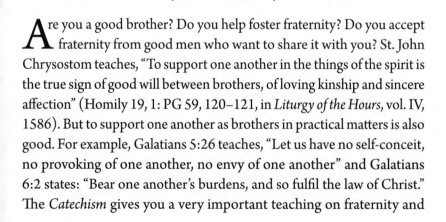

Are you a good brother? Do you help foster fraternity? Do you accept fraternity from good men who want to share it with you? St. John Chrysostom teaches, "To support one another in the things of the spirit is the true sign of good will between brothers, of loving kinship and sincere affection" (Homily 19, 1: PG 59, 120–121, in *Liturgy of the Hours*, vol. IV, 1586). But to support one another as brothers in practical matters is also good. For example, Galatians 5:26 teaches, "Let us have no self-conceit, no provoking of one another, no envy of one another" and Galatians 6:2 states: "Bear one another's burdens, and so fulfil the law of Christ." The *Catechism* gives you a very important teaching on fraternity and

---

[9] *Treatise on the Lord's Prayer*, in *Liturgy of the Hours*, vol. III, 377.

brotherhood: "All men are called to the same end: God himself. There is a certain resemblance between the unity of the divine persons and the fraternity that men are to establish among themselves in truth and love. Love of neighbor is inseparable from love for God" (1878). Think about it: your fraternity with others is to resemble the unity found between the Three Divine Persons: Father, Son, and Holy Spirit. That's quite a calling. Live it. (See days 14, 57, 122, 130, and 191.)

Day 9

The Demands of Virtue and Aiming toward Salvation

So put away all malice and all guile and insincerity and envy and all slander. Like newborn babes, long for the pure spiritual milk, that by it you may grow up to salvation; for you have tasted the kindness of the Lord. (1 Pet. 2:1–3)

It is deeply rewarding for men striving for salvation to follow in Christ's footsteps and obey God's commandments. (Pope St. John XXIII)[10]

Following God's commandments and striving for virtue should not make you sad, mad, depressed, or unpleasant to be around. Rather, others should see in you the virtues you're living and striving to attain and say to themselves, "I want that." "I want what he's got." Take Matthew 5:14–16 as your guide: "You are the light of the world. A city set on a hill cannot be hid. Nor do men light a lamp and put it under a bushel, but on a stand, and it gives light to all in the house. Let your light so shine before men, that they may see your good works and give glory to your Father who is in heaven."

As a dedicated Catholic Christian man, you should face the fact that some things are simply *not* virtuous, such as unjust anger, jealousy, envy, and failure to fulfill your Sunday Mass obligation. But what about those everyday things that you might do that are also not virtuous? For example, using a handicap parking space — when you're not handicapped yourself — for quicker access to the store; or parking so crooked in a regular

---

[10] Canonization homily for St. Martin de Porres, May 6, 1962, in *Liturgy of the Hours*, vol. IV, 1542.

parking space that you prevent someone else from using the empty parking spot right next to yours; or not using your turn signal when switching lanes in your vehicle. Such carelessness is not virtuous. Pay attention to your daily life and its activities, even in the little things. Strive for virtue and become a virtuous man — all the while working out your salvation (see Phil. 2:12). (See days 10, 43, 44, 52, 53, 69, 90, 109, and 130.)

Day 10

The Virtue of Diligence

A slack hand causes poverty, but the hand of the diligent makes rich. (Prov. 10:4)

We should then strive with the greatest zeal to be found among the number of those who await him [God], so that we may share in the promised gifts. How will this be, beloved? If our mind is fixed on God through faith, if we are diligent in seeking what is pleasing and acceptable to him, if we fulfill what is according to his blameless will and follow the way of truth, casting away from ourselves all that is unholy. (Pope St. Clement I)[11]

❧————————❧

Here's a good definition for the virtue of diligence: "Do what you're supposed to do, when you're supposed to do it, in the way it's supposed to be done." Anything less is slothfulness; anything more is workaholism. Balance leads you to virtue. Virtue leads you to joy. (See days 9, 43, 44, 52, 53, 64, 69, 90, 109, and 130.)

[11] *Letter to the Corinthians*, chap. 30, in *Liturgy of the Hours*, vol. IV, 453.

Day 11

The True Gospel

I am astonished that you are so quickly deserting him who called you in the grace of Christ and turning to a different gospel — not that there is another gospel, but there are some who trouble you and want to pervert the gospel of Christ. But even if we, or an angel from heaven, should preach to you a gospel contrary to that which we preached to you, let him be accursed. As we have said before, so now I say again, If any one is preaching to you a gospel contrary to that which you received, let him be accursed. Am I now seeking the favor of men, or of God? Or am I trying to please men? If I were still pleasing men, I should not be a servant of Christ. For I would have you know, brethren, that the gospel which was preached by me is not man's gospel. For I did not receive it from man, nor was I taught it, but it came through a revelation of Jesus Christ. (Gal. 1:6–12)

Dear brothers, the commands of the Gospel are nothing else than God's lessons, the foundations on which to build up hope, the supports for strengthening faith, the food that nourishes the heart. They are the rudder for keeping us on the right course, the protection that keeps our salvation secure. As they instruct the receptive minds of believers on earth, they lead safely to the kingdom of heaven. (St. Cyprian)[12]

Get to know the words of Jesus recorded in the Gospels of Matthew, Mark, Luke, and John. Start with Mark. It's the shortest (with only sixteen chapters); it's captivating yet fast-paced and tells of miracle after miracle performed by Jesus. Make a commitment now to read just one chapter a day. You'll finish in two weeks. (See days 20, 85, 188, and 200.)

---

[12] *Treatise on the Lord's Prayer*, in *Liturgy of the Hours*, vol. II, 104–105.

Day 12

The Truth

Have I then become your enemy by telling you the truth? (Gal. 4:16)

[T]he truth can be assaulted but never defeated or falsified. (St. Boniface)[13]

❖————————❖

During the homily for the canonization of the great Carmelite mystic, philosopher, and Auschwitz martyr St. Teresa Benedicta of the Cross (St. Edith Stein), Pope John Paul II summed up the nun's lived message of life in this way: "*Do not accept anything as the truth if it lacks love. And do not accept anything as love which lacks truth!* One without the other becomes a destructive lie" (October 11, 1998). Clearly, truth is tied to love, and love to truth. This is because God is truth and God is love (see John 14:6; 1 John 4:8, 16). And since you are made in God's image and according to His likeness (Gen. 1:26), you, too, are called to truth and love.

In John 17:17–19, Jesus prays to His Heavenly Father, "Sanctify them in the truth; thy word is truth. As thou didst send me into the world, so I have sent them into the world. And for their sake I consecrate myself, that they also may be consecrated in truth." Christ Himself founded the Church, His Bride. You can know the truth by way of the Church's teachings through Sacred Scripture and Tradition as upheld by the Magisterium (the teaching office of the Church), which is itself grounded in the apostolic college and guided by the Holy Spirit (see Matt. 16:18–19; John 16:13–15). As the apostle John teaches, "We are from God. Anyone who knows God listens to us; anyone who is not from God does not listen to us. By this we know the spirit of truth and the spirit of error" (1

---

[13] *Ep.* 78: MGH, *Epistolae*, 3, in *Liturgy of the Hours*, vol. III, 1456.

John 4:6). Your immersing yourself in God's truth and love through the teachings of Jesus Christ and His Bride, the Church, calls you to salvation through that same Church, which Christ Himself founded and which is "the pillar and bulwark of the truth" (1 Tim. 3:15). 1 Timothy 2:4–6 teaches, "[God our Savior] desires all men to be saved and to come to the knowledge of the truth. For there is one God, and there is one mediator between God and men, the man Christ Jesus, who gave himself as a ransom for all, the testimony to which was borne at the proper time." Live authentic truth. Live authentic love. (See days 33, 37, 107, 118, 122, 161, 163, 169, 174, and 182.)

Day 13

Trust in the Lord

Trust in the LORD, and do good; so you will dwell in the land, and enjoy security. Take delight in the LORD, and he will give you the desires of your heart. Commit your way to the LORD; trust in him, and he will act. He will bring forth your vindication as the light, and your right as the noonday. (Ps. 37:3–6)

Jesus, I trust in You. (St. Faustina Kowalska)[14]

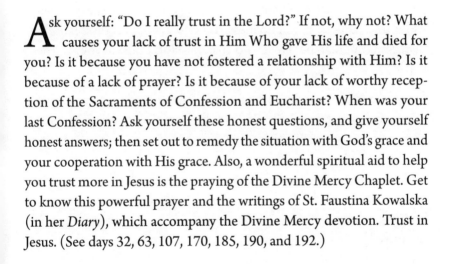

Ask yourself: "Do I really trust in the Lord?" If not, why not? What causes your lack of trust in Him Who gave His life and died for you? Is it because you have not fostered a relationship with Him? Is it because of a lack of prayer? Is it because of your lack of worthy reception of the Sacraments of Confession and Eucharist? When was your last Confession? Ask yourself these honest questions, and give yourself honest answers; then set out to remedy the situation with God's grace and your cooperation with His grace. Also, a wonderful spiritual aid to help you trust more in Jesus is the praying of the Divine Mercy Chaplet. Get to know this powerful prayer and the writings of St. Faustina Kowalska (in her *Diary*), which accompany the Divine Mercy devotion. Trust in Jesus. (See days 32, 63, 107, 170, 185, 190, and 192.)

[14] *Diary of St. Maria Faustina Kowalska: Divine Mercy in My Soul* [hereafter *Diary*] (Stockbridge, MA: Marian Press, 1987), no. 24.

Virtuous Living and Growing in Holiness

Finally, brethren, we beseech and exhort you in the Lord Jesus, that as you learned from us how you ought to live and to please God, just as you are doing, you do so more and more. For you know what instructions we gave you through the Lord Jesus. For this is the will of God, your sanctification: that you abstain from immorality; that each one of you know how to control his own body in holiness and honor, not in the passion of lust like heathen who do not know God; that no man transgress, and wrong his brother in this matter, because the Lord is an avenger in all these things, as we solemnly forewarned you. For God has not called us for uncleanness, but in holiness. Therefore whoever disregards this, disregards not man but God, who gives his Holy Spirit to you. (1 Thess. 4:1–8)

I see my mistake in feeling ashamed of repentance for my sins....

... [W]e must first die to sin, and then create in our lives on earth a harmony through virtuous deeds, if the grace of our devotion is to reach up to the Lord....

We must fashion our lives and shape our actions in the light of the things that are above. We must not allow [inordinate] pleasure to awaken bodily passions, which weigh our soul down instead of freeing it. (St. Ambrose)[15]

❖————————❖

Almighty God wants the best for you. Never forget this important truth. He is a God Who heals you from having taken bad roads in your past and offers you good roads for your present and future. This is

---

[15] *Explanations of the Psalms*, Ps. 1, in *Liturgy of the Hours*, vol. III, 348.

because God is more interested in your future than in your past. He's more interested in the kind of person you can *yet become* than in the person you *used to be*. While indeed taking your sins seriously — whether mortal or venial — God never takes those sins as the last word. Why? Because He has made you in His image and after His likeness (see Gen. 1:26), He calls you to a life of His sanctifying grace, and He is your God and is bigger than any sin you have ever committed — even the most hideous or wicked mortal sin. In short, God wants you to move forward in a life of His grace — especially His sanctifying grace, the ordinary channels of which are the seven sacraments of His Church. God's sanctifying grace is what makes you an actual partaker in His own divine life (see 2 Pet. 1:3–5). This means that a profound transformation of you — in your human nature — is possible through God's divine grace. So let God move you forward, and cooperate with Him in moving you forward. In short, make 1 Thessalonians 5:23 your goal: "May the God of peace himself sanctify you wholly; and may your spirit and soul and body be kept sound and blameless at the coming of our Lord Jesus Christ." (See days 8, 26, 43, 54, 57, 81, 93, 122, 130, 144, 152, 168, 191, 193, and 197.)

When Sadness Seems to Have the Upper Hand

> This day is holy to the LORD your God; do not mourn or weep. (Neh. 8:9)
>
> Throughout the whole period between the resurrection and ascension, God's providence was at work to instill this one lesson into the hearts of the disciples, to set this one truth before their eyes, that our Lord Jesus Christ, who was truly born, truly suffered and truly died, should be recognized as truly risen from the dead. The blessed apostles together with all the others had been intimidated by the catastrophe of the cross, and their faith in the resurrection had been uncertain; but now they were so strengthened by the evident truth that when their Lord ascended into heaven, far from feeling any sadness, they were filled with great joy. (Pope St. Leo the Great)[16]

The Christian man is not to be sad but must know how to carry his cross — whatever it might be — and carry it heroically. Remember: whenever the Catholic Church formally canonizes a saint, it is first and foremost because that saint — while still living on earth — practiced virtue to a heroic degree. He may not have done so *always*, but at some point, he began to embrace heroic virtue — even during times of suffering, trial, and tribulation in his life. As 2 Corinthians 4:8–10 teaches: "We are afflicted in every way, but not crushed; perplexed, but not driven to despair; persecuted, but not forsaken; struck down, but not destroyed; always carrying in the body the death of Jesus, so that the life of Jesus may also be manifested in our bodies." Christ's Paschal Mystery — His Passion, Death, Resurrection and Ascension into Heaven — reminds you of these truths. (See days 18, 40, 61, and 200.)

---

[16] *Sermo 1 de Ascensione*, in *Liturgy of the Hours*, vol. II, 899.

Humility amid Trials and Successes

Count it all joy, my brethren, when you meet various trials, for you know that the testing of your faith produces steadfastness. And let steadfastness have its full effect, that you may be perfect and complete, lacking in nothing. (James 1:2–4)

Our pilgrimage on earth cannot be exempt from trial. We progress by means of trial. No one knows himself except through trial, or receives a crown except after victory, or strives except against an enemy or temptations. (St. Augustine)[17]

G od's ways are not your ways. For example, when you encounter something that you deem a trial or tribulation — a difficult job or financial situation, an illness, a conflict with a family member or a friend — humble yourself and ask: "Is God permitting this particular situation in my life to help me understand that, through it, I am sharing in His Cross?" What is the lesson here? Remember that the Cross of Jesus led to Resurrection and new life. So, if you find yourself working amid difficult coworkers, is God teaching you how to get along better with others? If a difficult financial situation, is He possibly calling you to live more simply, to save more, and to have a greater solidarity with the poor? If an illness, is He calling you to unite yourself with others who are sick? If a conflict with a family member or a friend, is He leading you to reconcile and ask for forgiveness? What about situations involving your success and good fortune? How do you handle these? Are you humbled, or do you respond with puffed-up pride? Amid all these examples, one

---

[17] *Commentary on the Psalms*, Ps. 60, in *Liturgy of the Hours*, vol. II, 87.

thing is certain: the virtue of humility is needed to see things *as they really are*, to assess the reality of the situation at hand and not to reach beyond yourself. Again, God's ways are not your ways. Whatever the situation, humble yourself before Almighty God and ask Him for *clarity* regarding the situation, to see it as He sees it. Fr. John Hardon, SJ, gives us a great lesson on the virtue of humility as it applies to everyday living experiences (both the bad and the good!) when he teaches:

> [Humility is the] moral virtue that keeps a person from reaching beyond himself. It is the virtue that restrains the unruly desire for personal greatness and leads people to an orderly love of themselves based on a true appreciation of their position with respect to God and their neighbors. Religious humility recognizes one's total dependence on God; moral humility recognizes one's creaturely equality with others. Yet humility is not only opposed to pride; it is also opposed to immoderate self-abjection, which would fail to recognize God's gifts and use them according to his will.[18]

Remember what 1 Peter 5:5–7 states: "Clothe yourselves, all of you, with humility toward one another, for 'God opposes the proud, but gives grace to the humble' [Prov. 3:34]. Humble yourselves therefore under the mighty hand of God, that in due time he may exalt you. Cast all your anxieties on him, for he cares about you." So in times of trial and tribulation, success and good fortune, practice the virtue of humility. (See days 50, 60, 81, 87, 88, 102, 106, 120, 128,129, and 133.)

---

[18] Fr. John A. Hardon, SJ, *Modern Catholic Dictionary*, s.v. "Humility" (Bardstown, KY: Eternal Life, 1999), 260.

Day 17

Accountability

My brethren, if any one among you wanders from the truth and some one brings him back, let him know that whoever brings back a sinner from the error of his way will save his soul from death and will cover a multitude of sins. (James 5:19–20)

The doors are open for all who sincerely and wholeheartedly return to God; indeed, the Father is most willing to welcome back a truly repentant son or daughter.... Scripture says that for the Father and his angels in heaven the festal joy and gladness at the return of one repentant sinner is great beyond compare.

And so, if you are a thief and desire to be forgiven, steal no more. If you are a robber, return your gains with interest. If you have been a false witness, practice speaking the truth. If you are a perjurer, stop taking oaths. You must also curb all the other evil passions: anger, lust, grief, and fear. No doubt you will be unable all at once to root out passions habitually given way to, but this can be achieved by God's power, human prayers, the help of your brothers and sisters, sincere repentance, and constant practice. (St. Clement of Alexandria)[19]

A real man seeks someone to be accountable to for his negative and adverse — sometimes sinful — actions. He seeks out from trusted brothers, relatives, friends, and coworkers the help and counsel needed to avoid such behavior. He also understands the importance of confessing his sins regularly to a priest in the Sacrament of Penance. (See days 1, 5, 13, 24, 33, 34, 39, 49, 66, 87, 93, 94, 109, 116, 127, 155, 170, 175, 185, and 188.)

[19] *Homily on the Salvation of the Rich,* in *Journey with the Fathers: Commentaries on the Sunday Gospels, Year A,* ed. Edith Barnecut, OSB (New York: New City Press, 1992), 128–129.

Confidence

Therefore do not throw away your confidence, which has a great reward. For you have need of endurance, so that you may do the will of God and receive what is promised. (Heb. 10:35–36)

[T]hinking humble thoughts, exercising self-control, keeping ourselves far from all backbiting and slander, being righteous in deed, and not in word only....

Beloved, how blessed, how wonderful, are God's gifts! Life with immortality, glory with righteousness, truth with confidence, self-control with holiness: all these are the gifts that fall within our understanding. What then are those gifts that are in store for those who wait for him? Only the most holy Creator and Father of the ages knows their greatness and splendor. (Pope St. Clement I)[20]

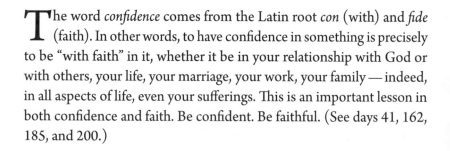

The word *confidence* comes from the Latin root *con* (with) and *fide* (faith). In other words, to have confidence in something is precisely to be "with faith" in it, whether it be in your relationship with God or with others, your life, your marriage, your work, your family — indeed, in all aspects of life, even your sufferings. This is an important lesson in both confidence and faith. Be confident. Be faithful. (See days 41, 162, 185, and 200.)

---

[20] *Letter to the Corinthians*, chaps. 30, 35, in *Liturgy of the Hours*, vol. IV, 452–453.

Day 19

The Athlete of God

Do you not know that in a race all the runners compete, but only one receives the prize? So run that you may obtain it. Every athlete exercises self-control in all things. They do it to receive a perishable wreath, but we an imperishable. Well, I do not run aimlessly, I do not box as one beating the air; but I pommel my body and subdue it, lest after preaching to others I myself should be disqualified. (1 Cor. 9:24–27)

[L]et unity, the greatest of all goods, be your preoccupation. Carry the burdens of all men as the Lord carries yours; have patience with all in charity.... Give yourself to prayer continually, ask for wisdom greater than you now have, keep alert with an unflagging spirit. Speak to each man individually, following God's example; bear the infirmities of all, like a perfect athlete of God. The greater the toil, the richer the reward.

... Exercise self-discipline, for you are God's athlete; the prize is immortality and eternal life, as you know full well....

Do not be overwhelmed by those who seem trustworthy and yet teach heresy. Remain firm, like the anvil under the hammer. The good athlete must take punishment in order to win.... Read the signs of the times....

[S]tand firm. (St. Ignatius of Antioch)[21]

As a committed athlete of God, you should watch over every aspect of your life, realizing that your body and soul are intimately and intricately united. In fact, the Church teaches that "the unity of soul and body is so profound that one has to consider the soul to be the 'form' of the body: i.e., it is because of its spiritual soul that the body made of

---

[21] *Letter to Polycarp*, chaps. 1, 3, in *Liturgy of the Hours*, vol. III, 564–565.

matter becomes a living, human body; spirit and matter, in man, are not two natures united, but rather their union forms a single nature [human nature]" (*CCC* 365, quoting the Council of Vienne [1312]: DS 902). In other words, as a human person, you don't have a body; you *are* a body. And as a human person, you don't have a soul; you *are* a soul. Again, both body and soul are intimately and intricately linked. So, from the exercises you do, to the spiritual and temporal practices in which you participate, to the diet on which you nourish yourself, to the virtues and true goods you pursue, as an athlete of God you are committed to run the race to one day attain Heaven — eternal beatitude, the Beatific Vision. Run like an athlete. (See days 33, 118, 138, and 200.)

Day 20

Gospel Lessons from God

For I am not ashamed of the gospel: it is the power of God for salvation to every one who has faith, to the Jew first and also to the Greek. For in it the righteousness of God is revealed through faith for faith; as it is written, "He who through faith is righteous shall live." (Rom. 1:16–17)

The more the Gospel is read, the more faith becomes alive. The Gospel is the book which serves all and for all. (Pope St. Pius X)[22]

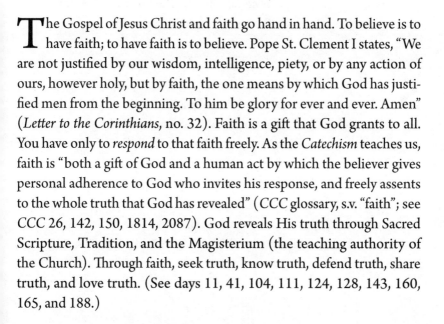

The Gospel of Jesus Christ and faith go hand in hand. To believe is to have faith; to have faith is to believe. Pope St. Clement I states, "We are not justified by our wisdom, intelligence, piety, or by any action of ours, however holy, but by faith, the one means by which God has justified men from the beginning. To him be glory for ever and ever. Amen" (*Letter to the Corinthians*, no. 32). Faith is a gift that God grants to all. You have only to *respond* to that faith freely. As the *Catechism* teaches us, faith is "both a gift of God and a human act by which the believer gives personal adherence to God who invites his response, and freely assents to the whole truth that God has revealed" (*CCC* glossary, s.v. "faith"; see *CCC* 26, 142, 150, 1814, 2087). God reveals His truth through Sacred Scripture, Tradition, and the Magisterium (the teaching authority of the Church). Through faith, seek truth, know truth, defend truth, share truth, and love truth. (See days 11, 41, 104, 111, 124, 128, 143, 160, 165, and 188.)

---

[22] Schroeder, *Every Day Is a Gift*, 37.

Day 21

The Body Is Holy

I appeal to you therefore, brethren, by the mercies of God, to present your bodies as a living sacrifice, holy and acceptable to God, which is your spiritual worship. Do not be conformed to this world but be transformed by the renewal of your mind, that you may prove what is the will of God, what is good and acceptable and perfect. (Rom. 12:1–2)

For what is more king-like than to find yourself ruler over your body after having surrendered your soul to God? And what is more priestly than to promise the Lord a pure conscience and to offer him in love unblemished victims on the altar of one's heart? (Pope St. Leo the Great)[23]

Sacred Scripture tells you that your body is a temple of the Holy Spirit: "Do you not know that your body is a temple of the Holy Spirit within you, which you have from God? You are not your own; you were bought with a price. So glorify God in your body" (1 Cor. 6:19–20). Your body *is* holy. It *is* a temple of God. For example, whenever you receive the Eucharist worthily in Holy Communion, your body becomes a living tabernacle housing the Eucharistic Lord for as long as the Sacred Species remain in you. What an honor Almighty God bestows upon you. Glorify God in your body. (See days 65, 92, 97, 99, 103, 114, 132, 144, 145, 155, and 199.)

[23] *Sermo* 4, 1–2: PL 54, 148–149, in *Liturgy of the Hours,* vol. IV, 1549–1550.

Work Out Your Salvation

Therefore, my beloved, as you have always obeyed, so now, not only as in my presence but much more in my absence, work out your own salvation with fear and trembling; for God is at work in you, both to will and to work for his good pleasure. Do all things without grumbling or questioning, that you may be blameless and innocent, children of God without blemish in the midst of a crooked and perverse generation, among whom you shine as lights in the world. (Phil. 2:12–15)

Do all your actions in accord with the right light of your reason. In all things, seek your salvation, the edification of others, and the praise and glory of God. (St. Bonaventure)[24]

When St. Paul tells you to work out your salvation with "fear," he's referring to a *filial* fear (from the Latin *filius*, meaning "son"). Here, St. Paul is referring to the fear of a child who doesn't want to disappoint the parent precisely because he knows the parent *loves* him. This is the basis for *perfect contrition*, wherein you are sorry for your sins most of all because they have offended God, Whom you should love above all things. It is not a *servile* fear, which is a fear that is afraid of forthcoming punishment. This latter is slavish, but it can still form the basis for *imperfect contrition*. Imperfect contrition is when you are sorry for your sins most of all because of the punishment they threaten you with: temporal punishment for venial sin and eternal punishment for mortal sin. Once mortal sin has been confessed in the Sacrament of Reconciliation, however, it then merits temporal punishment. Filial fear is about reciprocal

---

[24] Schroeder, *Every Day Is a Gift*, 104.

love — that is, a love freely given, freely received, and freely given back. It's a reciprocal love that is so strong it makes you "tremble." This is why St. Peter Chrysologus teaches, "God's desire [is] to be loved rather than feared, to be a father rather than a Lord. God appeals to us in his mercy to avoid having to punish us in his severity" (*Sermo* 108, in *Liturgy of the Hours*, vol. II, 770). You are to have a filial fear toward God precisely because you know that God loves you and wants the best for you, and so you freely return that love to God. All of this is conveyed well by Romans 8:15–17, which states, "For you did not receive the spirit of slavery to fall back into fear, but you have received the spirit of sonship. When we cry, 'Abba! Father!' it is the Spirit himself bearing witness with our spirit that we are children of God, and if children, then heirs, heirs of God and fellow heirs with Christ, provided we suffer with him in order that we may also be glorified with him." And Deuteronomy 10:12, too, assures you, "And now … what does the LORD your God require of you, but to fear the LORD your God, to walk in all his ways, to love him, to serve the LORD your God with all your heart and with all your soul." (See days 20, 73, 141, and 147.)

The Blessed Man

Blessed is the man who walks not in the counsel of the wicked, nor stands in the way of sinners, nor sits in the seat of scoffers; but his delight is in the law of the LORD, and on his law he meditates day and night. He is like a tree planted by streams of water, that yields its fruit in its season, and its leaf does not wither. In all that he does, he prospers. (Ps. 1:1–3)

And so I say: "Woe to the man who trusts in men rather than in Christ." Whether you like it or not, you will grow apart from men, but Christ is faithful and always with you, for Christ provides all things. Let us always give thanks to him. Amen. (St. John of God)[25]

Invite and allow Jesus Christ into your life as never before. Do this with purposeful, willed, and deliberate intention. Begin to build every aspect of your life on the foundation of Jesus Christ, your Savior; that is, your family life, your friendships, your work, your faith, and your recreation and leisure. Then, navigate these areas *through* Him and *with* Him and *in* Him. Ignite the God-given power of your baptismal priesthood. (See days 24, 67, 72, 105, 150, and 200.)

---

[25] Letter, in *Liturgy of the Hours*, vol. II, 1705.

Day 24

Striving for a Blameless Life

Blessed are those whose way is blameless, who walk in the law of the LORD! Blessed are those who keep his testimonies, who seek him with their whole heart, who also do no wrong, but walk in his ways! (Ps. 119:1–3)

Whoever is in Christ is a new creation; the old has passed away [2 Cor. 5:17]. Now by the "new creation" Paul means the indwelling of the Holy Spirit in a heart that is pure and blameless, free of all malice, wickedness or shamefulness. For when a soul has come to hate sin and has delivered itself as far as it can to the power of virtue, it undergoes a transformation by receiving the grace of the Spirit. Then, it is healed, restored and made wholly new. Indeed, the two texts: *Purge out the old leaven that you may be a new one* [1 Cor. 5:7], and: *Let us celebrate the festival, not with the old leaven but with the unleavened bread of sincerity and truth* [1 Cor. 5:8], support those passages which speak about the new creation. (St. Gregory of Nyssa)[26]

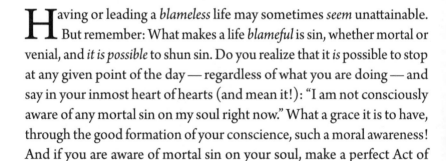

Having or leading a *blameless* life may sometimes *seem* unattainable. But remember: What makes a life *blameful* is sin, whether mortal or venial, and *it is possible* to shun sin. Do you realize that it *is* possible to stop at any given point of the day — regardless of what you are doing — and say in your inmost heart of hearts (and mean it!): "I am not consciously aware of any mortal sin on my soul right now." What a grace it is to have, through the good formation of your conscience, such a moral awareness! And if you are aware of mortal sin on your soul, make a perfect Act of

---

[26] *Book on Christian formation*, in *Liturgy of the Hours*, vol. IV, 337–338.

Contrition immediately and then get to the Sacrament of Reconciliation (Confession) as soon as is reasonably possible. An Act of Contrition is "perfect" when you are sorry for your sins "most of all" (primarily) because they have offended Almighty God, and secondarily because they threaten you with punishment: eternal punishment for mortal sin and temporal punishment for venial sin. An Act of Contrition is "imperfect" when you are sorry for your sins primarily because of the punishment they threaten you with, and secondarily because they have offended God. As for your venial sins? Try your best to shun those as well. Make a good Act of Contrition and continue to strive for perfection in the moral life, thanking God all the while for such an opportunity. (See Matthew 5:48: "You, therefore, must be perfect, as your heavenly Father is perfect.") (See days 49, 58, 87, 91, and 185.)

Your Existence

Before I formed you in the womb I knew you, and before you were born I consecrated you. (Jer. 1:5)

Recognize to whom you owe the fact that you exist, that you breathe, that you understand, that you are wise, and, above all, that you know God and hope for the kingdom of heaven and the vision of glory, now darkly and as in a mirror but then with greater fullness and purity. You have been made a son of God, coheir with Christ. (St. Gregory of Nazianzen)[27]

Even *before* God created the world and the cosmos — the entire universe — He knew you. Your life is a gift, and it happens only once. The Church teaches that "when 'the single course of our earthly life' is completed, we shall not return to other earthly lives: 'It is appointed for men to die once.' There is no 'reincarnation' after death" (*CCC* 1013, quoting *Lumen Gentium* 48 § 3 and Hebrews 9:27). Converse *daily* with God, Who made you in His image, after His likeness (Gen. 1:26). He knows you through and through and desires to save you. He desires intimate friendship with you. (See days 4, 7, 26, 52, 162, 185, and 200.)

---

[27] *Oratio 14 De pauperum amore*, in *Liturgy of the Hours*, vol. II, 96.

The Image and Likeness of God

Then God said, "Let us make man in our image, after our likeness; and let them have dominion over the fish of the sea, and over the birds of the air, and over the cattle, and over all the earth, and over every creeping thing that creeps upon the earth." So God created man in his own image, in the image of God he created him; male and female he created them. (Gen. 1:26–27)

You were made in the image of God. If then you wish to resemble him, follow his example. Since the very name you bear as Christians is a profession of love for men, imitate the love of Christ. (St. Asterius of Amasea)[28]

Remember that God is love (1 John 4:8, 16). Some of the Church Fathers teach that for humans, being made in the "image" of God refers to intellective and rational ability, and being made after God's "likeness" refers to the ability to partake in His saving sanctifying grace. No other creature in the corporeal world is afforded this dignity by the Creator except the human person. What a message this is to defend human life — and human nature — on all fronts, from conception until natural death. Defend God. Defend human life. (See days 14, 34, 43, 144, 152, 168, and 197.)

---

[28] Homily 13, in *Liturgy of the Hours*, vol. II, 122.

Day 27

Fraternal Charity

If any one says, "I love God," and hates his brother, he is a liar; for he who does not love his brother whom he has seen, cannot love God whom he has not seen. (1 John 4:20)

Since you do not yet see God, you merit the vision of God by loving your neighbor. By loving your neighbor, you prepare your eyes to see God. Saint John says clearly: *If you do not love your brother whom you see, how will you love God whom you do not see!* [see 1 John 4:20]. (St. Augustine)[29]

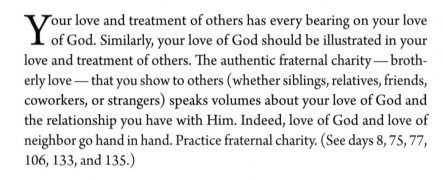

Your love and treatment of others has every bearing on your love of God. Similarly, your love of God should be illustrated in your love and treatment of others. The authentic fraternal charity — brotherly love — that you show to others (whether siblings, relatives, friends, coworkers, or strangers) speaks volumes about your love of God and the relationship you have with Him. Indeed, love of God and love of neighbor go hand in hand. Practice fraternal charity. (See days 8, 75, 77, 106, 133, and 135.)

---

[29] *Treatise on John,* in *Liturgy of the Hours,* vol. I, 512.

Day 28

Reaping What You Sow

Do not be deceived; God is not mocked, for whatever a man sows, that he will also reap. For he who sows to his own flesh will from the flesh reap corruption; but he who sows to the Spirit will from the Spirit reap eternal life. (Gal. 6:7–8)

The world rages, the flesh is heavy, and the devil lays his snares, but I do not fall, for my feet are planted on firm rock. (St. Bernard)[30]

❖————————❖

God knows of your efforts to work on personal holiness and of your striving to advance in the spiritual life. This should be a very comforting thought for you if you remain diligent in your efforts to pursue faithfully the good, the true, and the beautiful in concrete daily actions (see CCC 1803). Do not grow lax in your efforts. If you do, you run the risk of pursuing the bad, the false, and the ugly. (See days 7, 30, 43, 58, 80, 103, 106, 130, 164, 180, and 196.)

[30] *Sermo* 61 on the Song of Songs, in *Liturgy of the Hours*, vol. III, 125.

Day 29

God Is Love

So we know and believe the love God has for us. God is love, and he who abides in love abides in God, and God abides in him. (1 John 4:16)

If God is love, charity should know no limit, for God cannot be confined. (Pope St. Leo the Great)[31]

If "God is love," as St. John the Evangelist tells us, above, and we humans are made in God's image and after His likeness (see Gen. 1:26), then we can say confidently that the most fundamental and innate vocation of the human person is to love. You are called to love. It's important, too, that you let yourself be loved. St. Mother Teresa of Calcutta sums all this up when she says, "When God created us, he created us out of love. There is no other explanation because God is love. And he has created us to love and to be loved. If we could remember that all the time, there would be no wars, no violence, no hatred in the world. So beautiful. So simple."[32] (See days 101, 122, 127, 177, and 187.)

[31] *Sermo 10 in Quadragesima*, in *Liturgy of the Hours*, vol. II, 295.
[32] *Where There Is Love, There Is God*, ed. Brian Kolodiejchuk, M.C. (New York: Image, 2012), 6.

Day 30

Do Good

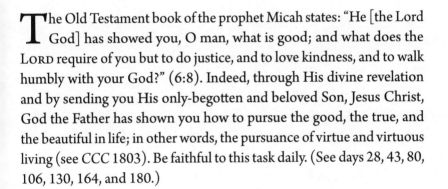

And let us not grow weary in well-doing, for in due season we shall reap, if we do not lose heart. So then, as we have opportunity, let us do good to all men, and especially to those who are of the household of faith. (Gal. 6:9–10)

We must be ready and eager for every opportunity to do good, and put our whole heart into it. (Pope St. Clement I)[33]

The Old Testament book of the prophet Micah states: "He [the Lord God] has showed you, O man, what is good; and what does the Lord require of you but to do justice, and to love kindness, and to walk humbly with your God?" (6:8). Indeed, through His divine revelation and by sending you His only-begotten and beloved Son, Jesus Christ, God the Father has shown you how to pursue the good, the true, and the beautiful in life; in other words, the pursuance of virtue and virtuous living (see *CCC* 1803). Be faithful to this task daily. (See days 28, 43, 80, 106, 130, 164, and 180.)

[33] *Letter to the Corinthians,* no. 33, in *Liturgy of the Hours,* vol. III, 76.

Seeking Wisdom

Happy is the man who finds wisdom, and the man who gets understanding, for the gain from it is better than gain from silver and its profit better than gold. She is more precious than jewels, and nothing you desire can compare with her. (Prov. 3:13–15)

God is man's glory. Man is the vessel which receives God's action and all his wisdom and power. (St. Irenaeus)[34]

T he Letter of James in the New Testament sums up the supernatural virtue of wisdom (one of the seven gifts of the Holy Spirit) in this way: "The wisdom from above is first pure, then peaceable, gentle, open to reason, full of mercy and good fruits, without uncertainty or insincerity" (3:17–18). Now *that's* a multifaceted divine gift worth *seeking* and *receiving* and *living*. Seek God's wisdom in all things. And while you're at it, be sure to seek *all* seven gifts of the Holy Spirit: wisdom, understanding, counsel, fortitude, knowledge, piety, and fear of the Lord (see Isa. 11:1–3). (See days 44, 66, 71, 136, and 137.)

---

[34] *Against Heresies*, bk. 3, chap. 20, in *Liturgy of the Hours*, vol. I, 337.

Day 32

Trusting in the Lord

Blessed is the man who trusts in the LORD, whose trust is the LORD. He is like a tree planted by water, that sends out its roots by the stream, and does not fear when heat comes, for its leaves remain green, and is not anxious in the year of drought, for it does not cease to bear fruit. (Jer. 17:7–8)

When a soul sees and realizes the gravity of its sins, when the whole abyss of the misery into which it immersed itself is displayed before its eyes, let it not despair, but with trust let it throw itself into the arms of My mercy, as a child into the arms of its beloved mother. These souls have a right of priority to My compassionate heart; they have first access to My mercy. Tell them that no soul that has called upon My mercy has been disappointed or brought to shame. I delight particularly in a soul which has placed its trust in My goodness. (Jesus to St. Faustina Kowalska)[35]

To trust in Jesus means to have faith in Him and in God's omnipotent mercy. Do you have the faith it takes to trust that the Lord Jesus Christ is indeed your Savior and desires to save you — despite your moral failings, weaknesses, and temperament and personality quirks? In fact, He desires to give you now, through your strong trust in Him, a share in the peace and tranquility that only He can give. Trust in the Sacred, Merciful, and Eucharistic Heart of Jesus. Trust in the mercy of God. Remember what Ephesians 2:4–7 teaches you: "But God, who is rich in mercy, out of the great love with which he loved us, even when we were dead through our trespasses, made us alive together with Christ (by

[35] *Diary*, no. 1541.

grace you have been saved), and raised us up with him, and made us sit with him in the heavenly places in Christ Jesus, that in the coming ages he might show the immeasurable riches of his grace in kindness toward us in Christ Jesus." (See days 13, 107, 190, and 192.)

Being a Temple of God

Do you not know that your body is a temple of the Holy Spirit within you, which you have from God? You are not your own; you were bought with a price. So glorify God in your body. (1 Cor. 6:19–20)

If we are indeed the temple of God and if the Spirit of God lives in us, then what every believer has within himself is greater than what he admires in the skies. (Pope St. Leo the Great)[36]

❦————————————❧

How you treat your body — a temple of the Holy Spirit — says a lot about whether you are leaning toward a life of virtue or of vice. Noteworthy bodily practices such as fasting regularly, eating right, good hygiene, and exercising can help you to "train" your body, which — through its five senses acting on the tugs of concupiscence — can seem unruly at times and even lead you into vices such as pornography and morally illicit relationships. These noteworthy bodily practices, coupled with spiritual practices for the soul — such as monthly Confession, weekly Eucharist, and daily Rosary and Divine Mercy Chaplet (even while power walking!) — can help make your body a *more worthy* temple for the indwelling of the Holy Spirit. (See days 12, 19, 37, 118, 122, and 185.)

---

[36] *Sermo in Nativitate Domini* 7, in *Liturgy of the Hours*, vol. III, 192.

Day 34

The Dignity of Human Nature

So God created man in his own image, in the image of God he created him; male and female he created them. And God blessed them, and God said to them, "Be fruitful and multiply, and fill the earth and subdue it; and have dominion over the fish of the sea and over the birds of the air and over every living thing that moves upon the earth." ... And God saw everything that he had made, and behold, it was very good. (Gen. 1:27–28, 31)

Rouse yourself, man, and recognize the dignity of your nature. Remember that you were made in God's image; though corrupted in Adam, that image has been restored in Christ. (Pope St. Leo the Great)[37]

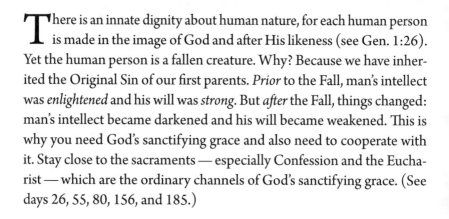

There is an innate dignity about human nature, for each human person is made in the image of God and after His likeness (see Gen. 1:26). Yet the human person is a fallen creature. Why? Because we have inherited the Original Sin of our first parents. *Prior* to the Fall, man's intellect was *enlightened* and his will was *strong*. But *after* the Fall, things changed: man's intellect became darkened and his will became weakened. This is why you need God's sanctifying grace and also need to cooperate with it. Stay close to the sacraments — especially Confession and the Eucharist — which are the ordinary channels of God's sanctifying grace. (See days 26, 55, 80, 156, and 185.)

---

[37] *Sermo in Nativitate Domini* 7, in *Liturgy of the Hours*, vol. III, 191.

Day 35

Using Things as They Should Be Used

As each has received a gift, employ it for one another, as good stewards of God's varied grace. (1 Pet. 4:10)

Use creatures as they should be used: the earth, the sea, the sky, the air, the springs and the rivers. Give praise and glory to their Creator for all that you find beautiful and wonderful in them. See with your bodily eyes the light that shines on earth, but embrace with your whole soul and all your affections *the true light which enlightens every man who comes into this world* (John 1:9). (Pope St. Leo the Great)[38]

Good stewardship is about using your gifts, talents, and material goods wisely. Whether employing well your natural leadership skills or your automotive mechanical skills, teaching a youth catechism class at your parish, or cleaning out your garage, closets, and cupboards to donate unused clothing and household items to a local charity, you'd be surprised at how much you can build up the Kingdom of God — and your neighbor — by using things wisely and by being faithful to your daily duties and vocational tasks at hand according to your state in life.

Fr. Jean-Baptiste Rauzan, the founder of the Fathers of Mercy, instructs on how to be faithful to this vision when he states:

So, then, do every act with exactness, do it at its proper time, in the most perfect manner possible and without regard for that which follows it: have direction of intention at the outset; an offering and

---

[38] *Sermo in Nativitate Domini 7*, in *Liturgy of the Hours*, vol. III, 191–192.

thanksgiving at the end; and a raising up of the mind and tender aspirations during the course of the action.[39]

Use created things wisely yourself, and employ created things wisely for others' use as well. (See days 74, 106, 153, 175, 176, and 177.)

---

[39] Fr. Albert Delaporte, SPM, *The Life of the Very Reverend Father Jean-Baptiste Rauzan*, trans. Rev. Patrick G. Branigan, SPM, unpublished translation for internal community use only, bk. 5, 14.

Day 36

Building Up Others

We who are strong ought to bear with the failings of the weak, and not to please ourselves; let each of us please his neighbor for his good, to edify him. (Rom. 15:1–2)

If you truly want to help the soul of your neighbor, approach God first with all your heart. Ask Him simply to fill you with love, the greatest of all virtues; with it you can accomplish what you desire. (St. Vincent Ferrer)[40]

Stop and think about this: out of all Ten Commandments, only three have to do with love of God, while seven have to do with love of neighbor. What do you think about that? The *majority* of the Ten Commandments have to do with love of neighbor! This fact should speak volumes to you about the emphasis that you are to place on love of neighbor and not only on love of God. After all, is not your neighbor made in the image and likeness of God, as you are? Yes, he is. As the Letter to the Romans states: "Owe no one anything, except to love one another; for he who loves his neighbor has fulfilled the law.... Love does no wrong to a neighbor; therefore love is the fulfilling of the law" (13:8, 10). So build up your neighbor — and love him. (See days 8, 27, 57, 76, 86, 106, 128, 141, and 188.)

---

[40] Schroeder, *Every Day Is a Gift*, 54.

Day 37

Flesh and Spirit

> But I say, walk by the Spirit, and do not gratify the desires of the flesh. For the desires of the flesh are against the Spirit, and the desires of the Spirit are against the flesh; for these are opposed to each other, to prevent you from doing what you would. (Gal. 5:16–17)
>
> God ... shows that spiritual grace is repelled by uncleanness of the flesh and by the stain of more serious sin. (St. Ambrose)[41]

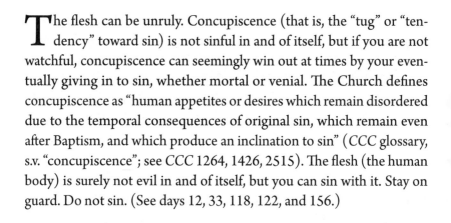

T he flesh can be unruly. Concupiscence (that is, the "tug" or "tendency" toward sin) is not sinful in and of itself, but if you are not watchful, concupiscence can seemingly win out at times by your eventually giving in to sin, whether mortal or venial. The Church defines concupiscence as "human appetites or desires which remain disordered due to the temporal consequences of original sin, which remain even after Baptism, and which produce an inclination to sin" (*CCC* glossary, s.v. "concupiscence"; see *CCC* 1264, 1426, 2515). The flesh (the human body) is surely not evil in and of itself, but you can sin with it. Stay on guard. Do not sin. (See days 12, 33, 118, 122, and 156.)

---

[41] *On the Mysteries*, no. 10, in *Liturgy of the Hours*, vol. III, 488.

Day 38

Living in Union with Christ

As therefore you received Christ Jesus the Lord, so live in him, rooted and built up in him and established in the faith, just as you were taught, abounding in thanksgiving. See to it that no one makes a prey of you by philosophy and empty deceit, according to human tradition, according to the elemental spirits of the universe, and not according to Christ. For in him the whole fulness of deity dwells bodily, and you have come to fulness of life in him, who is the head of all rule and authority. (Col. 2:6–10)

In proportion to God's need of nothing is man's need for communion with God. (St. Irenaeus)[42]

Concerning God, St. Irenaeus also teaches that "[h]e who stands in need of no one gave communion with himself to those who need him."[43] St. Irenaeus thus makes it very clear: Without God, you can do nothing (see John 15:5). Jesus Christ is God — the Second Person of the Most Holy Trinity. He wants you to have union with Him and the Father and the Holy Spirit. Pray to the Blessed Trinity. Draw close to the Blessed Trinity. Indeed, foster a *Trinitarian spirituality*. (See days 9, 10, 43, 44, 53, 69, 84, 90, 109, 130, 187, and 200.)

---

[42] *Against Heresies*, bk. 4, chap. 13, in *Liturgy of the Hours*, vol. II, 78.
[43] *Against Heresies*, bk. 4, chap. 14, in *Liturgy of the Hours*, vol. II, 177.

Day 39

Sin and Guilt

I confess my iniquity, I am sorry for my sin. (Ps. 38:18)

If there is any slave of sin here present, he should at once prepare himself through faith for the rebirth into freedom that makes us God's adopted children. He should lay aside the wretchedness of slavery to sin, and put on the joyful slavery of the Lord, so as to be counted worthy to inherit the kingdom of heaven. By acknowledging your sins, strip away your former self, seduced as it is by destructive desires, and put on the new self, renewed in the likeness of its Creator. (St. Cyril of Jerusalem)[44]

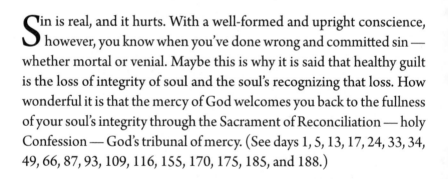

Sin is real, and it hurts. With a well-formed and upright conscience, however, you know when you've done wrong and committed sin — whether mortal or venial. Maybe this is why it is said that healthy guilt is the loss of integrity of soul and the soul's recognizing that loss. How wonderful it is that the mercy of God welcomes you back to the fullness of your soul's integrity through the Sacrament of Reconciliation — holy Confession — God's tribunal of mercy. (See days 1, 5, 13, 17, 24, 33, 34, 49, 66, 87, 93, 109, 116, 155, 170, 175, 185, and 188.)

[44] Catechetical instruction 1, in *Liturgy of the Hours*, vol. III, 445.

Prayer Is Conversation with God

As he was setting out on his journey, a man ran up and knelt before him, and asked him, "Good Teacher, what must I do to inherit eternal life?" (Mark 10:17)

Prayer and converse with God is a supreme good: it is a partnership and union with God. As the eyes of the body are enlightened when they see light, so our spirit, when it is intent on God, is illumined by his infinite light. I do not mean the prayer of outward observance but prayer from the heart, not confined to fixed times or periods but continuous throughout the day and night. (St. John Chrysostom)[45]

The great Carmelite reformer and mystic St. Teresa of Ávila teaches that "mental prayer in my opinion is nothing else than an intimate sharing between friends; it means taking time frequently to be alone with Him who we know loves us" (*The Book of Her Life*, chap. 8, 5). So converse with Almighty God — your Triune God: Father, Son, and Holy Spirit — just as you would with a dear friend. Converse with God about your hopes, joys, sufferings, and trials. Do this often. Let God be your friend, and *you* be a friend of God. (See days 50, 77, 78, 146, 184, 194, 197, and 198.)

---

[45] Supp. Hom. 6 *De precatione*, in *Liturgy of the Hours*, vol. II, 68–69.

Day 41

Where Your Heart and Treasure Are

In this you rejoice, though now for a little while you may have to suffer various trials, so that the genuineness of your faith, more precious than gold which though perishable is tested by fire, may redound to praise and glory and honor at the revelation of Jesus Christ. Without having seen him you love him; though you do not now see him you believe in him and rejoice with unutterable and exalted joy. As the outcome of your faith you obtain the salvation of your souls. (1 Pet. 1:6–9)

Where a man's heart is, there is his treasure also. God is not accustomed to refusing a good gift to those who ask for one. Since he is good, and especially to those who are faithful to him, let us hold fast to him with all our soul, our heart, our strength, and so enjoy his light and see his glory and possess the grace of supernatural joy. Let us reach out with our hearts to possess that good, let us exist in it and live in it, let us hold fast to it, that good which is beyond all we can know or see and is marked by perpetual peace and tranquility, a peace which is beyond all we can know or understand. (St. Ambrose)[46]

＊━━━━━━━━＜

Amid your having to "suffer various trials" throughout your life, keep fighting the good fight of faith. Your reward for remaining faithful to God and all that He has revealed to you through Scripture, Tradition, and the Magisterium will be great. Never doubt this. Remain steadfast. Remain faithful. Then you will hear Jesus say, like the master in the parable of the talents, "Well done, good and faithful servant; you have been faithful over a little, I will set you over much; enter into the joy of your master" (Matt. 25:21). (See days 20, 104, 111, 124, 143, 160, 165, and 188.)

[46] *Flight from the World*, chap. 6, no. 36, in *Liturgy of the Hours*, vol. II, 203.

Day 42

Hearing and Listening

They have ears, but do not hear. (Ps. 115:6)

If you do not close your ear to others you open God's ear to yourself. (St. Peter Chrysologus)[47]

Proverbs 4:1–2 teaches, "Hear, O sons, a father's instruction, and be attentive, that you may gain insight; for I give you good precepts: do not forsake my teaching." Indeed, just as you desire to hear God speaking to you, you must realize that His spoken word to you can be delivered through other human beings; for example, a father instructing his son; a mother instructing her daughter; a friend verbally guiding another friend with sound advice; a confessor guiding a penitent; a spiritual director guiding a spiritual directee. Be attentive to the ways in which God speaks to you. He often uses other people as His instruments. (See days 51, 107, 169, and 187.)

---

[47] *Sermo* 43, in *Liturgy of the Hours*, vol. II, 231.

Day 43

Virtue and Vice

Make every effort to supplement your faith with virtue, and virtue with knowledge, and knowledge with self-control, and self-control with steadfastness, and steadfastness with godliness, and godliness with brotherly affection, and brotherly affection with love. For if these things are yours and abound, they keep you from being ineffective or unfruitful in the knowledge of our Lord Jesus Christ. For whoever lacks these things is blind and shortsighted and has forgotten that he was cleansed from his old sins. (2 Pet. 1:5–9)

However much you may cultivate your heart, clear the soil of your nature, root out vices, sow virtues. (St. Peter Chrysologus)[48]

The *Catechism* teaches that "a virtue is an habitual and firm disposition to do the good. It allows the person not only to perform good acts, but to give the best of himself. The virtuous person tends toward the good with all his sensory and spiritual powers; he pursues the good and chooses it in concrete actions" (1803). But it also teaches that "sin creates a proclivity to sin; it engenders vice by repetition of the same acts. This results in perverse inclinations which cloud conscience and corrupt the concrete judgment of good and evil. Thus sin tends to reproduce itself and reinforce itself" (1865). But there's hope. The *Catechism* quotes St. Gregory of Nyssa: "The goal of a virtuous life is to become like God" (1803, *De beatitudinibus*, 1: *PG* 44, 1200D). This is a powerful statement that should inspire you to a commitment to pursue and achieve virtue and shun vice in every facet of your daily lived experience. (See days 9, 10, 14, 26, 28, 30, 44, 52, 53, 69, 80, 90, 106, 109, 129, 130, 144, 152, 156, 164, 168, 195, and 197.)

[48] *Sermo 43*, in *Liturgy of the Hours*, vol. II, 232.

Day 44

Cardinal Virtues

And if any one loves righteousness, her labors are virtues; for she teaches self-control and prudence, justice and courage; nothing in life is more profitable for men than these. (Wisd. 8:7)

There are three ways for wisdom or prudence to abound in you: if you confess your sins, if you give thanks and praise, and if your speech is edifying. (St. Bernard)[49]

Based in Sacred Scripture, Catholic moral tradition teaches that "four virtues play a pivotal role [in the moral life] and accordingly are called 'cardinal'; all the others are grouped around them. They are: prudence, justice, fortitude, and temperance. 'If anyone loves righteousness, [Wisdom's] labors are virtues; for she teaches temperance and prudence, justice, and courage' (Wisd. 8:7)" (CCC 1805). The Latin root of the word *cardinal* is *cardo*, meaning "hinge." The Latin adjective *cardinalis* means "serving as a hinge." In other words, the success of your moral life "hinges" (or "pivots") on these four virtues: temperance (self-control), prudence, justice, and fortitude (courage). This is a lesson worth remembering so as to advance in holiness in your vocation and state in life. (See days 9, 10, 31, 43, 52, 53, and 130.)

---

[49] *Sermo de diversis* 15, in *Liturgy of the Hours*, vol. III, 204.

Day 45

Spiritual Blindness

Jesus said to him, "What do you want me to do for you?" And the blind man said to him, "Master, let me receive my sight." And Jesus said to him, "Go your way; your faith has made you well." And immediately he received his sight and followed him on the way. (Mark 10:51–52)

God is seen by those who have the capacity to see him, provided that they keep the eyes of their mind open. All have eyes, but some have eyes that are shrouded in darkness, unable to see the light of the sun. Because the blind cannot see it, it does not follow that the sun does not shine. The blind must trace the cause back to themselves and their eyes. In the same way, you have eyes in your mind that are shrouded in darkness because of your sins and evil deeds. (St. Theophilus of Antioch)[50]

The blind man had physical blindness, but he possessed the spiritual "sight" of faith. That spiritual sight of faith led to his being cured of physical blindness. Do not be blind to the light of faith. God's (divine) revelation will lead you to this faith, rooted in truth. Revelation is "God's communication of himself, by which he makes known the mystery of his divine plan, a gift of self-communication which is realized by deeds and words over time, and most fully by sending us his own divine Son, Jesus Christ" (CCC glossary, s.v. "revelation"; see CCC 50). Pursue this revelation and be faithful to it. Cooperate with it. Let it lead you to the light of faith and truth. (See days 4, 43, 115, and 126.)

[50] From the book addressed to Autolycus, bk. 1, 2.7, in *Liturgy of the Hours*, vol. II, 240.

Day 46

Standing Strong in Time of Trial and Temptation

No temptation has overtaken you that is not common to man. God is faithful, and he will not let you be tempted beyond your strength, but with the temptation will also provide the way of escape, that you may be able to endure it. (1 Cor. 10:13)

Whenever we suffer some affliction, we should regard it both as a punishment and as a correction. Our holy Scriptures themselves do not promise us peace, security and rest. On the contrary, the Gospel makes no secret of the troubles and temptations that await us, but it also says that *he who perseveres to the end will be saved* [Matt. 24:13]. (St. Augustine)[51]

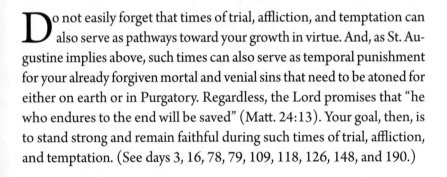

Do not easily forget that times of trial, affliction, and temptation can also serve as pathways toward your growth in virtue. And, as St. Augustine implies above, such times can also serve as temporal punishment for your already forgiven mortal and venial sins that need to be atoned for either on earth or in Purgatory. Regardless, the Lord promises that "he who endures to the end will be saved" (Matt. 24:13). Your goal, then, is to stand strong and remain faithful during such times of trial, affliction, and temptation. (See days 3, 16, 78, 79, 109, 118, 126, 148, and 190.)

---

[51] *Sermo Caillau-Saint Yves* 2, 92, in *Liturgy of the Hours*, vol. IV, 134.

Today Is the Day of Salvation

Working together with him, then, we entreat you not to accept the grace of God in vain. For he says, "At the acceptable time I have listened to you, and helped you on the day of salvation." Behold, now is the acceptable time; behold, now is the day of salvation. (2 Cor. 6:1–2)

[W]e must carefully seek after our own salvation; otherwise, one who is bent on deceiving us will insinuate himself and turn us aside from the path that leads to life. (attributed to Barnabas)[52]

※━━━━━━━━━━━━※

Today is the day of salvation — your salvation. Strive diligently to remain in a state of God's sanctifying grace; that is, with no known mortal sin on your soul. How do you know that today won't be the day you'll die? You don't. So make an effort to live each day "eternity minded" — not in a morose or macabre way, no, but in joyful, anticipation of the Heaven that awaits those who remain faithful to Almighty God and who endeavor to know, love, and serve Him (see 1 Cor. 2:9). (See days 125, 126, 136, 147, and 187.)

---

[52] Letter, chap. 2, in *Liturgy of the Hours*, vol. IV, 61.

Day 48

Works of Mercy

"For I was hungry and you gave me food, I was thirsty and you gave me drink, I was a stranger and you welcomed me, I was naked and you clothed me, I was sick and you visited me, I was in prison and you came to me." Then the righteous will answer him, "Lord, when did we see thee hungry and feed thee, or thirsty and give thee drink? And when did we see thee a stranger and welcome thee, or naked and clothe thee? And when did we see thee sick or in prison and visit thee?" And the King will answer them, "Truly, I say to you, as you did it to one of the least of these my brethren, you did it to me." (Matt. 25:35–40)

As we prepare to celebrate the greatest of all mysteries, by which the blood of Jesus Christ did away with our sins, let us first of all make ready the sacrificial offerings of works of mercy....

Let us now extend to the poor and those afflicted in different ways a more open-handed generosity, so that God may be thanked through many voices and the relief of the needy supported by our fasting. No act of devotion on the part of the faithful gives God more pleasure than that which is lavished on his poor. Where he finds charity with its loving concern, there he recognizes the reflection of his own fatherly care. (Pope St. Leo the Great)[53]

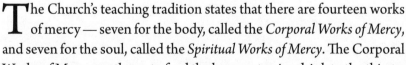

The Church's teaching tradition states that there are fourteen works of mercy — seven for the body, called the *Corporal Works of Mercy*, and seven for the soul, called the *Spiritual Works of Mercy*. The Corporal Works of Mercy are these: to feed the hungry, to give drink to the thirsty,

[53] *Sermo 10 in Quadragesima*, in *Liturgy of the Hours*, vol. II, 295–296.

to clothe the naked, to visit the imprisoned, to shelter the homeless, to visit the sick, and to bury the dead. The Spiritual Works of Mercy are these: to admonish the sinner, to instruct the ignorant, to counsel the doubtful, to comfort the sorrowful, to bear wrongs patiently, to forgive all injuries, and to pray for the living and the dead. As a dedicated Catholic man, and according to your abilities and means, you are called to remain active in these important works of mercy, which aid your neighbor. The fourteen works of mercy can help you to foster an *other-centered* outlook, thus safeguarding you from an inordinate *self-centered* outlook. (See days 32, 72, 74, and 93.)

Day 49

Repentance

The time is fulfilled, and the kingdom of God is at hand; repent, and believe in the gospel. (Mark 1:15)

God's will is to save us, and nothing pleases him more than our coming back to him with true repentance. The heralds of truth and the ministers of divine grace have told us this from the beginning, repeating it in every age. Indeed, God's desire for our salvation is the primary and preeminent sign of his infinite goodness. (St. Maximus the Confessor)[54]

The word *repentance* comes from the Latin word *paenitere*, meaning "to make sorry." Whenever you repent, you are telling Almighty God — Father, Son, and Holy Spirit — that you are sorry for your sins, both venial and mortal. This is why the twice-daily examination of conscience — the *particular examen* at midday and the *general examen* at the end of the day — is such a wonderful practice in the spiritual life. During these examens, you are telling God that you are sorry for any sins you committed that day (both particularly and generally), and at the same time, you are renewing your sorrow for past sins committed, even past mortal sins that have already been confessed, so as to experience continued healing from them. The daily examination of conscience takes only about two minutes, and it ends with an Act of Contrition. The Acts of the Apostles states that God "commands all men everywhere to repent" (17:30). Indeed, He does. Be a good man of God and repent. (See days 24, 58, 87, and 185.)

---

[54] Epistle 11, in *Liturgy of the Hours*, vol. II, 304.

Day 50

Seek the Lord Your God

But from there you will seek the LORD your God, and you will find him, if you search after him with all your heart and with all your soul. When you are in tribulation, and all these things come upon you in the latter days, you will return to the LORD your God and obey his voice, for the LORD your God is a merciful God; he will not fail you or destroy you. (Deut. 4:29–31)

Escape from your everyday business for a short while, hide for a moment from your restless thoughts. Break off from your cares and troubles and be less concerned about your tasks and labors. Make a little time for God and rest a while in him.

Enter into your mind's inner chamber. Shut out everything but God and whatever helps you to seek him; and when you have shut the door, look for him. Speak now to God and say with your whole heart: *I seek your face; your face, Lord, I desire* [Ps. 27:8]. (St. Anselm)[55]

❖━━━━━━━━━❖

Our Blessed Lord commands in Matthew 7:7, "Ask and it will be given to you; seek and you will find; knock and the door will be opened to you." Think about it: God is calling you to communicate with Him with cognizant, willed, deliberate, and purposeful intention. What an honor this is. Don't miss the opportunity — daily — to communicate and converse with God as a close friend and dear confidant. Seek the Lord your God. (See days 31, 40, 136, 161, and 200.)

[55] *Proslogion*, chap. 1, in *Liturgy of the Hours*, vol. I, 184.

Day 51

Don't Worry

And he said to his disciples, "Therefore I tell you, do not be anxious about your life, what you shall eat, nor about your body, what you shall put on. For life is more than food, and the body more than clothing. Consider the ravens: they neither sow nor reap, they have neither storehouse nor barn, and yet God feeds them. Of how much more value are you than the birds! And which of you by being anxious can add a cubit to his span of life? If then you are not able to do as small a thing as that, why are you anxious about the rest? Consider the lilies, how they grow; they neither toil nor spin; yet I tell you, even Solomon in all his glory was not arrayed like one of these. But if God so clothes the grass which is alive in the field today and tomorrow is thrown into the oven, how much more will he clothe you, O men of little faith! And do not seek what you are to eat and what you are to drink, nor be of anxious mind. For all the nations of the world seek these things; and your Father knows that you need them. Instead, seek his kingdom, and these things shall be yours as well. (Luke 12:22–31)

The business of this life should not preoccupy us with its anxiety and pride, so that we no longer strive with all the love of our heart to be like our Redeemer, and to follow his example. (Pope St. Leo the Great)[56]

It takes faith not to worry and not to be preoccupied with things — not to be anxious or inordinately stressed out. True enough, you do have to do what is required of you in faithfulness to your daily duty to achieve your desired outcomes in situations with peace of mind, but even then

---

[56] *Sermo 15 De passione Domini*, in *Liturgy of the Hours*, vol. II, 314.

there may be things that go awry or get in the way and sabotage your plans and those desired outcomes. At such times, undue worry can set in. Then you should remember this counsel attributed to St. Pio of Pietrelcina (Padre Pio): "Pray, hope, and don't worry. Worry is useless. God is merciful and will hear your prayer."

So turn to God for assistance, guidance, and peace of mind during such times. And remember: God will answer your prayer in His way, *not* your way — unless these two ways are indeed compatible. As the Lord's Prayer states, "Thy kingdom come, Thy will be done" (Matt. 6:10). It's not, "*My* kingdom come, *my* will be done." Pray, hope, and don't worry. (See days 42, 60, 107, and 169.)

Day 52

True Friendship

A faithful friend is a sturdy shelter: he that has found one has found a treasure. There is nothing so precious as a faithful friend, and no scales can measure his excellence. A faithful friend is an elixir of life; and those who fear the Lord will find him. Whoever fears the Lord directs his friendship aright. (Sir. 6:14–17)

Every virtue can attract the friendship of others to us. For every virtue is a good, and anything good is lovable to all and renders lovable all who possess it. Friendship blossoms, grows, and is strengthened in the measure that virtue develops. (St. Thomas Aquinas)[57]

The wise man seeks out other wise men. The virtuous man seeks out other virtuous men. What's the old adage? It goes something like this: "Garbage in, garbage out. Virtue in, virtue out." And there's another one: "Show me your friends, and I'll show you your life." Seek out other godly men in your life who aren't afraid to show their love for God and neighbor, men who also strive for virtue and virtuous living. Strong, holy friendships develop when friends possess characteristics such as these and support one another in the journey of life. (See days 9, 10, 43, 44, 53, 69, 84, 90, 109, 130, and 200.)

[57] Schroeder, *Every Day Is a Gift*, 140.

Day 53

The Three Theological Virtues

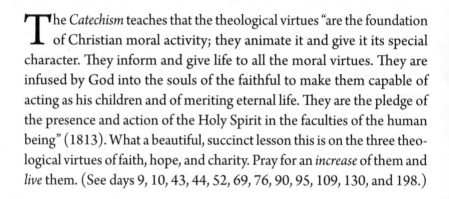

So faith, hope, love abide, these three; but the greatest of these is love. (1 Cor. 13:13)

Faith, hope and love bring safely to God the person who prays, that is, the person who believes, who hopes, who desires, and who ponders what he is asking of the Lord in the Lord's Prayer. (St. Augustine)[58]

❧————————❧

The *Catechism* teaches that the theological virtues "are the foundation of Christian moral activity; they animate it and give it its special character. They inform and give life to all the moral virtues. They are infused by God into the souls of the faithful to make them capable of acting as his children and of meriting eternal life. They are the pledge of the presence and action of the Holy Spirit in the faculties of the human being" (1813). What a beautiful, succinct lesson this is on the three theological virtues of faith, hope, and charity. Pray for an *increase* of them and *live* them. (See days 9, 10, 43, 44, 52, 69, 76, 90, 95, 109, 130, and 198.)

[58] Epistle 130, in *Liturgy of the Hours*, vol. IV, 422.

Eternity in Heaven

Let not your hearts be troubled; believe in God, believe also in me. In my Father's house are many rooms; if it were not so, would I have told you that I go to prepare a place for you? And when I go and prepare a place for you, I will come again and will take you to myself, that where I am you may be also. (John 14:1–3)

When Christ has already given us the gift of his death, who is to doubt that he will give the saints the gift of his own life? Why does our human frailty hesitate to believe that mankind will one day live with God? (St. Augustine)[59]

———————✦———————

Heaven is real. And God promises admittance there for all who remain faithful to Him. Do not let the devil tell you otherwise. (See days 14, 73, 81, 95, and 198.)

[59] *Sermo Guelferbytanus* 3, in *Liturgy of the Hours*, vol. II, 432.

Day 55

The Fickleness of Human Nature

Now when he was in Jerusalem at the Passover feast, many believed in his name when they saw the signs which he did; but Jesus did not trust himself to them, because he knew all men and needed no one to bear witness of man; for he himself knew what was in man. (John 2:23–25)

Men like nothing better than discussing and minding the business of others, passing superfluous comments at random and criticizing people behind their backs. (St. Columban)[60]

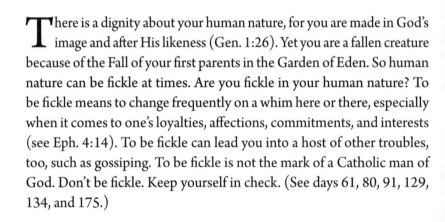

There is a dignity about your human nature, for you are made in God's image and after His likeness (Gen. 1:26). Yet you are a fallen creature because of the Fall of your first parents in the Garden of Eden. So human nature can be fickle at times. Are you fickle in your human nature? To be fickle means to change frequently on a whim here or there, especially when it comes to one's loyalties, affections, commitments, and interests (see Eph. 4:14). To be fickle can lead you into a host of other troubles, too, such as gossiping. To be fickle is not the mark of a Catholic man of God. Don't be fickle. Keep yourself in check. (See days 61, 80, 91, 129, 134, and 175.)

[60] Instr. 11, in *Liturgy of the Hours*, vol. IV, 1582–1583.

Day 56

Love of the World versus Love of God

Do not love the world or the things in the world. If any one loves the world, love for the Father is not in him. For all that is in the world, the lust of the flesh and the lust of the eyes and the pride of life, is not of the Father but is of the world. And the world passes away, and the lust of it; but he who does the will of God abides for ever. (1 John 2:15–17)

Even the most intimate bonds of friendship and the closest affinity of minds cannot truly lay claim to this peace if they are not in agreement with the will of God. Alliances based on evil desires, covenants of crime and pacts of vice — all lie outside the scope of this peace. Love of the world cannot be reconciled with love of God, and the man who does not separate himself from the children of this generation cannot join the company of the sons of God. (Pope St. Leo the Great)[61]

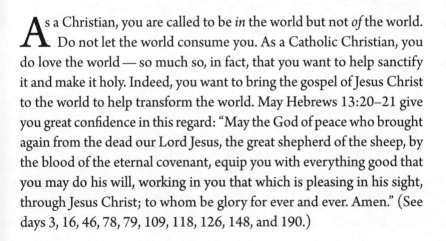

As a Christian, you are called to be *in* the world but not *of* the world. Do not let the world consume you. As a Catholic Christian, you do love the world — so much so, in fact, that you want to help sanctify it and make it holy. Indeed, you want to bring the gospel of Jesus Christ to the world to help transform the world. May Hebrews 13:20–21 give you great confidence in this regard: "May the God of peace who brought again from the dead our Lord Jesus, the great shepherd of the sheep, by the blood of the eternal covenant, equip you with everything good that you may do his will, working in you that which is pleasing in his sight, through Jesus Christ; to whom be glory for ever and ever. Amen." (See days 3, 16, 46, 78, 79, 109, 118, 126, 148, and 190.)

---

[61] *Sermo 95*, in *Liturgy of the Hours*, vol. IV, 226.

Day 57

The Ten Commandments

And one of the scribes came up and heard them disputing with one another, and seeing that he answered them well, asked him, "Which commandment is the first of all?" Jesus answered, "The first is, 'Hear, O Israel: The Lord our God, the Lord is one; and you shall love the Lord your God with all your heart, and with all your soul, and with all your mind, and with all your strength.' The second is this, 'You shall love your neighbor as yourself.' There is no other commandment greater than these." (Mark 12:28–31)

Through the Decalogue [the Ten Commandments] [God] prepared man for friendship with himself and for harmony with his neighbor. This was to man's advantage, because God needed nothing from man.

This raised man to glory, for it gave him what he did not have, friendship with God. But it brought no advantage to God, for God did not need man's love. (St. Irenaeus)[62]

In the above passage from St. Mark's Gospel, Jesus really gives the inquisitive scribe *all* Ten Commandments, albeit in an abbreviated form. Romans 13:9 hints at this when it states, "The commandments, 'You shall not commit adultery, You shall not kill, You shall not steal, You shall not covet,' and any other commandment, are summed up in this sentence, 'You shall love your neighbor as yourself.'" God gave you the Ten Commandments to help you draw closer to Him and to your neighbor. Remember that the first three Commandments deal with love of God, while the remaining seven Commandments deal with love of neighbor.

---

[62] *Against Heresies*, bk. 4, chap. 16, in *Liturgy of the Hours*, vol. II, 195–196.

Remember this: the *majority* of the Ten Commandments have to do with love of neighbor. What, then, is God trying to tell you? That the Ten Commandments are all about love of God *and* love of neighbor — with no less an emphasis on the latter. So act accordingly and love accordingly. 1 John 3:23–24 assures us: "This is his commandment, that we should believe in the name of his Son Jesus Christ and love one another, just as he has commanded us. All who keep his commandments abide in him, and he in them." And Ecclesiastes 12:13 sums it up this way: "Fear God, and keep his commandments; for this is the whole duty of man." (See days 8, 14, 36, 76, 86, 122, 128, 130, 141, 173, 188, and 191.)

Day 58

Mortal Sin

If any one sees his brother committing what is not a mortal sin, he will ask, and God will give him life for those whose sin is not mortal. There is sin which is mortal; I do not say that one is to pray for that. All wrongdoing is sin, but there is sin which is not mortal. (1 John 5:16–17)

Two things alone I fear: mortal sin which kills the soul, and dying in mortal sin.... I fear that some of you may fall victims of your own negligence of your spiritual welfare. Death skips no one. (St. John Bosco)[63]

❧————————❧

Mortal sin in a person's life is a very real possibility. The *Catechism* teaches, "For a *sin* to be *mortal*, three conditions must together be met: 'Mortal sin is sin whose object is grave matter and which is also committed with full knowledge and deliberate consent'" (1857, quoting *Reconciliatio et Paenitentia*, 17 § 12). The *Catechism* also teaches that "God predestines no one to go to hell; for this, a willful turning away from God (a mortal sin) is necessary, and persistence in it until the end" (1037; cf. Council of Orange II [529]: DS 397; Council of Trent [1547]: 1567). Pray to God daily that you never fall into mortal sin — the devil's death trap. And if you do fall into mortal sin, make a perfect Act of Contrition immediately and get to the Sacrament of Penance as soon as is reasonably possible. (See days 7, 24, 28, 49, 87, 103, 106, and 196.)

---

[63] From a November 1858 talk to a group of boys, as quoted in Rev. Giovanni Battista Lemoyne, SDB, *The Biographical Memoirs of Saint John Bosco*, vol. VI, 1858–1861, trans. Rev. Diego Borgatello, SDB (New Rochelle: Salesiana Publishers, 1971), 40.

Day 59

The Cross

So they took Jesus, and he went out, bearing his own cross, to the place called the place of a skull, which is called in Hebrew Golgotha. There they crucified him, and with him two others, one on either side, and Jesus between them. (John 19:17–18)

Whoever wishes to live perfectly should do nothing but disdain what Christ disdained on the cross and desire what he desired, for the cross exemplifies every virtue.

　… And if he gave his life for us, then it should not be difficult to bear whatever hardships arise for his sake. (St. Thomas Aquinas)[64]

Regarding your participation in Christ's sacrifice on the Cross, the Church teaches the following: "The cross is the unique sacrifice of Christ, the 'one mediator between God and men.' … He calls his disciples to 'take up [their] cross and follow [him],' for 'Christ also suffered for [us], leaving [us] an example so that [we] should follow in his steps" (CCC 618, quoting 1 Tim. 2:5; Matt. 16:24; 1 Pet. 2:21). What is your cross that you need to "take up"? Whether big or small, permanent or temporary — whatever it is — take up your cross valiantly and follow Christ. As Pope St. Leo the Great teaches: "Through the Cross, the faithful receive strength from weakness, glory from dishonor, life from death."[65] (See days 67, 82, 83, 95, 96, 133, and 143.)

---

[64] *Collatio 6 super Credo in Deum*, in *Liturgy of the Hours*, vol. III, 1335.
[65] *Sermo 8 de passione Domini*, in *Liturgy of the Hours*, vol. II, 359.

Day 60

Anxiety and Distress Are Useless

Rejoice in the Lord always; again I will say, Rejoice. Let all men know your forbearance. The Lord is at hand. Have no anxiety about anything, but in everything by prayer and supplication with thanksgiving let your requests be made known to God. And the peace of God, which passes all understanding, will keep your hearts and your minds in Christ Jesus. (Phil. 4:4–7)

There is no reason for us to be in a state of great anxiety when evils threaten; we must remember that God is very near us as our protector. *The Lord is at hand for those who are troubled in heart, and he will save those who are downcast in spirit. The tribulations of the just are many, and the Lord will rescue them from them all.* If we do our best to obey and keep his commandments, he does not delay in giving us what he has promised. (St. Ambrose)[66]

At every Mass you attend, right after you pray the Lord's Prayer aloud with the congregation, the priest celebrant asks the Lord God on behalf of the congregation that "we may be always free from sin and safe from all distress, as we await the blessed hope and the coming of our Savior, Jesus Christ."[67] These, then, are the three major themes that Holy Mother Church places before you in the celebration of Mass just before you receive the "source and summit of the Christian life," the Most Holy Eucharist (see *Lumen Gentium* 11, CCC 1324): to be *free from sin*, to be *safe from all distress*, and to *await the blessed hope* of Christ's Second Coming. Let these powerful themes from Holy Mass cast anxiety and distress out of your life. (See days 51, 65, 92, 114, 142, and 155.)

[66] Treatise on the Letter to the Philippians, in *Liturgy of the Hours*, vol. IV, 335.
[67] *Roman Missal*, English translation according to the Third Typical Edition (Totowa, NJ: Catholic Book Publishing, 2011), 517.

Day 61

State of Sanctifying Grace

Therefore, since we are justified by faith, we have peace with God through our Lord Jesus Christ. Through him we have obtained access to this grace in which we stand, and we rejoice in our hope of sharing the glory of God. More than that, we rejoice in our sufferings, knowing that suffering produces endurance, and endurance produces character, and character produces hope, and hope does not disappoint us, because God's love has been poured into our hearts through the Holy Spirit who has been given to us. (Rom. 5:1–5)

If I am not [in a state of grace], may it please God to put me in it; if I am [in a state of grace], may it please God to keep me there. (St. Joan of Arc)[68]

The Church's universal *Catechism* teaches that sanctifying grace is the "grace which heals our human nature wounded by sin by giving us a share in the divine life of the Trinity. It is a habitual, supernatural gift which continues the work of sanctifying us — of making us 'perfect,' holy, and Christlike" (*CCC* glossary, s.v. "sanctifying grace"; see *CCC* 1999). Only mortal sin removes you from a state of sanctifying grace. Don't fall into a state of mortal sin. That is a trap set by the devil. (See days 81, 97, 168, 185, 187, 189, and 197.)

---

[68] Quoted in *CCC* 2005. This statement is St. Joan's response to a question set as a trap by her ecclesiastical judges, who asked her whether she was in a state of God's grace.

Day 62

Drawing Closer to God

Submit yourselves therefore to God. Resist the devil and he will flee from you. Draw near to God and he will draw near to you. Cleanse your hands, you sinners, and purify your hearts, you men of double mind.... Humble yourselves before the Lord and he will exalt you. (James 4:7–8, 10)

[T]he man who cleanses his heart of every created thing and every evil desire will see the image of the divine nature in the beauty of his own soul....

When the mists of sin no longer cloud the eye of your soul, you see that blessed vision clearly in the peace and purity of your own heart. That vision is nothing else than the holiness, the purity, the simplicity and all the other glorious reflections of God's nature, through which God himself is seen. (St. Gregory of Nyssa)[69]

The great Doctor of the Church St. Cyril of Alexandria tells us, "After Christ had completed his mission on earth, it still remained necessary for us to become sharers in the divine nature of the Word. We had to give up our own life and be so transformed that we would begin to live an entirely new kind of life that would be pleasing to God."[70] God's desire for you is to embrace virtue and shun vice; to do good and avoid evil; to pursue activity that works toward your betterment and not toward your detriment. By doing so *daily*, you can draw closer to Him — *daily*. Remember that Almighty God calls you to Himself, and intimately so. Give Him your life — the very life He has given you. In your prayer each day, give back to the Giver the gift He has given you. (See days 7, 41, 52, 144, 152, 162, 184, 197 and 200.)

[69] *Orat. 6 De beatitudinibus*, in *Liturgy of the Hours*, vol. III, 413–414.
[70] *Commentary on the Gospel of John*, bk. 10, in *Liturgy of the Hours*, vol. II, 990.

Day 63

Loving One's Enemies

But I say to you that hear, Love your enemies, do good to those who hate you, bless those who curse you, pray for those who abuse you. (Luke 6:27–28)

The perfection of brotherly love lies in the love of one's enemies. We can find no greater inspiration for this than grateful remembrance of the wonderful patience of Christ....

... Further, if [someone] wishes to savor the joy of brotherly love with greater perfection and delight, he must extend even to his enemies the embrace of true love. (St. Aelred)[71]

To love your enemies can be one of the toughest imperatives that Jesus gives you. Why? Because it will take a firm and deliberate act of your will to overcome what your feelings, passions, and emotions tell you about your enemies. Fortunately, however, your spiritual life advances based on such directives from your will, and not so much from your feelings, passions, and emotions. These "willed directives" of yours are founded on God's grace and your cooperation with it. Through prayer and spiritual training, your inordinate feelings, passions, and emotions become subject to your grace-guided and willed directives. (See days 13, 75, 135, 170, and 198.)

[71] *Mirror of Love*, bk. 3, 5, in *Liturgy of the Hours*, vol. II, 131–132.

Best-Laid Plans

We know that in everything God works for good with those who love him, who are called according to his purpose. (Rom. 8:28)

And when night comes, and you look back over the day and see how fragmentary everything has been, and how much you planned that has gone undone, and all the reasons you have to be embarrassed and ashamed: just take everything exactly as it is, put it in God's hands and leave it with Him. Then you will be able to rest in Him — really rest — and start the next day as a new life. (attributed to St. Teresa Benedicta of the Cross [St. Edith Stein])

Have you ever had a day when *nothing* goes as you had planned? This is evidence of the maxim "Man proposes, but God disposes." Even the phrase "best-laid plans" implies the impracticality — futility, even — of making plans when the possibility of carrying them out fully is sometimes uncertain. Nevertheless, God *does* want you to plan and plan *well*. This is the part of your cultivating the virtue of diligence in your life. Diligence is the capital virtue found halfway between the extremes of sloth and workaholism. Just be prepared for the reality that "things may not always go as planned," so when *that* happens, your response to it will be tempered, virtuous, and grace-filled. (See days 4, 7, 10, 18, 19, 191, and 200.)

Sharing in the Fruits of the Mass

Jesus said to them, "Truly, truly, I say to you, unless you eat the flesh of the Son of man and drink his blood, you have no life in you; he who eats my flesh and drinks my blood has eternal life, and I will raise him up at the last day. For my flesh is food indeed, and my blood is drink indeed. He who eats my flesh and drinks my blood abides in me, and I in him. As the living Father sent me, and I live because of the Father, so he who eats me will live because of me." (John 6:53–57)

This sacrifice [of the Mass] is so pleasing and acceptable to God that as soon as he has seen it he must immediately have pity on us and extend clemency to all who are truly repentant....

Moreover, it is eternal. It is offered ... each day for our consolation, and indeed at every hour and moment as well, so that we may have the strongest reason for comfort. That is why the Apostle adds: *He has secured an eternal redemption* [Heb. 9:12].

All who have embarked on true contrition and penance for the sins they have committed, and are firmly resolved not to commit sins again for the future but to persevere constantly in that pursuit of virtues which they have now begun, all these become sharers in this holy and eternal sacrifice [of the Mass]. (St. John Fisher)[72]

What a gift the Holy Sacrifice of the Mass is! It brings into your midst the Most Holy Eucharist — the "source and summit of the Christian life" (see *Lumen Gentium* 11; *CCC* 1324). The Eucharist is the most precious Body, Blood, Soul, and Divinity of your Lord Jesus

---

[72] *Commentary on the Psalms*, Ps. 129, in *Liturgy of the Hours*, vol. II, 351.

Christ under sacramental forms. Know this with absolute certainty: your faithful attendance and participation in Sunday Mass — a holy day of obligation — and your worthy reception of the Eucharist at it are most pleasing to Almighty God. (See days 21, 60, 72, 82, 92, 97, 99, 103, 114, 132, 142, 143, 144, 145, 155, and 199.)

Stumbling Blocks

For Jews demand signs and Greeks seek wisdom, but we preach Christ crucified, a stumbling block to Jews and folly to Gentiles, but to those who are called, both Jews and Greeks, Christ the power of God and the wisdom of God. (1 Cor. 1:22–24)

Remove all obstacles and stumbling blocks so that you will be able to go straight along the road to eternal life. Through a sincere faith prepare yourselves so that you may be free to receive the Holy Spirit. Through your penance begin to wash your garments; then, summoned to the spouse's bedchamber, you will be found spotless. (St. Cyril of Jerusalem)[73]

What are the stumbling blocks in your life that prevent you from making a greater commitment to Jesus Christ and His Bride, the Church? (see Eph. 5:21–33; John 19:31–35). What prevents you from monthly Confession? Weekly Eucharist? What makes you "stumble" when it comes to a steadfast commitment to lead your family in *daily* prayer — for example, in the family Rosary or the Divine Mercy Chaplet? Or in a prayer before and after meals? Is it vice? Is it a particular issue, a dependency, or an addiction? Are you simply embarrassed to *lead* in these things? Whatever it may be, clear away the stumbling blocks. (See days 31, 44, 88, 89, 96, 100, 108, 121, 125, 179, 182, and 185.)

---

[73] *Catecheses*, Cat. 3, in *Liturgy of the Hours*, vol. II, 1714.

Day 67

Living a Sacrificial Life

Through him then let us continually offer up a sacrifice of praise to God, that is, the fruit of lips that acknowledge his name. Do not neglect to do good and to share what you have, for such sacrifices are pleasing to God. (Heb. 13:15–16)

I give unceasing thanks to my God, who kept me faithful *in the day of my testing* [see 1 Cor. 10:13]. Today I can offer him sacrifice with confidence, giving myself as *a living victim* to Christ [see Rom. 8:18; 14:8], my Lord, who *kept me safe through all my trials* [see Rev. 3:10]. I can say now: *Who am I, Lord,* and what is my calling, that you worked through me with such divine power? [see 2 Sam. 7:18].... God showed me how to have faith in him for ever, as one who is never to be doubted. (St. Patrick)[74]

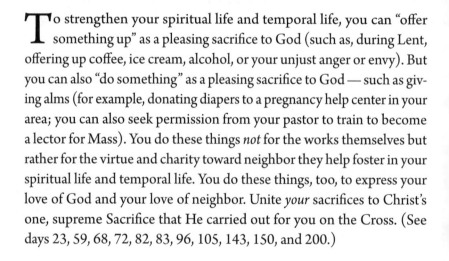

To strengthen your spiritual life and temporal life, you can "offer something up" as a pleasing sacrifice to God (such as, during Lent, offering up coffee, ice cream, alcohol, or your unjust anger or envy). But you can also "do something" as a pleasing sacrifice to God — such as giving alms (for example, donating diapers to a pregnancy help center in your area; you can also seek permission from your pastor to train to become a lector for Mass). You do these things *not* for the works themselves but rather for the virtue and charity toward neighbor they help foster in your spiritual life and temporal life. You do these things, too, to express your love of God and your love of neighbor. Unite *your* sacrifices to Christ's one, supreme Sacrifice that He carried out for you on the Cross. (See days 23, 59, 68, 72, 82, 83, 96, 105, 143, 150, and 200.)

---

[74] *Confession of St. Patrick,* no. 34, in *Liturgy of the Hours,* vol. II, 1710–1711.

Day 68

Vine and Branches

I am the vine, you are the branches. He who abides in me, and I in him, he it is that bears much fruit, for apart from me you can do nothing. (John 15:5)

The Lord calls himself the vine and those united to him branches in order to teach us how much we shall benefit from our union with him, and how important it is for us to remain in his love. By receiving the Holy Spirit, who is the bond of union between us and Christ, our Savior, those who are joined to him, as branches are to a vine, share in his own nature.

On the part of those who come to the vine, their union with him depends upon a deliberate act of the will; on his part, the union is effected by grace. Because we had good will, we made the act of faith that brought us to Christ, and received from him the dignity of adoptive sonship that made us his own kinsmen, according to the words of Saint Paul: *He who is joined to the Lord is one spirit with him* [1 Cor. 6:17]. (St. Cyril of Alexandria)[75]

Branches are pruned, at least annually, so that the vine (the primary plant and stem) may more readily send its growth nutrients to the branches that are freshened by their pruning. This sounds like the goal of the annual liturgical season of Lent: to forgo those areas in life that are keeping you from a greater relationship with Almighty God. But in reality, you should *always* be ready to be "pruned" of those things that are subtly making their way into your life and are not pleasing to Almighty God. What are examples of such things that are not pleasing to Almighty

---

[75] *Commentary on the Gospel of John*, bk. 10, in *Liturgy of the Hours*, vol. II, 833.

God? Internet pornography, addictions of all sorts, immoral and unnatural lifestyles, foul language, using the Lord's name in vain, lying, cheating, an aversion to the sick and the poor. Everyone's "list" is different, yet with some similarities. Begin to prune *now*. (See days 23, 25, 51, 52, 67, 162, 184, 185, and 200.)

Day 69

A Real Man Is a Virtuous Man

Let no evil talk come out of your mouths, but only such as is good for edifying, as fits the occasion, that it may impart grace to those who hear. And do not grieve the Holy Spirit of God, in whom you were sealed for the day of redemption. Let all bitterness and wrath and anger and clamor and slander be put away from you, with all malice, and be kind to one another, tenderhearted, forgiving one another, as God in Christ forgave you. (Eph. 4:29–32)

All holiness and perfection of soul lies in our love for Jesus Christ our God, who is our redeemer and our supreme good. It is part of the love of God to acquire and to nurture all the virtues which make a man perfect. (St. Alphonsus Liguori)[76]

An important point for men to remember is that the Latin word for "man" (as male) is *vir*. *Vir* is a Latin word that provides the etymology for the Latin word *virtus*, implying power, ability, and strength. *Virtus*, in English, is *virtue*. The important lesson here: to be *manly* is precisely to be *virtuous*. Do not forget this. (See days 9, 10, 43, 44, 52, 53, 90, 109, and 130.)

---

[76] *Tract. de praxis amandi Iesum Christum*, in *Liturgy of the Hours*, vol. IV, 1264.

Day 70

Righteous Anger versus Unrighteous Anger

Be angry but do not sin; do not let the sun go down on your anger, and give no opportunity to the devil. (Eph. 4:26–27)

May you never know anger, but be patient, long-suffering, persevering and chaste. May he [Christ] grant you a place among his saints....
... Pray, too, for our rulers, for our leaders, and for all those in power, even for those who persecute and hate you, and for those who are enemies of the cross. (St. Polycarp)[77]

There is such a thing as righteous anger (that is, just anger). But there is also such a thing as unrighteous anger (that is, unjust anger). For example, it is right and just for a man to be angry if, when he comes home from work, he finds a thief robbing his house. But it is neither right nor just for a man to become unjustly angered by the fact that his favorite sports team lost a game — and in the process of that unjust anger, makes everyone around him miserable. It is neither right nor just, either, to hold an ongoing, years-long grudge against your brother-in-law because he never returned your chainsaw. This is called "brooding over injuries," and it can be mortally sinful — if not venially sinful — depending on whether the situation at hand constitutes grave matter. The devil is very cunning (see Gen. 3:1). He likes to throw unrighteous, unjust anger into the mix of everyday life and living. Know the difference between righteous and unrighteous anger. (See days 93, 106, 129, and 195.)

---

[77] *Letter to the Philippians*, chap. 12, in *Liturgy of the Hours*, vol. IV, 331.

Day 71

Custody of the Eyes

The eye is the lamp of the body. So, if your eye is sound, your whole body will be full of light; but if your eye is not sound, your whole body will be full of darkness. If then the light in you is darkness, how great is the darkness! (Matt. 6:22–23)

A person's soul should be clean, like a mirror reflecting light. If there is rust on the mirror his face cannot be seen in it. In the same way, no one who has sin within him can see God.

But if you will you can be healed. Hand yourself over to the doctor, and he will open the eyes of your mind and heart. Who is to be the doctor? It is God, who heals and gives life through his Word and wisdom. (St. Theophilus of Antioch)[78]

The bodily sense of sight is particularly important to you as a man. This is because your sense of sight is essential to your roles as provider, protector, and defender of yourself, your loved ones, your friends, and your society and culture. Moreover, your role of defender extends to things that you do not want to see hurt, disrupted, or abused, such as truth, goodness, and moral virtue. The devil knows how important the sense of sight is for men, so he tries in every way to tempt you through sight and to draw you into sin by contorted, twisted ways. Guard your sight. Practice custody of the eyes by controlling what you permit yourself to see. (See days 45, 107, 131, 146, 167, 175, and 180.)

---

[78] From the book addressed to Autolycus, bk. 1, in *Liturgy of the Hours*, vol. II, 241.

Baptismal Priesthood and Ministerial Priesthood

Come to him, to that living stone, rejected by men but in God's sight chosen and precious; and like living stones be yourselves built into a spiritual house, to be a holy priesthood, to offer spiritual sacrifices acceptable to God through Jesus Christ.... You are a chosen race, a royal priesthood, a holy nation, God's own people, that you may declare the wonderful deeds of him who called you out of darkness into his marvelous light. Once you were no people but now you are God's people; once you had not received mercy but now you have received mercy. (1 Pet. 2:4–5, 9–10)

Listen now to what the Apostle urges us to do. *I appeal to you,* he says, *to present your bodies as a living sacrifice* [Romans 12:1]. By this exhortation of his, Paul has raised all men to priestly status.

How marvelous is the priesthood of the Christian, for he is both the victim that is offered on his own behalf, and the priest who makes the offering. He does not need to go beyond himself to seek what he is to immolate to God: with himself and in himself he brings the sacrifice he is to offer God for himself. The victim remains and the priest remains, always one and the same. Immolated, the victim still lives: the priest who immolates cannot kill. Truly it is an amazing sacrifice in which a body is offered without being slain and blood is offered without being shed....

Paul says: *I appeal to you by the mercy of God to present your bodies as a sacrifice, living and holy.* The prophet said the same thing: *Sacrifice and offering you did not desire, but you have prepared a body for me* [Heb. 10:5; see Ps. 40:6]. Each of us is called to be both a sacrifice to God and his priest. Do not forfeit what divine authority confers on you. Put on the garment of holiness, gird yourself with the belt of chastity. Let Christ be your helmet, let the cross on your forehead be your unfailing protection. Your breastplate should be the knowledge of God that he himself has given you.

Keep burning continually the sweet-smelling incense of prayer. Take up the sword of the Spirit. Let your heart be an altar. Then, with full confidence in God, present your body for sacrifice. God desires not death, but faith; God thirsts not for blood, but for self-surrender; God is appeased not by slaughter, but by the offering of your free will. (St. Peter Chrysologus)[79]

In Catholic theology are two priesthoods: the ministerial priesthood and the baptismal priesthood. The former is a sacrament — the Sacrament of Holy Orders. The latter is *not* a sacrament, but it is intimately bound to the Sacrament of Baptism. Both of these priesthoods, although different in *kind*, share in the threefold office of Jesus Christ as Priest, Prophet, and King. This is why, at every Mass you attend, you hear the priest celebrant say at the Offertory, that is, at the offering of the gifts of bread and wine, "Pray, brethren (brothers and sisters), that *my sacrifice and yours* may be acceptable to God, the almighty Father" (*Roman Missal*, 382, emphasis added). Only a priest can offer a sacrifice. And the laity sitting in the pews during Mass are, indeed, exercising their baptismal priesthood (see Rev. 1:5–6; 5:9–10). Your personal needs and intentions that you bring to Mass are offered in sacrifice — with yourself. It is important for you to know this liturgical reality and spirituality of the Holy Sacrifice of the Mass. Pope St. Leo the Great, writing as a ministerial priest about the baptismal priesthood, sums this all up by teaching: "For all, regenerated in Christ, are made kings by the sign of the cross; they are consecrated priests by the oil of the Holy Spirit [at Baptism], so that beyond the special service of our ministry as priests, all spiritual and mature Christians know that they are a royal race and sharers in the office of the priesthood."[80] (See days 23, 65, 67, 82, 97, 105, 143, 144, 145, 150, and 200.)

---

[79] *Sermo* 108, in *Liturgy of the Hours*, vol. II, 771–772.
[80] *Sermo* 4, in *Liturgy of the Hours*, vol. IV, 1549.

Christ Died for You

For if we have been united with him in a death like his, we shall certainly be united with him in a resurrection like his. We know that our old self was crucified with him so that the sinful body might be destroyed, and we might no longer be enslaved to sin. For he who has died is freed from sin. But if we have died with Christ, we believe that we shall also live with him. For we know that Christ being raised from the dead will never die again; death no longer has dominion over him. The death he died he died to sin, once for all, but the life he lives he lives to God. So you also must consider yourselves dead to sin and alive to God in Christ Jesus. (Rom. 6:5–11)

Perhaps someone can be found who will dare to die for a good man; but for the unjust man, for the wicked one, the sinner, who would be willing to die except Christ alone who is so just that he justifies even the unjust? (St. Augustine)[81]

Jesus Christ died for you because He wants you one day to be in Heaven with Him for all eternity with the Father and the Holy Spirit. Pray daily for your salvation — and *not* in a way that is scrupulous and based on *servile fear* (the fear of impending punishment). No. Rather, pray daily for salvation in a way that is filled with faith, hope, love, and trust based on *filial fear* (the fear that doesn't want to disappoint precisely because of reciprocal love and honor). (See days 22, 141, 147, and 200.)

---

[81] *Sermo* 23A, in *Liturgy of the Hours,* vol. IV, 189.

Be a Giver of Alms

Beware of practicing your piety before men in order to be seen by them; for then you will have no reward from your Father who is in heaven. Thus, when you give alms, sound no trumpet before you, as the hypocrites do in the synagogues and in the streets, that they may be praised by men. Truly, I say to you, they have their reward. But when you give alms, do not let your left hand know what your right hand is doing, so that your alms may be in secret; and your Father who sees in secret will reward you. (Matt. 6:1–4)

The giver of alms should be free from anxiety and full of joy. His gain will be greatest when he keeps back least for himself. The holy apostle Paul tells us: *He who provides seed for the sower will also provide bread for eating; he will provide you with more seed, and will increase the harvest of your goodness* [2 Cor. 9:10], in Christ Jesus our Lord, who lives and reigns with the Father and the Holy Spirit for ever and ever. Amen. (Pope St. Leo the Great)[82]

The Old Testament book of Tobit teaches, "Prayer is good when accompanied by fasting, almsgiving, and righteousness. A little with righteousness is better than much with wrongdoing. It is better to give alms than to treasure up gold. For almsgiving delivers from death, and it will purge away every sin. Those who perform deeds of charity and of righteousness will have fulness of life; but those who commit sin are the enemies of their own lives" (12:8–10). In Catholic theology, the "three eminent good works" to be practiced to help you overcome your

---

[82] *Sermo 10 in Quadragesima*, in *Liturgy of the Hours*, vol. II, 296.

sinfulness are prayer, fasting, and almsgiving. Why? Because they help to make you more other-centered and less self-centered. These good works are done not for their own sake but, rather, because of the charity they help foster between you and your neighbor. They also strengthen your love of God. Make prayer, fasting and almsgiving a strong part of your spiritual life *and* temporal life. (See days 32, 35, 48, 72, and 93.)

Day 75

The Ability to Love and Be Loved

We love, because he first loved us. If any one says, "I love God," and hates his brother, he is a liar; for he who does not love his brother whom he has seen, cannot love God whom he has not seen. And this commandment we have from him, that he who loves God should love his brother also. (1 John 4:19–21)

As soon as the living creature (that is, man) comes to be, a power of reason is implanted in us like a seed, containing within it the ability and the need to love. When the school of God's law admits this power of reason, it cultivates it diligently, skillfully nurtures it, and with God's help brings it to perfection....

... Since we received a command to love God, we possess from the first moment of our existence an innate power and ability to love....

... What desire is as urgent and overpowering as the desire implanted by God in a soul that is completely purified of sin and cries out in its love: *I am wounded by love* [Song of Sol. 2:5]? The radiance of the divine beauty is altogether beyond the power of words to describe. (St. Basil the Great)[83]

The most fundamental and innate vocation of the human person is to love. The problem is, there are some people who do not know how to love others because they do not love God or themselves. St. Aelred, the famous abbot, states: "If someone wishes to love himself, he must not allow himself to be corrupted by indulging his sinful nature. If he wishes to resist the promptings of his sinful nature he must enlarge the whole horizon of his love and contemplate the loving gentleness of the

---

[83] *Detailed Rules for Monks*, resp. 2, 1, in *Liturgy of the Hours*, vol. III, 59–60.

humanity of the Lord."[84] Love God and love yourself; through these, you will learn to love others, even your enemies. (See days 27, 63, 76, 135, 158, and 173.)

[84] *Mirror of Love*, bk. 3, 5, in *Liturgy of the Hours*, vol. II, 132.

Love of God and Love of Neighbor

"You shall love the Lord your God with all your heart, and with all your soul, and with all your mind, and with all your strength.... You shall love your neighbor as yourself." There is no other commandment greater than these. (Mark 12:30–31)

The most certain sign, in my opinion, as to whether or not we are observing these two laws [that is, love of God and love of neighbor] is whether we observe well the love of neighbor. We cannot know whether or not we love God, although there are strong indications for recognizing that we do love Him; but we can know whether we love our neighbor. And be certain that the more advanced you see you are in love for your neighbor the more advanced you will be in the love of God. (St. Teresa of Avila)[85]

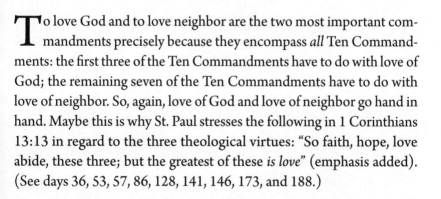

To love God and to love neighbor are the two most important commandments precisely because they encompass *all* Ten Commandments: the first three of the Ten Commandments have to do with love of God; the remaining seven of the Ten Commandments have to do with love of neighbor. So, again, love of God and love of neighbor go hand in hand. Maybe this is why St. Paul stresses the following in 1 Corinthians 13:13 in regard to the three theological virtues: "So faith, hope, love abide, these three; but the greatest of these *is love*" (emphasis added). (See days 36, 53, 57, 86, 128, 141, 146, 173, and 188.)

---

[85] *Interior Castle*, Fifth Mansion, 3, 8.

Day 77

The Vision of God

And after six days Jesus took with him Peter and James and John his brother, and led them up a high mountain apart. And he was transfigured before them, and his face shone like the sun, and his garments became white as light. (Matt. 17:1–2)

The blessedness of seeing God is justly promised to the pure of heart. For the eye that is unclean would not be able to see the brightness of the true light, and what would be happiness to clear minds would be a torment to those that are defiled. Therefore, let the mists of worldly vanities be dispelled, and the inner eye be cleansed of all the filth of wickedness, so that the soul's gaze may feast serenely upon the great vision of God. (Pope St. Leo the Great)[86]

You may discern a "vision of God" and His greatness manifested in a multiplicity of ways within creation — for example, when gazing upon a beautiful mountain range, when observing a first-time mother with her newborn baby, or while partaking in the celebration of the Eucharist in a grand cathedral. You might even have a vision of God while working with the sick, the poor, or the downtrodden. God can also manifest Himself to you in the stillness of prayer and silence, in contemplation, within the quietness of your own heart. Your task is to discover the "vision of God" in this multiplicity of ways and draw closer to Him each time, every day, thus strengthening both your communication and your relationship with Him. Look for God. (See days 27, 40, 71, 78, 133, and 135.)

[86] *Sermo 95*, in *Liturgy of the Hours*, vol. IV, 225.

Day 78

Prayer and Converse with God

He was praying in a certain place, and when he ceased, one of his disciples said to him, "Lord, teach us to pray, as John taught his disciples." And he said to them, "When you pray, say: 'Father, hallowed be thy name. Thy kingdom come. Give us each day our daily bread; and forgive us our sins, for we ourselves forgive every one who is indebted to us; and lead us not into temptation.'" (Luke 11:1–4)

Our spirit should be quick to reach out toward God, not only when it is engaged in meditation; at other times also, when it is carrying out its [daily] duties, caring for the needy, performing works of charity, [and] giving generously in the service of others, our spirit should long for God and call him to mind, so that these works may be seasoned with the salt of God's love, and so make a palatable offering to the Lord of the universe. Throughout the whole of our lives we may enjoy the benefit that comes from prayer if we devote a great deal of time to it. (St. John Chrysostom)[87]

※————————————※

Set times for organized, vocal, or meditative prayer are good because they can lead you to commit to daily prayer times and routines; prayers such as the Our Father and the Glory Be, the Divine Mercy Chaplet and the Rosary, and *Lectio Divina* (a contemplative way of reading Sacred Scripture — the Bible) can be included here too. But don't forget that prayer can also simply be conversation with God — a conversation from your heart to God. In fact, St. Clement of Alexandria said just that:

---

[87] *Hom. 6 De precatione*, in *Liturgy of the Hours*, vol. II, 69.

"Prayer is conversation with God."[88] So, when it comes to prayer, it's not a question of either-or but, rather, both-and: prayerful "conversation with God" may be *both* a more rote, set, and organized style of vocal or meditative prayer *and* a heart-to-heart conversation as you would have with a dear parent or a close friend. (See days 27, 40, 77, 133, and 135.)

[88] Paul Thigpen, *A Dictionary of Quotes from the Saints* (Ann Arbor, MI: Servant Publications, 2001), 170.

Temptation

And lead us not into temptation, but deliver us from evil. (Matt. 6:13)

As the pilot of a vessel is tried in the storm; as the wrestler is tried in the ring; the soldier in the battle, and the hero in adversity: so is the Christian tried in temptation. (St. Basil the Great)[89]

A second-century homily gives these insightful words: "For the sake of eternal life, my brothers, let us do the will of the Father who called us, resisting the temptations that lead us into sin and striving earnestly to advance in virtue. Let us revere God for fear of the evils that spring from impiety."[90] Now, *that's* a lesson worth learning from: a holy reverence for God and a pious devotional life can help you advance in virtue and strengthen you against temptation. (See days 3, 16, 46, 78, 109, 118, 126, 148, and 190.)

[89] Thigpen, *A Dictionary of Quotes*, 228.
[90] Quoted in *Liturgy of the Hours*, vol. IV, 516.

Day 80

Pursue Good, True, and Beautiful Things

Finally, brethren, whatever is true, whatever is honorable, whatever is just, whatever is pure, whatever is lovely, whatever is gracious, if there is any excellence, if there is anything worthy of praise, think about these things. What you have learned and received and heard and seen in me, do; and the God of peace will be with you. (Phil. 4:8–9)

Virtue is a very wonderful thing for us. It is the good of life, the fruit of a clear conscience, and the peace of the innocent. (St. Ambrose)[91]

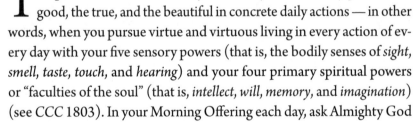

The peace of God resides in you when you habitually pursue the good, the true, and the beautiful in concrete daily actions — in other words, when you pursue virtue and virtuous living in every action of every day with your five sensory powers (that is, the bodily senses of *sight, smell, taste, touch,* and *hearing*) and your four primary spiritual powers or "faculties of the soul" (that is, *intellect, will, memory,* and *imagination*) (see *CCC* 1803). In your Morning Offering each day, ask Almighty God to grant you clarity to know what is good, true, and beautiful in every circumstance of every day and the grace to pursue it courageously with these nine great gifts of the body-soul composite that you are in your human nature. (See days 3, 28, 30, 118, 126, 134, 156, 164, 180, and 191.)

---

[91] Schroeder, *Every Day Is a Gift*, 181.

Day 81

Rising to the Heights

If then you have been raised with Christ, seek the things that are above, where Christ is, seated at the right hand of God. Set your minds on things that are above, not on things that are on earth. (Col. 3:1–2)

If we follow Christ closely we shall be allowed, even on this earth, to stand as it were on the threshold of the heavenly Jerusalem, and enjoy the contemplation of that everlasting feast, like the blessed apostles, who in following the Savior as their leader, showed, and still show, the way to obtain the same gift from God. (St. Athanasius)[92]

Almighty God desires the absolute best for you in this life. Even amid any trials, sufferings, or tribulations you might experience, the triune Godhead — Father, Son, and Holy Spirit — desires that you "rise to the heights" with His sanctifying grace to guide you as a faithful son striving for spiritual perfection so as to obtain salvation in Heaven. Regular reception of the Sacraments of Reconciliation and Eucharist — which, in turn, can help you to cultivate a strong spiritual life — are just two examples of how you can grow in love, holiness, and God's sanctifying grace. (See days 5, 14, 26, 34, 47, 61, 81, 97, 168, 185, 187, 189, 197, and 198.)

---

[92] Easter letter, Ep. 14, in *Liturgy of the Hours*, vol. II, 342.

Day 82

The Perfect Sacrifice

Now as they were eating, Jesus took bread, and blessed, and broke it, and gave it to the disciples and said, "Take, eat; this is my body." And he took a cup, and when he had given thanks he gave it to them, saying, "Drink of it, all of you; for this is my blood of the covenant, which is poured out for many for the forgiveness of sins." (Matt. 26:26–28)

Hold fast to this and never doubt it: the only-begotten Son, God the Word, becoming man offered himself for us to God as a fragrant offering and sacrifice. In the time of the old testament, patriarchs, prophets and priests sacrificed animals in his honor, and in honor of the Father and the Holy Spirit as well. Now in the time of the new testament the holy catholic Church throughout the world never ceases to offer the sacrifice of bread and wine, in faith and love, to him and to the Father and the Holy Spirit, with whom he shares one godhead.

Those animal sacrifices foreshadowed the flesh of Christ which he would offer for our sins, though himself without sin, and the blood which he would pour out for the forgiveness of our sins. In this sacrifice there is thanksgiving for, and commemoration of, the flesh of Christ that he offered for us, and the blood that the same God poured out for us. (St. Fulgentius of Ruspe)[93]

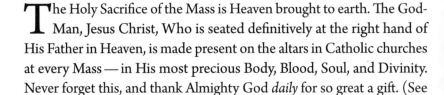

The Holy Sacrifice of the Mass is Heaven brought to earth. The God-Man, Jesus Christ, Who is seated definitively at the right hand of His Father in Heaven, is made present on the altars in Catholic churches at every Mass — in His most precious Body, Blood, Soul, and Divinity. Never forget this, and thank Almighty God *daily* for so great a gift. (See days 59, 65, 67, 72, 83, 96, 97, 143, 144, and 145.)

[93] Treatise on faith addressed to Peter, chap. 22, 62, in *Liturgy of the Hours*, vol. II, 384.

Day 83

Sacrificing Yourself to God

When Jesus had received the vinegar, he said, "It is finished"; and he bowed his head and gave up his spirit. (John 19:30)

[W]e must sacrifice ourselves to God, each day and in everything we do, accepting all that happens to us for the sake of the Word, imitating his passion by our sufferings, and honoring his blood by shedding our own. We must be ready to be crucified. (St. Gregory Nazianzen)[94]

In Catholic circles, have you ever heard the phrase "offer it up"? There's a lot of wisdom to it. Any well-written Morning Offering prayer, for example, will make some mention of offering up your prayers, sufferings, sorrows, joys, and good works of that day for the praise of Almighty God — as well as to make reparation for sin (your own and others') and for the conversion of sinners and the union of all Christians — in short, for the sanctification and salvation of the world. Pray daily a worthy Morning Offering that includes these elements, and offer these pleasing sacrifices to Almighty God. (See days 59, 67, 80, 82, 96, 143, 147, and 158.)

---

[94] *Oratio* 45, in *Liturgy of the Hours*, vol. II, 393.

Day 84

Choose Your Friends Wisely

There are friends who pretend to be friends, but there is a friend who sticks closer than a brother. (Prov. 18:24)

This is what truly perfect, stable and lasting friendship is, a tie that envy cannot spoil, nor suspicion weaken, nor ambition destroy. A friendship so tempted yielded not an inch, was buffeted but did not collapse. In the face of so many insults, it remained unshaken. *Go*, therefore, *and do likewise* [see Luke 10:37]. (St. Aelred)[95]

As you learned in the Scripture passage for day 52, above, the book of Sirach 6:14–17 teaches, "A faithful friend is a sturdy shelter: he that has found one has found a treasure. There is nothing so precious as a faithful friend, and no scales can measure his excellence. A faithful friend is an elixir of life; and those who fear the Lord will find him. Whoever fears the Lord directs his friendship aright." With true friends, virtue is reciprocally learned. In other words, your true friends should lead you to grow in virtue, and, as a true friend yourself, you should lead others to grow in virtue. True friendship does *not* lend itself to sinful or immoral behavior. This truth is taught in 1 Corinthians 15:33:"Do not be deceived: 'Bad company ruins good morals.'" Choose your friends wisely. (See days 23, 25, 52, 56, 57, 158, and 197.)

---

[95] *Treatise on Spiritual Friendship*, bk. 3, in *Liturgy of the Hours*, vol. III, 400.

Day 85

Encouragement

Since we belong to the day, let us be sober, and put on the breastplate of faith and love, and for a helmet the hope of salvation. For God has not destined us for wrath, but to obtain salvation through our Lord Jesus Christ, who died for us so that whether we wake or sleep we might live with him. Therefore encourage one another and build one another up, just as you are doing. (1 Thess. 5:8–11)

The Gospel of God's love for man, the Gospel of the dignity of the person and the Gospel of life are a single and indivisible Gospel. (Pope St. John Paul II)[96]

❖──────────❖

Humans are social beings by nature. We are not meant to be isolated beings. Genesis 2:18, for example, teaches that "it is not good that the man should be alone." Also, when Jesus teaches His disciples to pray, note that He gives them the Lord's Prayer (the Our Father) in the first person *plural* — not in the first person *singular*. He teaches you to pray, "Give *us* this day *our* daily bread" — not "Give *me* this day *my* daily bread." St. Anthony of the Desert made his hermit monks prove that they could first live *in community* before he would let them go out and live a life of solitude and prayer alone in a hermitage — and even then, there were times throughout the liturgical year when the hermits had to rejoin community life for a set time, for example, at Christmas and Easter. The lesson, here, is this: as social beings, we need to *encourage one another* toward holiness, to become great saints. Holiness is not an isolated task. Remember: God, neighbor, love, and life. (See days 95, 101, 149, and 191.)

---

[96] Encyclical *Evangelium Vitae* (March 25, 1995), no. 2.

Day 86

Increasing Your Love

And it is my prayer that your love may abound more and more, with knowledge and all discernment, so that you may approve what is excellent, and may be pure and blameless for the day of Christ, filled with the fruits of righteousness which come through Jesus Christ, to the glory and praise of God. (Phil. 1:9–11)

[W]hen our mind is strong and free from all anxiety, it is able to taste the riches of divine consolation, and to preserve, through love, the memory of this taste. This teaches us what is best with absolute certainty. As Saint Paul says: *My prayer is that your love may increase more and more in knowledge and insight, and so enable you to choose what is best* [Phil. 1:9–10]. (Diadochus of Photice)[97]

❧────────────❧

Growing in love for both God and neighbor is a prominent theme throughout the New Testament. For example, 1 Thessalonians 3:12–13 reads: "May the Lord make you increase and abound in love to one another and to all men, as we do to you, so that he may establish your hearts unblamable in holiness before our God and Father, at the coming of our Lord Jesus with all his saints." Regardless of your past or present moral failings or state of affairs, no matter your temperament or personality, *never* let the devil tell you that you cannot grow more and more in love. God's Word tells you otherwise. (See days 27, 36, 57, 76, 87, 89, 93, 94, 95, 120, 128, 141, and 188.)

---

[97] *On Spiritual Perfection*, chap. 6, in *Liturgy of the Hours*, vol. III, 155.

Day 87

Willingly Boast of Your Weaknesses

He said to me, "My grace is sufficient for you, for my power is made perfect in weakness." I will all the more gladly boast of my weaknesses, that the power of Christ may rest upon me. For the sake of Christ, then, I am content with weaknesses, insults, hardships, persecutions, and calamities; for when I am weak, then I am strong. (2 Cor. 12:9–10)

Your weaknesses and deficiencies ought to make you humble, but you should also throw all of them into the fire of the love of God, where they will be devoured and consumed like a straw mattress thrown into a great furnace. (St. Paul of the Cross)[98]

N ever wallow in the mire of self-discouragement and say that "there is no hope for me" amid your weaknesses, trials, and tribulations. This would be a lie of the Evil One. Rather, take your cue from the words of the two St. Pauls quoted above. Acknowledge your faults, imperfections, and crosses of every kind — in a word, your *weaknesses* — all the while striving for holiness and perfection through grace in Jesus Christ. If your weaknesses involve mortally sinful matter, get up each time after a fall. Immediately make a perfect Act of Contrition and then go to Confession as soon as is reasonably possible. Seek out spiritual direction to overcome vice. Strive to overcome even habitual venial sin. (See days 24, 49, 58, and 185.)

[98] Thigpen, *A Dictionary of Quotes*, 245.

Signs and Persecutions

Then he said to them, "Nation will rise against nation, and kingdom against kingdom; there will be great earthquakes, and in various places famines and pestilences; and there will be terrors and great signs from heaven. But before all this they will lay their hands on you and persecute you, delivering you up to the synagogues and prisons, and you will be brought before kings and governors for my name's sake. This will be a time for you to bear testimony. Settle it therefore in your minds, not to meditate beforehand how to answer; for I will give you a mouth and wisdom, which none of your adversaries will be able to withstand or contradict. You will be delivered up even by parents and brothers and kinsmen and friends, and some of you they will put to death; you will be hated by all for my name's sake. But not a hair of your head will perish. By your endurance you will gain your lives." (Luke 21:10–19)

To enter the kingdom of God we must endure many tribulations [Acts 14:22]. If there are many persecutions, there are many testings; where there are many crowns of victory, there are many trials of strength. It is then to your advantage if there are many persecutors; among many persecutions you may more easily find a path to victory. (St. Ambrose)[99]

❖━━━━━━━━━❖

As a faithful Catholic Christian, you are not exempt from trial and persecution. You already know this. Jesus tells you this plainly in the above passage from the Gospel of St. Luke. Jesus also tells you that there will be signs. Some of those signs, mentioned above, can be said to be taking place now or can be said to have already taken place. Even

---

[99] Exposition of Psalm 118, chap. 20, in *Liturgy of the Hours*, vol. III, 1309.

your nonbelieving family members may cause conflict with you when you attempt to stand up for the truths of Jesus Christ and His Bride, the Church; this, too, is a sign and type of persecution. With steadfast faith, always be ready for such signs and persecutions. (See days 66, 89, 90, 100, 108, 121, 125, 179, and 182.)

Day 89

Red Martyrdom and White Martyrdom

Consider him who endured from sinners such hostility against himself, so that you may not grow weary or fainthearted. In your struggle against sin you have not yet resisted to the point of shedding your blood. (Heb. 12:3–4)

[W]e read in the Proverbs of Solomon: *If you sit down to eat at the table of a ruler, observe carefully what is set before you; then stretch out your hand, knowing that you must provide the same kind of meal yourself* [see Prov. 23]. What is this ruler's table if not the one at which we receive the body and blood of him who laid down his life for us?....

At this table of the Lord we do not commemorate the martyrs in the same way as we commemorate others who rest in peace. We do not pray for the martyrs as we pray for those others, rather, they pray for us, that we may follow in their footsteps. They practiced the perfect love of which the Lord said there could be none greater. They provided "the same kind of meal" [body and blood given] as they had themselves received at the Lord's table....

... Inasmuch, then, as they shed their blood for their brothers, the martyrs provided "the same kind of meal" as they had received at the Lord's table. Let us then love one another as Christ also loved us and gave himself up for us. (St. Augustine)[100]

St. Ambrose teaches, "As there are many kinds of persecution, so there are many kinds of martyrdom. Every day you are a witness to Christ.... How many hidden martyrs there are, bearing witness to Christ each day

[100] *Treatise on John, Tract. 84, in Liturgy of the Hours*, vol. II, 449–451.

and acknowledging Jesus as the Lord!"[101] As a faithful Catholic, are you ready and willing to face either a red martyrdom or white martyrdom for the truth of Jesus Christ? A red martyrdom is a martyrdom of blood; that is, of actually dying for the Faith, of dying for Jesus Christ and His Bride, the Church, which is the "pillar and bulwark of the truth" (see Eph. 5:21–33; John 19:31–35; 1 Tim. 3:15–16). A white martyrdom is the martyrdom of enduring trials, tribulations, and persecutions — sometimes constant — because of your faith in and defense of Jesus Christ and His Bride, the Church. As a committed Catholic man of God, you should always be ready for either martyrdom — or *both*. Pray daily to have the strength for this and to *stand firm and be strong* (see 1 Cor. 16:13). (See days 66, 88, 90, 100, 108, 121, 125, 128, 151, 179, and 182.)

---

[101] *Sermo* 20, in *Liturgy of the Hours*, vol. IV, 1475–1476.

Day 90

Heroic Suffering and Heroic Virtue

Then Jesus, crying with a loud voice, said, "Father, into thy hands I commit my spirit!" And having said this he breathed his last. (Luke 23:46)

[W]e are heirs of God, coheirs with Christ [Rom. 8:17]. A coheir of Christ is one who is glorified along with Christ. The one who is glorified along with him is one who, by suffering for him, suffers along with him.

To encourage us in suffering, [St.] Paul adds that all our sufferings are small in comparison with the wonderful reward that will be revealed in us; our labors do not deserve the blessings that are to come. We shall be restored to the likeness of God, and counted worthy of seeing him face to face. (St. Ambrose)[102]

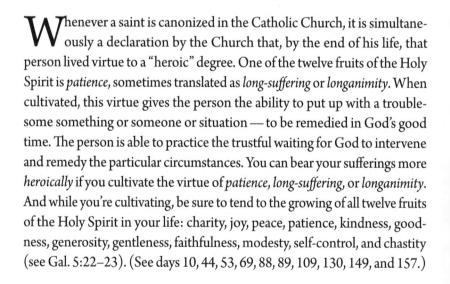

Whenever a saint is canonized in the Catholic Church, it is simultaneously a declaration by the Church that, by the end of his life, that person lived virtue to a "heroic" degree. One of the twelve fruits of the Holy Spirit is *patience*, sometimes translated as *long-suffering* or *longanimity*. When cultivated, this virtue gives the person the ability to put up with a troublesome something or someone or situation — to be remedied in God's good time. The person is able to practice the trustful waiting for God to intervene and remedy the particular circumstances. You can bear your sufferings more *heroically* if you cultivate the virtue of *patience, long-suffering,* or *longanimity.* And while you're cultivating, be sure to tend to the growing of all twelve fruits of the Holy Spirit in your life: charity, joy, peace, patience, kindness, goodness, generosity, gentleness, faithfulness, modesty, self-control, and chastity (see Gal. 5:22–23). (See days 10, 44, 53, 69, 88, 89, 109, 130, 149, and 157.)

---

[102] Epistle 35, in *Liturgy of the Hours*, vol. III, 183–184.

Day 91

Perfection

You, therefore, must be perfect, as your heavenly Father is perfect. (Matt. 5:48)

It is quite true, my very dear friends, that God has made man's spirit unstable and changeable in order that man would not abide in evildoing, and also that, once in possession of the good, he would not stop short, but would step up from one good to a higher one, and to a loftier one still. Thus, advancing from virtue to virtue, he might reach the summit of perfection. (St. Anthony Zaccaria)[103]

In one real sense, Christian perfection simply means "never giving up" and striving always to do better "next time." God does not ask you to be successful each time but only to be faithful each time in getting back up and back on track on the road that leads to Him. Remember, in the fourteen Stations of the Cross, Jesus falls three times (i.e., in Stations 3, 7, and 9). These falls of Jesus are caused by real bodily fatigue during His walking the Way of the Cross to Calvary, for He had a real human nature just like yours in every way but without sin (see Heb. 4:15). So, with that fully human nature that He possessed, He also had a real human body subject to extreme exhaustion. But for *you*, however, the three falls of Jesus are *also symbolic* of moral falls. Each time, Jesus got back up — you know this by virtue of Stations 4, 8, and 10. So, when you fall, get back up. In all aspects of your life, strive for perfection: Never give up. And always get back up. (See days 24, 87, 89, 99, 134, and 200.)

---

[103] Letter 2, to Mr. Bartolomeo Ferrari and Mr. Giacomo Antonio Morigia, January 4, 1531, Barnabites, https://www.barnabites.com/letter-2/.

Day 92

Striving for Peace with All

Strive for peace with all men, and for the holiness without which no one will see the Lord. (Hebrews 12:14)

[T]he sacred heart [of Jesus] is an inexhaustible fountain and its sole desire is to pour itself out into the hearts of the humble so as to free them and prepare them to lead lives according to his good pleasure.

... Are you making no progress in prayer? Then you need only offer God the prayers which the Savior has poured out for us in the sacrament of the altar. Offer God his fervent love in reparation for your sluggishness. In the course of every activity, pray as follows: "My God, I do this or I endure that in the heart of your Son and according to his holy counsels. I offer it to you in reparation for anything blameworthy or imperfect in my actions." Continue to do this in every circumstance of life....

But above all preserve peace of heart. (St. Margaret Mary Alacoque)[104]

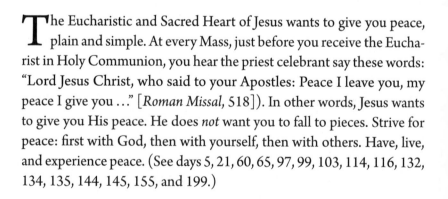

The Eucharistic and Sacred Heart of Jesus wants to give you peace, plain and simple. At every Mass, just before you receive the Eucharist in Holy Communion, you hear the priest celebrant say these words: "Lord Jesus Christ, who said to your Apostles: Peace I leave you, my peace I give you ..." [*Roman Missal*, 518]). In other words, Jesus wants to give you His peace. He does *not* want you to fall to pieces. Strive for peace: first with God, then with yourself, then with others. Have, live, and experience peace. (See days 5, 21, 60, 65, 97, 99, 103, 114, 116, 132, 134, 135, 144, 145, 155, and 199.)

---

[104] *Vie et Oeuvres* 2, in *Liturgy of the Hours*, vol. IV, 1488–1489.

Day 93

The Mercy of God

And he arose and came to his father. But while he was yet at a distance, his father saw him and had compassion, and ran and embraced him and kissed him. (Luke 15:20)

Confession heals, confession justifies, confession grants pardon of sin. All hope consists in confession. In confession there is a chance for mercy. Believe it firmly. Do not doubt, do not hesitate, never despair of the mercy of God. Hope and have confidence in confession. (St. Isidore of Seville)[105]

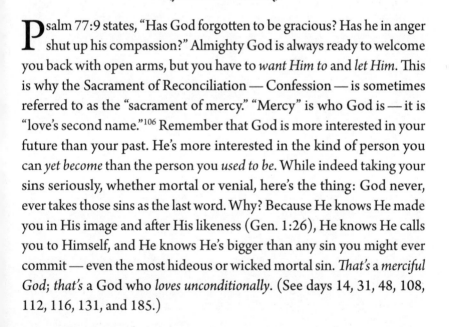

Psalm 77:9 states, "Has God forgotten to be gracious? Has he in anger shut up his compassion?" Almighty God is always ready to welcome you back with open arms, but you have to *want Him to* and *let Him*. This is why the Sacrament of Reconciliation — Confession — is sometimes referred to as the "sacrament of mercy." "Mercy" is who God is — it is "love's second name."[106] Remember that God is more interested in your future than your past. He's more interested in the kind of person you can *yet become* than the person you *used to be*. While indeed taking your sins seriously, whether mortal or venial, here's the thing: God never, ever takes those sins as the last word. Why? Because He knows He made you in His image and after His likeness (Gen. 1:26), He knows He calls you to Himself, and He knows He's bigger than any sin you might ever commit — even the most hideous or wicked mortal sin. *That's a merciful God; that's* a God who *loves unconditionally*. (See days 14, 31, 48, 108, 112, 116, 131, and 185.)

---

[105] Quoted in Mike Aquilina, *The Way of the Fathers: Praying with the Early Christians* (Huntington, IN: Our Sunday Visitor, 1999), 67.

[106] Pope St. John Paul II, encyclical *Dives in Misericordia* (November 30, 1980), no. 7.

Turning Back to God

"Our transgressions and our sins are upon us, and we waste away because of them; how then can we live?" … As I live, says the Lord GOD, I have no pleasure in the death of the wicked, but that the wicked turn from his way and live; turn back, turn back from your evil ways. (Ezek. 33:10–11)

The world hates Christians, so why give your love to it instead of following Christ, who loves you and has redeemed you?

… What man, stationed in a foreign land, would not want to return to his own country as soon as possible? Well, we look upon paradise [Heaven] as our country, and a great crowd of our loved ones awaits us there, a countless throng of parents, brothers and children longs for us to join them. Assured though they are of their own salvation, they are still concerned about ours. What joy both for them and for us to see one another and embrace! O the delight of that heavenly kingdom where there is no fear of death! O the supreme and endless bliss of everlasting life! (St. Cyprian)[107]

I t is never too late to turn back wholeheartedly to God with great love and a desire to do His will. Allow Him to show you, personally, the steadfastness of a Father's care and commitment for a son whom He loves with a love that knows no limits or bounds. Think of the Heaven that awaits you for being faithful to God while on earth. Also, pray for the salvation of your loved ones who have died. Pray for the blessed repose of their souls by having a Mass celebrated for them, or by praying a Rosary

[107]Sermon on man's mortality, chap. 18, in *Liturgy of the Hours*, vol. IV, 604.

or a Divine Mercy Chaplet for them. If their souls are in Purgatory, they can surely use these prayers. If their souls are already in Heaven, Catholic tradition holds that God will then apply your prayers where and to whom they are needed. Either way, ask your loved ones, also, to intercede for you — on your behalf — before the throne of Almighty God. Indeed, it is a holy and pious practice to pray for the dead (see 2 Macc. 12:43–46). (See days 5, 17, 127, and 200.)

Day 95

No Greater Love Than This

Greater love has no man than this, that a man lay down his life for his friends. (John 15:13)

If you seek an example of love: *"Greater love than this no man has, than to lay down his life for his friends"* [John 15:13]. Such a man was Christ on the cross. And if he gave his life for us, then it should not be difficult to bear whatever hardships arise for his sake. (St. Thomas Aquinas)[108]

The greatest love that you can have for another person in *this life* — that is, while living on earth — is to be willing to lay down your life for that person (see John 15:13). But the greatest love that you can have for another person even *beyond* this earthly life is to want to one day see that person in Heaven for all eternity. You wish and will that person's salvation. Never forget this. As a committed Catholic Christian, all those with whom you may have had a "falling out" — for however long (such as a parent, sibling, relative, friend, or coworker) — are called to enjoy an eternity with God in Heaven, just as you are. And by your lived example, you are meant to help them get there. Heal those broken relationships *now*. Do not let them go on any longer. (See days 53, 59, 86, 87, 89, 94, and 198.)

---

[108] *Collatio 6 super Credo in Deum,* in *Liturgy of the Hours,* vol. III, 1335.

Day 96

The Catholic Church Glories in the Cross of Jesus Christ

Far be it from me to glory except in the cross of our Lord Jesus Christ, by which the world has been crucified to me, and I to the world. (Gal. 6:14)

The Catholic Church glories in every deed of Christ. Her supreme glory, however, is the cross. Well aware of this, [St.] Paul says: *God forbid that I glory in anything but the cross of our Lord Jesus Christ!* (St. Cyril of Jerusalem)[109]

If the Cross is a major point of focus for the life of Christ's Bride, the Church (see Eph. 5:21–33; John 19:31–35), and you are a member of that Church, then the Cross should be a major focus in your life also. Contemplate the Cross. Meditate on what Jesus did in going to the Cross and dying on it — for you. The Sorrowful Mysteries of the Rosary provide a powerful point of reference for such meditation. Pray the Sorrowful Mysteries of the Rosary today and glory in the Cross of Jesus Christ, as the Church and St. Paul do. You'll be in good company if you do. (See days 59, 66, 67, 97, 100, 133, 134, 188, 191, and 197.)

---

[109] *Catecheses,* Cat. 13, in *Liturgy of the Hours,* vol. III, 157.

Jesus Christ as the Sacrificial Lamb

The next day he [John] saw Jesus coming toward him, and said, "Behold, the Lamb of God, who takes away the sin of the world!" (John 1:29)

In the Mosaic law a sacrificial lamb banished the destroyer. But now *it is the Lamb of God who takes away the sin of the world*. Will he not free us from our sins even more? The blood of an animal, a sheep, brought salvation. Will not the blood of the only-begotten Son bring us greater salvation? (St. Cyril of Jerusalem)[110]

At every Mass you attend, following the chanting or singing or reciting of the Agnus Dei (Lamb of God), just before the Rite of Communion, you hear the priest celebrant say these words, while showing the congregation the consecrated Eucharistic Host and the chalice, which contains the Lord's Precious Blood: "Behold the Lamb of God, behold him who takes away the sins of the world. Blessed are those called to the supper of the Lamb." After this, the congregation responds with words similar to the faithful centurion who felt unworthy that Jesus should enter his home and heal his paralyzed servant who was in great distress (see Matt. 8:5–13): "Lord, I am not worthy that you should enter under my roof, but only say the word and my soul shall be healed" (*Roman Missal*, 521). Like the faithful centurion, you too are not worthy — *even when you are* in a state of sanctifying grace with no known mortal sin on your soul. But your Lord Jesus Christ still comes to you to communicate His love to you — indeed, His very self to you — in Holy Communion, in the Most Holy Eucharist. (See days 21, 65, 72, 82, 92, 96, 99, 103, 114, 132, 134, 143, 144, 145, 155, 188, 191, 197, and 199.)

---

[110] *Catecheses*, Cat. 13, in *Liturgy of the Hours*, vol. III, 158.

Day 98

The Name "Christian"

And in Antioch the disciples were for the first time called Christians. (Acts 11:26)

Just beg for me the courage and endurance not only to speak but also to will what is right, so that I may not only be called a Christian, but prove to be one. For if I prove myself to be a Christian by martyrdom, then people will call me one, and my loyalty to Christ will be apparent when the world sees me no more.... Christianity shows its greatness when it is hated by the world. (St. Ignatius of Antioch)[111]

The above quote from St. Ignatius of Antioch serves as a good lead-in for you to answer the age-old question "What's in a name?" You should also want to ask the opposite question, "What's *not* in a name?" For the committed Catholic, the following are not in the name "Christian": embarrassment, lukewarmness or tepidity, indifference, disloyalty, deceit or duplicitous living. You get the point. Be a *committed* Christian—a committed Catholic Christian. Go all in. And call other men to do the same. St. Gregory of Nyssa gives you this encouragement: "If we truly think of Christ as our source of holiness, we shall refrain from anything wicked or impure in thought or act and thus show ourselves to be worthy bearers of his name. For the quality of holiness is shown not by what we say but by what we do in life."[112] Remember, too, what St. Peter teaches so valiantly regarding the Christian name when he writes: "But rejoice in so far as you share Christ's sufferings, that you may also rejoice and be glad when his glory is revealed. If you are reproached for the name

---

[111] *Letter to the Romans*, 3, in *Liturgy of the Hours*, vol. III, 324.
[112] *Treatise on Christian Perfection*, in *Liturgy of the Hours*, vol. IV, 107–108.

of Christ, you are blessed, because the spirit of glory and of God rests upon you.... Yet if one suffers as a Christian, let him not be ashamed, but under that name let him glorify God" (1 Pet. 4:13–14, 16). Nor forget what St. Luke the Evangelist writes in Acts 4:10, 12 regarding "the name of Jesus Christ of Nazareth": "There is salvation in no one else, for there is no other name under heaven given among men by which we must be saved." (See days 26, 55, 100, 103, 106, 107, 166, and 182.)

One Body in Christ, One Body of Christ

In Christ Jesus you are all sons of God, through faith. For as many of you as were baptized into Christ have put on Christ. There is neither Jew nor Greek, there is neither slave nor free, there is neither male nor female; for you are all one in Christ Jesus. (Gal. 3:26–28)

[Y]ou are one with Jesus as the body is one with the head. You must, then, have one breath with him, one soul, one life, one will, one mind, one heart. And he must be your breath, heart, love, life, your all. These great gifts in the follower of Christ originate from baptism. They are increased and strengthened through confirmation and by making good use of other graces that are given by God. Through the holy eucharist they are brought to perfection. (St. John Eudes)[113]

❖━━━━━━━━━❖

Are you one with Christ, your Head? As a baptized member of His Body, the Church, of which He is the Head, are you united with that Head? Are you united with the Church? Ideally, the multiple members of a body have union with their head for proper functioning. For example, St. Paul teaches in 1 Corinthians 12:12–14, 27: "For just as the body is one and has many members, and all the members of the body, though many, are one body, so it is with Christ. For by one Spirit we were all baptized into one body — Jews or Greeks, slaves or free — and all were made to drink of one Spirit. For the body does not consist of one member but of many.... Now you are the body of Christ and individually members of it." Heed these great lessons from St. Paul and St. John Eudes: be one with Christ, your Head, and one with His Body, the Church. Pope

---

[113] *Treatise on the Admirable Heart of Jesus*, bk. 1, 5, in *Liturgy of the Hours*, vol. IV, 1332.

Benedict XVI sums all this up beautifully by adding a strong tie-in to the Eucharist and your duty to live in conformity with Christ:

[St. Paul's] original definition of the Church as the "Body of Christ", which we do not find in other Christian authors of the first century, is well known (cf. 1 Cor 12:27; Eph 4:12; 5:30; Col 1:24).

We find the deepest root of this surprising designation of the Church in the Sacrament of the Body of Christ. St Paul said: "Because there is one bread, we who are many are one body" (1 Cor 10:17). In the same Eucharist, Christ gives us his Body and makes us his Body. Concerning this, St Paul said to the Galatians: "You are all one in Christ" (Gal 3:28). By saying all this, Paul makes us understand that not only does the belonging of the Church to Christ exist, but also a certain form of equality and identification of the Church with Christ himself.

From this, therefore, derive the greatness and nobility of the Church, that is, of all of us who are part of her: from our being members of Christ, an extension as it were of his personal presence in the world. And from this, of course, stems our duty to truly live in conformity with Christ. (General Audience, November 22, 2006)

(See days 21, 65, 92, 97, 100, 101, 103, 114, 132, 144, 145, 155, and 199.)

Genuine Care among the Bodily Members of Christ

For the body does not consist of one member but of many. If the foot should say, "Because I am not a hand, I do not belong to the body," that would not make it any less a part of the body. And if the ear should say, "Because I am not an eye, I do not belong to the body," that would not make it any less a part of the body. If the whole body were an eye, where would be the hearing? If the whole body were an ear, where would be the sense of smell? But as it is, God arranged the organs in the body, each one of them, as he chose. If all were a single organ, where would the body be? As it is, there are many parts, yet one body. The eye cannot say to the hand, "I have no need of you," nor again the head to the feet, "I have no need of you." On the contrary, the parts of the body which seem to be weaker are indispensable, and those parts of the body which we think less honorable we invest with the greater honor, and our unpresentable parts are treated with greater modesty, which our more presentable parts do not require. But God has so adjusted the body, giving the greater honor to the inferior part, that there may be no discord in the body, but that the members may have the same care for one another. If one member suffers, all suffer together; if one member is honored, all rejoice together. (1 Cor. 12:14–26)

There are many rooms in the Father's house because the body has many members. (St. Irenaeus)[114]

Always remember: as a baptized member of the Body of Christ, you are always working with and praying for the *other members* of

---

[114] *Against Heresies*, bk. 3, chap. 19, in *Liturgy of the Hours*, vol. III, 151.

that Body as well, both living and deceased. You are not isolated in your Christianity. You are not isolated in your Catholicism. You believe in the Church Triumphant and Her members in Heaven; you believe in the Church Militant and Her members still living on earth and *fighting the good fight of faith* (see 1 Tim. 6:12); and you believe in the Church Suffering (also known as the Church Penitent and the Church Purgative) and Her members in Purgatory. Regarding the Church Militant, your time, talent, and treasure are meant to assist in building up the Body of Christ, the Church. Never be envious or jealous of another member's proper functioning within the Body. Each has his own calling, gifts, and tasks that are meant to serve the Lord and His Bride, the Church (see Eph. 5:21–33; John 19:31–35). (See days 66, 88, 89, 96, 99, 101, 108, 121, 125, 179, and 182.)

Day 101

Love Is the Goal of the Body of Christ

If I speak in the tongues of men and of angels, but have not love, I am a noisy gong or a clanging cymbal. And if I have prophetic powers, and understand all mysteries and all knowledge, and if I have all faith, so as to remove mountains, but have not love, I am nothing. If I give away all I have, and if I deliver my body to be burned, but have not love, I gain nothing. (1 Cor. 13:1–3)

The spiritual building up of the body of Christ is achieved through love.... And there can be no more effective way to pray for this spiritual growth than for the Church, itself Christ's body, to make the offering of his body and blood in the sacramental form of bread and wine. *For the cup we drink is a participation in the blood of Christ, and the bread we break is a participation in the body of Christ. Because there is one loaf, we who are many are one body, since we all share the same bread* [1 Cor. 10:16–17]. And so we pray that, by the same grace which made the Church Christ's body, all its members may remain firm in the unity of that body through the enduring bond of love. (St. Fulgentius of Ruspe)[115]

In chapter 13 of his First Letter to the Corinthians, St. Paul talks about the importance of authentic love that is founded on truth, rooted in Jesus Christ. Just before that, in chapter 12, St. Paul teaches about the Body of Christ having many functioning members, each with its own gifts and tasks to help build up that Body in the midst of the modern world. But none of what is mentioned in chapter 12 means anything at all if a member of the Body of Christ does not also possess the love of

---

[115] From a book addressed to Monimus, bk. 2, in *Liturgy of the Hours*, vol. II, 652.

Christ. And it is the Most Holy Eucharist — Christ truly present in the consecrated Host — that helps all who receive it worthily to build up the Body of Christ in that love of *Christ Himself.* This is because, "in the blessed Eucharist is contained the whole spiritual good of the Church, namely Christ himself, our Pasch" (*CCC* 1324, quoting *Presbyterorum Ordinis* 5). Receive the Eucharist worthily and frequently, and help to build up the Body of Christ in the love of Christ. (See days 99, 100, 143, 145, and 177.)

The Virgin Mother of God

In the sixth month the angel Gabriel was sent from God to a city of Galilee named Nazareth, to a virgin betrothed to a man whose name was Joseph, of the house of David; and the virgin's name was Mary. And he came to her and said, "Hail, full of grace, the Lord is with you!" But she was greatly troubled at the saying, and considered in her mind what sort of greeting this might be. And the angel said to her, "Do not be afraid, Mary, for you have found favor with God. And behold, you will conceive in your womb and bear a son, and you shall call his name Jesus. He will be great, and will be called the Son of the Most High; and the Lord God will give to him the throne of his father David, and he will reign over the house of Jacob for ever; and of his kingdom there will be no end." (Luke 1:26–33)

It was fitting that the Virgin should give birth only to God; and it was also fitting that God should be born only of the Virgin. Accordingly, the Creator of mankind, in order that he might become a man by being born of a human being, had to seek out from among all mankind and designate as his mother a woman he knew would be worthy of him and pleasing to him. And so he chose a sinless virgin, that he might be born sinless and free of all stain. He chose a humble virgin, from whom he might come forth meek and humble of heart, to display a most necessary and salutary model of these virtues for all mankind. Thus, He allowed a virgin to conceive, in whom he had earlier inspired a vow of virginity, and required of her the merit of humility.

Otherwise, how could the angel afterward pronounce her full of grace, if she had the slightest good quality which did not come from grace? Thus she, who was to conceive and bring forth the holy of holies, must be sanctified physically and so she received the gift of virginity;

that she might be sanctified spiritually, she received the gift of humility. (St. Bernard)[116]

Do you have a relationship with God's own Mother? John the Apostle did. From the Cross, Jesus gave John to Mary, and He likewise gave Mary to John. The Gospel of St. John states, "When Jesus saw his mother, and the disciple whom he loved standing near, he said to his mother, 'Woman, behold, your son!' Then he said to the disciple, 'Behold, your mother!' And from that hour the disciple took her to his own home" (19:26–27). This is a model for you to follow in your own relationship with the Virgin Mother of God. Take her into your home as John did. Talk to her. Confide in her. Love her. Seek her maternal intercession in your struggles with the world, the flesh, and the devil. Put a blessed image of her in your home and in your place of work and ask her to lead you and your loved ones ever closer to her divine Son, Jesus Christ. She is thus the *Theotokos* — "God bearer." (See days 5, 103, 116, 135, 136, 159, 163, 182, and 196.)

---

[116] Homily 2, in praise of the Virgin Mother, in *Liturgy of the Hours*, vol. IV, 130.

Day 103

Emmanuel: God with Us

All this took place to fulfil what the Lord had spoken by the prophet: "Behold, a virgin shall conceive and bear a son, and his name shall be called Emmanuel" (which means, God with us). (Matt. 1:22–23)

The Lord himself has given us a sign here below and in the heights of heaven, a sign that man did not ask for because he never dreamt that such a thing would be possible. A virgin was with a child and she bore a son who is called Emmanuel, which means "God with us." (St. Irenaeus)[117]

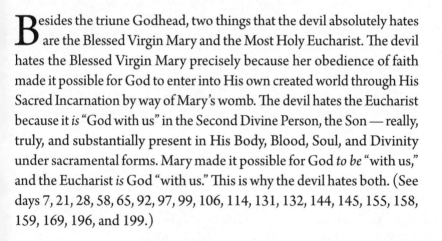

Besides the triune Godhead, two things that the devil absolutely hates are the Blessed Virgin Mary and the Most Holy Eucharist. The devil hates the Blessed Virgin Mary precisely because her obedience of faith made it possible for God to enter into His own created world through His Sacred Incarnation by way of Mary's womb. The devil hates the Eucharist because it *is* "God with us" in the Second Divine Person, the Son — really, truly, and substantially present in His Body, Blood, Soul, and Divinity under sacramental forms. Mary made it possible for God *to be* "with us," and the Eucharist *is* God "with us." This is why the devil hates both. (See days 7, 21, 28, 58, 65, 92, 97, 99, 106, 114, 131, 132, 144, 145, 155, 158, 159, 169, 196, and 199.)

---

[117] *Against Heresies*, bk. 3, chap. 19, in *Liturgy of the Hours*, vol. III, 151.

Day 104

Cooperating with God toward Salvation

And you, child, will be called the prophet of the Most High; for you will go before the Lord to prepare his ways, to give knowledge of salvation to his people in the forgiveness of their sins. (Luke 1:76–77)

Let us work for the food which does not perish — our salvation. (St. Bernard)[118]

Hebrews 5:9 states, "Being made perfect he [Jesus] became the source of eternal salvation to all who obey him." Know this: your Lord and Savior, Jesus Christ, *desires* your salvation. He is the *source* of your salvation. He gives you *knowledge* of your salvation. He wants you to *achieve* your salvation by cooperating with Him through your obedience to His revealed truth — a truth that is safeguarded by His one, holy, catholic, and apostolic Church through the deposit of faith. According to the *Catechism*, the deposit of faith is "the heritage of faith contained in Sacred Scripture and Tradition, handed on in the Church from the time of the Apostles, from which the Magisterium [the teaching authority of the Church] draws all that it proposes for belief as being divinely revealed" (*CCC* glossary, s.v. "deposit of faith"; see CCC 84; cf. 1202). Cooperate with God, and work out your salvation (see Phil. 2:12). (See days 20, 41, 111, 124, 128, 143, 160, 165, 188, and 194.)

---

[118] *Sermo de diversis* 15, in *Liturgy of the Hours*, vol. III, 203.

Day 105

The Purpose of the Apostolic Life

Jesus came and said to them, "All authority in heaven and on earth has been given to me. Go therefore and make disciples of all nations, baptizing them in the name of the Father and of the Son and of the Holy Spirit, teaching them to observe all that I have commanded you; and lo, I am with you always, to the close of the age." (Matt. 28:18–20)

The most resplendent manifestation of God's glory is the salvation of souls, whom Christ redeemed by shedding his blood. To work for the salvation and sanctification of as many souls as possible, therefore, is the preeminent purpose of the apostolic life. (St. Maximilian Kolbe)[119]

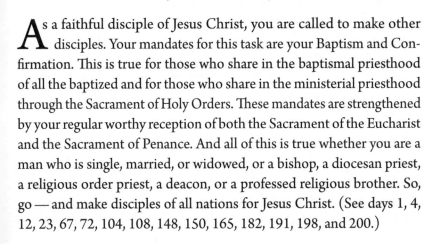

As a faithful disciple of Jesus Christ, you are called to make other disciples. Your mandates for this task are your Baptism and Confirmation. This is true for those who share in the baptismal priesthood of all the baptized and for those who share in the ministerial priesthood through the Sacrament of Holy Orders. These mandates are strengthened by your regular worthy reception of both the Sacrament of the Eucharist and the Sacrament of Penance. And all of this is true whether you are a man who is single, married, or widowed, or a bishop, a diocesan priest, a religious order priest, a deacon, or a professed religious brother. So, go — and make disciples of all nations for Jesus Christ. (See days 1, 4, 12, 23, 67, 72, 104, 108, 148, 150, 165, 182, 191, 198, and 200.)

---

[119] *Letters of St. Maximilian Mary Kolbe*, in *Liturgy of the Hours Supplement* (New York: Catholic Book Publishing, 1992), 11.

Day 106

Darkness and Light

Yet I am writing you a new commandment, which is true in him and in you, because the darkness is passing away and the true light is already shining. He who says he is in the light and hates his brother is in the darkness still. He who loves his brother abides in the light, and in it there is no cause for stumbling. (1 John 2:8–10)

May you consider truly good whatever leads to your goal and truly evil whatever makes you fall away from it. Prosperity and adversity, wealth and poverty, health and sickness, honors and humiliations, life and death, in the mind of the wise man, are not to be sought for their own sake, nor avoided for their own sake. But if they contribute to the glory of God and your eternal happiness, then they are good and should be sought. If they detract from this, they are evil and must be avoided. (St. Robert Bellarmine)[120]

The devil likes the darkness, but the committed Christian likes the light. There is no doubt about it: the devil likes to set traps for you in any number of ways or conditions, always playing on your weaknesses. And in doing so, he can also upset and even ruin your relationships with others. Just look at the seven capital sins and how they can not only bring you down *personally* but also bring down your relationships with others *socially* (for example, by having greed or envy toward another). So how do you combat this? You counteract the seven capital sins in your life by practicing each one's opposite corresponding virtue (that is, the seven capital virtues) in concrete actions throughout the day (see CCC 1803).

---

[120] *On the Ascent of the Mind to God*, Grad. 1, in *Liturgy of the Hours*, vol. IV, 1412–1413.

In other words, counteract pride with humility; greed or avarice with generosity; lust with chastity; anger with meekness or patience; gluttony with temperance; envy with kindness or fraternal love toward others; and sloth or acedia with diligence. Own this truth: a large part of your spiritual life should be disengaging the devil's daily traps. (See days 7, 28, 30, 35, 43, 58, 80, 103, 129, 130, 164, and 196.)

Seeing Things through the Eyes of Christian Faith

Then turning to the disciples he [Jesus] said privately, "Blessed are the eyes which see what you see! For I tell you that many prophets and kings desired to see what you see, and did not see it, and to hear what you hear, and did not hear it." (Luke 10:23–24)

When we entrust all the troubles of our earthly existence confidently to the divine heart [of Jesus], we are relieved of them. Then our soul is free to participate in the divine life. Then we walk by the side of the Savior on the path that He traveled on this earth during His earthly existence and still travels in His mystical afterlife. Indeed, with the eyes of faith, we penetrate into the secret depths of His hidden life within the pale of the Godhead. (St. Teresa Benedicta of the Cross [St. Edith Stein])[121]

Sometimes it may prove difficult for you to see things clearly, whether in your personal or professional life. At such times, it will take faith for you to "see things as God sees them" and to trust Him to get you through the conundrum — the difficulty or problem — at hand. Turn to Christ in such moments and ask Him to guide you with His vision of things — as He sees them — for your benefit. By doing so, you can arrive at the way of handling a situation in a way pleasing to God. Pope Francis provides this wonderful meditation on the subject:

> In faith, Christ is not simply the one in whom we believe, the supreme manifestation of God's love; he is also the one with whom

---

[121] "The Ethos of Women's Professions," in *Essays on Woman*, ed. Dr. Lucy Gelber and Romaeus Leuven, OCD, trans. Freda Mary Oben, 2nd ed., vol. 2 of *The Collected Works of Edith Stein* (Washington, D.C.: ICS Publications, 1996).

we are united precisely in order to believe. Faith does not merely gaze at Jesus, but sees things as Jesus himself sees them, with his own eyes: it is a participation in his way of seeing. In many areas in our lives we trust others who know more than we do. We trust the architect who builds our home, the pharmacist who gives us medicine for healing, the lawyer who defends us in court. We also need someone trustworthy and knowledgeable where God is concerned. Jesus, the Son of God, is the one who makes God known to us (cf. John 1:18). Christ's life, his way of knowing the Father and living in complete and constant relationship with him, opens up new and inviting vistas for human experience. (encyclical *Lumen Fidei* [June 29, 2013], no. 18)

Get into the habit of fostering a more conscious awareness of seeing things through the eyes of your Savior, Jesus Christ. And trust in Jesus ever more to help you grow in that Faith amid the most ordinary circumstances of everyday life. (See days 12, 13, 32, 42, 98, 51, 161, 166, 169, 182, 190, and 192.)

Day 108

The Church Is the Bride of Christ

Since it was the day of Preparation, in order to prevent the bodies from remaining on the cross on the sabbath (for that sabbath was a high day), the Jews asked Pilate that their legs might be broken, and that they might be taken away. So the soldiers came and broke the legs of the first, and of the other who had been crucified with him; but when they came to Jesus and saw that he was already dead, they did not break his legs. But one of the soldiers pierced his side with a spear, and at once there came out blood and water. He who saw it has borne witness — his testimony is true, and he knows that he tells the truth — that you also may believe. (John 19:31–35)

Now the Bride of Christ wishes to use the medicine of mercy rather than taking up arms of severity.... The Catholic Church, as she holds high the torch of Catholic truth at this ecumenical Council, wants to show herself a loving Mother to all: patient, kind, moved by compassion and goodness toward her separated children. (Pope St. John XXIII)[122]

As a Catholic, you believe that the Bride of Christ, the Church, which Jesus founded and which you know by Her four marks (one, holy, catholic, and apostolic), was born from our Lord's side on the Cross, when blood and water flowed out, symbolic of both the Sacrament of the Eucharist and the Sacrament of Baptism. Indeed, Vatican II teaches in *Sacrosanctum Concilium*, its Constitution on the Sacred Liturgy: "For it was from the side of Christ as He slept the sleep of death upon the cross

---

[122] Opening Address of the Second Vatican Ecumenical Council, *Gaudet Mater Ecclesia* (October 11, 1962), nos. 2–3, as quoted in Pope Francis's Bull of Indiction of the Extraordinary Jubilee Year of Mercy, *Misericordia Vultus* (April 11, 2015), no. 4.

that there came forth 'the wondrous sacrament of the whole Church' "
(no. 5, quoting the prayer before the second lesson for Holy Saturday, as
it was in the Roman Missal before the restoration of Holy Week).

Just as Eve was fashioned from the side of Adam, so was the Church
fashioned from the side of Christ. And as a Bride, the Church is also a
Mother — "Holy Mother Church." Now, just as a natural mother would
want to see her children have a relationship with God as well as with
herself, so the Church desires the same from Her baptized members.
Sacred worship and devotional piety are a big part of the reality of this
relationship. Such things as attending Mass regularly, partaking in the
sacraments, and fostering devotion and piety all lend themselves to both
the vertical and horizontal communions found in the life of Christ's Bride,
the Church. About this, Pope Benedict XVI eloquently states:

> There is also a Pauline letter that presents the Church as Christ's
> Bride (Eph 5:21–33).... [St. Paul] did so to express the intimacy
> of the relationship between Christ and his Church, both in the
> sense that she is the object of the most tender love on the part
> of her Lord, and also in the sense that love must be mutual and
> that we too therefore, as members of the Church, must show him
> passionate faithfulness.
>
> Thus, in short, a relationship of communion is at stake: the so
> to speak *vertical* communion between Jesus Christ and all of us,
> but also the *horizontal* communion between all who are distin-
> guished in the world by the fact that they "call on the name of our
> Lord Jesus Christ" (1 Cor 1:2). This is our definition: we belong
> among those who call on the name of the Lord Jesus Christ.
> (General Audience, November 22, 2006).

Love the Church. Love Her as the Bride of Christ. Love Her as your
Holy Mother. (See days 66, 88, 89, 100, 121, 125, 142, 179, and 182.)

Strong Man versus Weak Man

Therefore gird up your minds, be sober, set your hope fully upon the grace that is coming to you at the revelation of Jesus Christ. As obedient children, do not be conformed to the passions of your former ignorance, but as he who called you is holy, be holy yourselves in all your conduct; since it is written, "You shall be holy, for I am holy." (1 Pet. 1:13–16)

In the case of the weak sheep, it is to be feared that the temptation, when it comes, may break him. The sick person, however, is already ill by reason of some illicit desire or other, and this is keeping him from entering God's path and submitting to Christ's yoke.

There are men who want to live a good life and have already decided to do so, but are not capable of bearing sufferings even though they are ready to do good. Now, it is part of the Christian's strength not only to do good works but also to endure evil. Weak men are those who appear to be zealous in doing good works but are unwilling or unable to endure the sufferings that threaten. Lovers of the world, however, who are kept from good works by some evil desire, lie sick and listless, and it is this sickness that deprives them of any strength to accomplish good works. (St. Augustine)[123]

St. Peter calls all to strive for holiness. A strong man is willing to "fight the good fight of faith" (1 Tim. 6:12) to attain holiness and strive for growth in virtue and sanctity in his daily life. The weak man is just that: weak. This does not mean that there is no hope for the weak man, but it does mean that the weak man needs to make an honest (sometimes

[123] *Sermo* 46 on pastors, in *Liturgy of the Hours*, vol. IV, 285–286.

gut-wrenching) evaluation of things; he needs to take inventory of his priorities in life. He needs to seek growth and advancement in his regular reception of the Sacrament of Penance — that is, holy Confession. He needs to discover that it is indeed a great thing to discover that "my confessions are *not* the same each time," as this means he is advancing in the spiritual life. He needs to discover the joy of no longer confessing those "same things over and over again" that he used to confess so frequently. Just as much, he needs to rejoice in finding new areas to confess that he hasn't confessed before — again, because he is advancing in the spiritual life. This is holiness: finding new areas in which to seek perfection. This is advancing in virtue and the spiritual life. (See days 9, 10, 43, 44, 52, 53, 69, 90, 128, 130, and 185.)

Give the Truth When Convenient and Inconvenient

I charge you in the presence of God and of Christ Jesus who is to judge the living and the dead, and by his appearing and his kingdom: preach the word, be urgent in season and out of season, convince, rebuke, and exhort, be unfailing in patience and in teaching. For the time is coming when people will not endure sound teaching, but having itching ears they will accumulate for themselves teachers to suit their own likings, and will turn away from listening to the truth and wander into myths. As for you, always be steady, endure suffering, do the work of an evangelist, fulfil your ministry. (2 Tim. 4:1–5)

But I listen to the Apostle who says: *'Preach the word; insist upon it, welcome and unwelcome'* [2 Tim. 4:2]. Welcome to whom? Unwelcome to whom? By all means welcome to those who desire it; unwelcome to those who do not. (St. Augustine)[124]

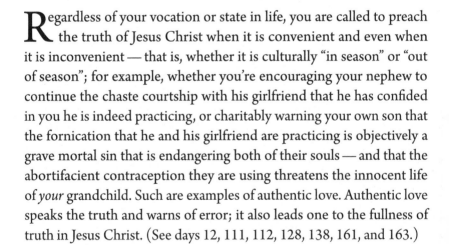

Regardless of your vocation or state in life, you are called to preach the truth of Jesus Christ when it is convenient and even when it is inconvenient — that is, whether it is culturally "in season" or "out of season"; for example, whether you're encouraging your nephew to continue the chaste courtship with his girlfriend that he has confided in you he is indeed practicing, or charitably warning your own son that the fornication that he and his girlfriend are practicing is objectively a grave mortal sin that is endangering both of their souls — and that the abortifacient contraception they are using threatens the innocent life of *your* grandchild. Such are examples of authentic love. Authentic love speaks the truth and warns of error; it also leads one to the fullness of truth in Jesus Christ. (See days 12, 111, 112, 128, 138, 161, and 163.)

---

[124] *Sermo* 46 on pastors, in *Liturgy of the Hours*, vol. IV, 290.

Day 111

Rash Judgment

Judge not, that you be not judged. For with the judgment you pronounce you will be judged, and the measure you give will be the measure you get. Why do you see the speck that is in your brother's eye, but do not notice the log that is in your own eye? (Matt. 7:1–3)

For what man can judge rightly concerning another? Our whole daily life is filled with rash judgments. (St. Augustine)[125]

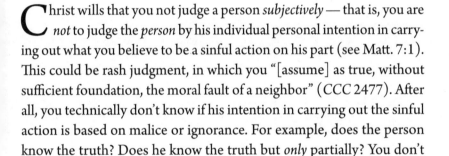

C hrist wills that you not judge a person *subjectively* — that is, you are *not* to judge the *person* by his individual personal intention in carrying out what you believe to be a sinful action on his part (see Matt. 7:1). This could be rash judgment, in which you "[assume] as true, without sufficient foundation, the moral fault of a neighbor" (CCC 2477). After all, you technically don't know if his intention in carrying out the sinful action is based on malice or ignorance. For example, does the person know the truth? Does he know the truth but *only* partially? You don't necessarily know the person's situation in full. So, again, you must not judge subjectively.

All that said, you can (and should) judge things *objectively* — that is, you can judge *acts* or *situations* that are being carried out, apart from their human subjects. How is it that you can do this? Because you know the truth as taught by Holy Mother Church through Her deposit of faith, by way of Sacred Scripture, Tradition, and the Magisterium. As the *Catechism* states so well, "Although we can judge that an act is in itself a grave offense, we must entrust judgment of persons to the justice and mercy

---

[125] *Sermo* 46 on pastors, in *Liturgy of the Hours*, vol. IV, 303.

of God" (*CCC* 1861). Indeed, if you did *not* make objective judgments, you would *not* be living your Faith — *nor* living the truth in Jesus Christ. But be careful of those subjective judgments. They can end up being rash judgments. (See days 20, 41, 104, 124, 143, 160, 165, and 188.)

Day 112

Affirming the Father and the Son and the Holy Spirit

I write to you, not because you do not know the truth, but because you know it, and know that no lie is of the truth. Who is the liar but he who denies that Jesus is the Christ? This is the antichrist, he who denies the Father and the Son. No one who denies the Son has the Father. He who confesses the Son has the Father also. Let what you heard from the beginning abide in you. If what you heard from the beginning abides in you, then you will abide in the Son and in the Father. And this is what he has promised us, eternal life. (1 John 2:21–25)

All who refuse to believe in him [Jesus Christ] must answer to God for the blood of his Son. (St. Polycarp)[126]

The message is clear from St. John: to deny the Son is simultaneously to deny the Father, who sent His only-begotten Son into the world to save the world (see 1 John 4:9–10; John 3:16). The devil desires you to deny *both* the Father and the Son. Why? Because doing so leads to denying the Holy Spirit as well and thus denying the triune Godhead. But instead of denying, affirm — *daily* — the complete rule over your life by the Most Holy Trinity: the Father, the Son, and the Holy Spirit. Acknowledge your triune God. Live a Trinitarian life *daily*. (See days 41, 51, 52, 113, 114, 162, and 200.)

---

[126] *Letter to the Philippians*, chap. 1, in *Liturgy of the Hours*, vol. IV, 315.

Day 113

Trinitarian Prayer and Trinitarian Power

And I will pray the Father, and he will give you another Counselor, to be with you for ever, even the Spirit of truth, whom the world cannot receive, because it neither sees him nor knows him; you know him, for he dwells with you, and will be in you. (John 14:16–17)

We acknowledge the Trinity, holy and perfect, to consist of the Father, the Son and the Holy Spirit. In this Trinity there is no intrusion of any alien element or of anything from outside, nor is the Trinity a blend of creative and created being. It is a wholly creative and energizing reality, self-consistent and undivided in its active power, for the Father makes all things through the Word and in the Holy Spirit, and in this way the unity of the holy Trinity is preserved. Accordingly, in the Church, one God is preached, one God who is *above all things and through all things and in all things* [Eph. 4:6]. God is *above all things* as Father, for he is principle and source; he is *through all things* through the Word; and he is *in all things* in the Holy Spirit. (St. Athanasius)[127]

❧————————☙

St. Turibius of Montenegro states that "God is the infinitely perfect being who is the most Holy Trinity" (*Compendium of the Catechism of the Catholic Church*, q. 40, 18). It has been said that if you sincerely involve the three Divine Persons in your daily life, you can accomplish more *by accident* compared with what you set out to do *on purpose*. God is very generous. He is a very loving, personal, merciful God. The Father, the Son, and the Holy Spirit want a personal relationship with you. As a Christian, you believe in a Trinitarian God: one God in three Divine

[127] Epistle 1, *ad Serapionem*, in *Liturgy of the Hours*, vol. III, 584.

Persons and yet three Divine Persons in one God. Indeed, the Most Holy Trinity is an inexhaustible mystery. But this should not stop you from prayerfully developing a loving, willed, purposeful relationship with the Blessed Trinity — cultivated with deliberate intention each and every day of your life. (See days 38, 112, 114, 123, 172, and 187.)

Day 114

To the Father, *through* the Son, *in* the Holy Spirit

The grace of the Lord Jesus Christ and the love of God and the fellowship of the Holy Spirit be with you all. (2 Cor. 13:14)

Notice at the conclusion of our prayer we never say, "through the Holy Spirit" but rather "through Jesus Christ, your Son, our Lord." Through the mystery of the Incarnation, Jesus Christ *became man, the mediator of God and man. He is a priest for ever according to the order of Melchizedek. By shedding his own blood he entered once and for all into the Holy Places. He did not enter a place made by human hands, a mere type of the true one* [1 Tim. 2:5–6; Heb. 7:17; 9:12, 24–28]; but, he entered heaven itself, where he is at God's right hand interceding for us. Quite correctly, then, the Church continues to reflect this mystery in her prayer.... This then is the reason why we offer prayer *to* God our Father, but *through* Jesus Christ our Lord [emphasis added]....

We do not, however, only say "your Son" when we conclude our prayer. We also say, "who lives and reigns with you *in* the unity of the Holy Spirit" [emphasis added]. In this way we commemorate the natural unity of the Father, Son and Holy Spirit. It is clear, then, that the Christ who exercises a priestly role on our behalf is the same Christ who enjoys a natural unity and equality with the Father and the Holy Spirit. (St. Fulgentius of Ruspe)[128]

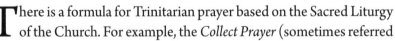

There is a formula for Trinitarian prayer based on the Sacred Liturgy of the Church. For example, the *Collect Prayer* (sometimes referred to as the *Opening Prayer*) of the Mass is always directed *to* the Father,

---

[128] Epistle 14, in *Liturgy of the Hours*, vol. III, 96–98.

through the Son, *in* the Holy Spirit. Indeed, the entire prayer of the Mass, which is the celebration of the Eucharist (and the celebration of any of the other six sacraments, for that matter), is Trinitarian in its orientation. This should say something about your personal prayer life — including your daily activity. Do those areas of your life — for example, your prayer, work, and recreation and leisure — have a Trinitarian orientation? Since your life is called to revolve around the Sacred Liturgy of the Church, especially the Eucharist, which is the "source and summit of the Christian faith" (*LG* 11; *CCC* 1324), be sure to orient all of your daily prayer and activity *to* the Father, *through* the Son, and *in* the Holy Spirit. (See days 21, 60, 65, 92, 97, 99, 103, 112, 113, 123, 131, 132, 142, 144, 145, 155, 158, 159, 169, 172, 187, 199, and 200.)

No Hypocrisy

And he [Jesus] said to them, "Well did Isaiah prophesy of you hypocrites, as it is written, 'This people honors me with their lips, but their heart is far from me.'" (Mark 7:6; see Isa. 29:13)

Whoever bids other folks to do right, but gives an evil example by acting the opposite way, is like a foolish weaver who weaves quickly with one hand and unravels the cloth just as quickly with the other. (St. Thomas More)[129]

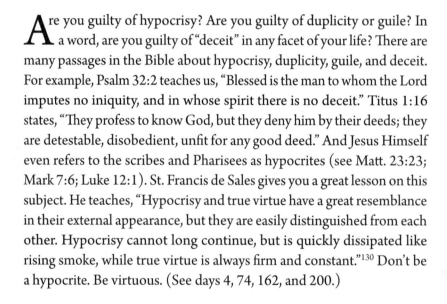

Are you guilty of hypocrisy? Are you guilty of duplicity or guile? In a word, are you guilty of "deceit" in any facet of your life? There are many passages in the Bible about hypocrisy, duplicity, guile, and deceit. For example, Psalm 32:2 teaches us, "Blessed is the man to whom the Lord imputes no iniquity, and in whose spirit there is no deceit." Titus 1:16 states, "They profess to know God, but they deny him by their deeds; they are detestable, disobedient, unfit for any good deed." And Jesus Himself even refers to the scribes and Pharisees as hypocrites (see Matt. 23:23; Mark 7:6; Luke 12:1). St. Francis de Sales gives you a great lesson on this subject. He teaches, "Hypocrisy and true virtue have a great resemblance in their external appearance, but they are easily distinguished from each other. Hypocrisy cannot long continue, but is quickly dissipated like rising smoke, while true virtue is always firm and constant."[130] Don't be a hypocrite. Be virtuous. (See days 4, 74, 162, and 200.)

---

[129] Thigpen, *A Dictionary of Quotes*, 123.
[130] Thigpen, *A Dictionary of Quotes*, 123.

Prodigal Children

And he arose and came to his father. But while he was yet at a distance, his father saw him and had compassion, and ran and embraced him and kissed him. And the son said to him, "Father, I have sinned against heaven and before you; I am no longer worthy to be called your son." But the father said to his servants, "Bring quickly the best robe, and put it on him; and put a ring on his hand, and shoes on his feet; and bring the fatted calf and kill it, and let us eat and make merry; for this my son was dead, and is alive again; he was lost, and is found." And they began to make merry. (Luke 15:20–24)

The faults of children are not always imputed to the parents, especially when they have instructed them and given good example. Our Lord, in His wondrous Providence, allows children to break the hearts of devout fathers and mothers. Thus the decisions your children have made don't make you a failure as a parent in God's eyes. You are entitled to feel sorrow, but not necessarily guilt. Do not cease praying for your children; God's grace can touch a hardened heart. Commend your children to the Immaculate Heart of Mary. When parents pray the Rosary, at the end of each decade they should hold the Rosary aloft and say to her, "With these beads bind my children to your Immaculate Heart," she will attend to their souls. (attributed to St. Louise de Marillac)[131]

Many devout Catholic parents experience aching hearts due to their "prodigal" sons and daughters who have left the Church for any number of reasons; for example, because of Church scandal, because they

---

[131] "St. Louise de Marillac," America Needs Fatima, June 30, 2015, https://americaneeds fatima.org/saint-of-the-day/st-louise-de-marillac.

themselves — the prodigals — have entered into immoral relationships or married outside the Church, or because they simply don't practice their Catholic Faith out of slothfulness. For such children in particular (or with *any* fallen-away Catholic loved one in general), you need to practice the theological virtue of hope. You must hope and pray that they will one day return (ideally, sooner rather than later) to their Catholic Faith and will no longer deprive themselves of the sacraments and the personal graces afforded by them — especially Confession and the Eucharist, which are the only two sacraments that can be received repeatedly with much frequency. And remember this: while you might have failed personally in the past in forming your children as devotedly in their Catholic Faith as you should have (for example, you did not see to it that they received what is usually their final Sacrament of Initiation: Confirmation), or perhaps did not provide a good example in practicing the Faith *regularly* (for example, you failed to ensure that Mass on Sunday — a holy day of obligation — was a mainstay in your household while your kids were growing up), there is always the need to *move forward*. Confess any sins you might have in failing to raise your kids in the Faith and move forward. Then pray and fast for your prodigal children and commend them especially to the Most Sacred Heart of Jesus and the Immaculate Heart of Mary by your own devotion to the Divine Mercy Chaplet and the Rosary and by your practicing the devotions of the nine First Fridays and five First Saturdays. (See days 5, 92, 93, 134, 135, and 185.)

We Must Forgive Others

Then Peter came up and said to him, "Lord, how often shall my brother sin against me, and I forgive him? As many as seven times?" Jesus said to him, "I do not say to you seven times, but seventy times seven." (Matt. 18:21–22)

If, then, we pray to the Lord to forgive us, we must in turn forgive. For we live under the eye of our Lord and God, and *we must all stand before the judgment seat of God, each to give an account of himself* [Rom. 14:10–12]. (St. Polycarp)[132]

It can be hard — sometimes *really* hard — to forgive another. Whether someone slighted you in a minor way or in a major way, it can be hard to forgive — even if the person who slighted you humbles himself and comes to you and asks you for forgiveness. While it is not wrong for you to seek just amends and resolutions when you have been slighted, you do need to forgive. You know this: You want to emulate your Savior in all things, right? So whenever you feel unforgiveness in your heart wanting to get the upper hand, think first of Jesus' words from the Cross regarding His persecutors and executioners: "Father, forgive them; for they know not what they do" (Luke 23:34). Jesus, Who is one with the Father (see John 10:30; 14:9–11), forgave them. And because Jesus is one with the Father, He asked the Father to forgive them also. Emulate your Savior and forgive others. (See days 16, 82, 104, 179, and 186.)

---

[132] *Letter to the Philippians*, chap. 6, in *Liturgy of the Hours*, vol. IV, 323.

What Constitutes Authentic Freedom

For you were called to freedom, brethren; only do not use your freedom as an opportunity for the flesh, but through love be servants of one another. For the whole law is fulfilled in one word, "You shall love your neighbor as yourself." (Gal. 5:13–14)

A spiritual man is one who no longer lives by the flesh, but is led by the Spirit of God, one called a son of God, remade in the likeness of God's Son. As the power of sight is active in a healthy eye, so the Holy Spirit is active in a purified soul. (St. Basil the Great)[133]

The body can often seem unruly and want to gain mastery over the soul. Sometimes the body, with its concupiscences (that is, the tendencies or tugs toward temptation and sin), seems to want to trample the sound reasoning of the soul. St. Paul says it best in Romans 7:15: "I do not understand my own actions. For I do not do what I want, but I do the very thing I hate." Remember: You are a body-soul composite; both body and soul are meant to coexist and work together. In fact, the soul is the very "form" of the body (see CCC 365); so, you have to attend to both and nourish both. A strong prayer life for the soul and a well-disciplined life for the body—like eating right and exercising—will assist you in "forming" your body and soul to function harmoniously together with the least amount of conflict in things both spiritual and temporal. For the dedicated Christian man, this is what constitutes authentic human freedom. (See days 12, 19, 33, 37, 80, 122, 126, 134, and 156.)

---

[133] *On the Holy Spirit*, chap. 26, in *Liturgy of the Hours*, vol. I, 503–504.

Day 119

Self-Love versus Love of God

He who loves his life loses it, and he who hates his life in this world will keep it for eternal life. (John 12:25)

There are Christians who are still puffed up with inordinate self-love. Such persons should not think that they have achieved renunciation of self or that they are really following Jesus Christ. (St. John of the Cross)[134]

There is such a thing as an *ordered* self-love and an *inordinate* self-love, as implied in the quotation from St. John of the Cross above. Ordered self-love is just that: *properly ordered*. Inordinate self-love is just that: *disordered* or "out of order." It has been said — somewhat humorously — that self-love can be so inordinate in a person that it actually dies fifteen minutes after the person does. The early Church bishop Diadochus of Photice, in his treatise *On Spiritual Perfection*, helps to identify these two types of self-love when he teaches:

> No one who is in love with himself is capable of loving God. The man who loves God is the one who mortifies his self-love for the sake of the immeasurable blessings of divine love. Such a man never seeks his own glory but only the glory of God. If a person loves himself he seeks his own glory, but the man who loves God loves the glory of his Creator....
>
> Anyone who loves God in the depths of his heart has already been loved by God. In fact, the measure of a man's love for God depends upon how deeply aware he is of God's love for him....

---

[134] Schroeder, *Every Day Is a Gift*, 52.

Once the love of God has released him from self-love, the flame of divine love never ceases to burn in his heart and he remains united to God by an irresistible longing.[135]

Be sure you practice an ordered self-love, not an inordinate self-love. (See days 4, 115, 162, and 197.)

[135] Quoted in *Liturgy of the Hours,* vol. III, 101–102.

Day 120

On Serving the Lord

Let love be genuine; hate what is evil, hold fast to what is good; love one another with brotherly affection; outdo one another in showing honor. Never flag in zeal, be aglow with the Spirit, serve the Lord. Rejoice in your hope, be patient in tribulation, be constant in prayer. (Rom. 12:9–12)

Do not be anxious. Rouse yourself to serve the Lord with steadfastness, attentiveness, and meekness. That is the true way to serve Him. (St. Francis de Sales)[136]

In 1 Thessalonians 1:9, St. Paul acknowledges how the members of the church at Thessalonica "turned to God from idols, to serve a living and true God." Two chapters later in the same letter, St. Paul prays that "the Lord make you [the members of the church at Thessalonica] increase and abound in love to one another and to all men ... so that he may establish your hearts unblamable in holiness before our God and Father, at the coming of our Lord Jesus with all his saints" (3:12–13). This is the goal of serving the Lord — that it lead to the love and service of neighbor.

Show me fifty committed Catholic men standing in a room, and I will show you *well over fifty ways* in which those individual men can truly serve the Lord and give love and provide service to their neighbors. But each man must do this in ways that are appropriate to his own vocation and state in life (whether single, married, widowed, divorced and living chastely, bishop, diocesan priest, religious order priest, deacon, or

---

[136] *Roses Among Thorns: Simple Advice for Renewing Your Spiritual Journey*, trans. Christopher O. Blum (Manchester, NH: Sophia Institute Press, 2014), 5.

consecrated brother in religious life). He must also employ his natural gifts and talents — whether more physical or intellectual in nature — and be sound in virtue and virtuous living. Such ideals promote a life "unblamable in holiness." (See days 86, 167, 183, and 200.)

Persecutors and Persecutions

Blessed are those who are persecuted for righteousness' sake, for theirs is the kingdom of heaven. Blessed are you when men revile you and persecute you and utter all kinds of evil against you falsely on my account. Rejoice and be glad, for your reward is great in heaven, for so men persecuted the prophets who were before you. (Matt. 5:10–12)

The persecutors who are visible are not the only ones. There are also invisible persecutors, much greater in number. This is more serious. Like a king bent on persecution, sending orders to persecute to his many agents, and establishing different persecutors in each city or province, the devil directs his many servants in their work of persecution, whether in public or in the souls of individuals. Of this kind of persecution Scripture says: *All who wish to live a holy life in Christ Jesus suffer persecution* [2 Tim. 3:12]. "All" suffer persecution; there is no exception. Who can claim exemption if the Lord himself endured the testing of persecution? How many there are today who are secret martyrs for Christ, giving testimony to Jesus as Lord! The Apostle knew this kind of martyrdom, this faithful witnessing to Christ; he said: *This is our boast, the testimony of our conscience* [2 Cor. 1:12]. (St. Ambrose)[137]

❖————————❖

L uke 6:22–23 teaches, "Blessed are you when men hate you, and when they exclude you and revile you, and cast out your name as evil, on account of the Son of man! Rejoice in that day, and leap for joy, for behold, your reward is great in heaven; for so their fathers did to the prophets." And Mark 13:9 states, "They will deliver you up to councils; and you will

---

[137] *Exposition on Psalm* 118, chap. 20, in *Liturgy of the Hours*, vol. III, 1309.

be beaten in synagogues; and you will stand before governors and kings for my sake, to bear testimony before them." Further, Mark 13:13 states, "You will be hated by all for my name's sake. But he who endures to the end will be saved." St. Paul, too, gives a glimpse of the faithful Christian's lot when he states, "When reviled, we bless; when persecuted, we endure; when slandered, we try to conciliate" (1 Cor. 4:12–13). And yet Pope St. Leo the Great gives us great hope when he teaches that "no type of cruelty can tear down the religion established by the mystery of Christ's cross. The Church is not diminished by persecutions, but rather increased."[138]

So, are you ready to suffer persecutions for the sake of Jesus Christ and His truth, as taught and upheld by His Bride, the Church? Hopefully so. And know that Jesus Christ is fully aware of your enduring persecutions on account of His name. St. Ambrose puts it this way: "In a little space, after a brief moment, when you have escaped from the hands of your persecutors without yielding to the powers of this world, Christ will come to you, and he will not allow you to be tested for long."[139] (See days 66, 88, 89, 100, 108, 125, 179, and 182.)

---

[138] *Sermo 82, in natali apostolorum Petri et Pauli,* in *Liturgy of the Hours,* vol. IV, 1570.

[139] *On Virginity,* chap. 12, in *Liturgy of the Hours,* vol. I, 1244.

Day 122

Unity, Order, Harmony, and Peace

Finally, all of you, have unity of spirit, sympathy, love of the brethren, a tender heart and a humble mind. Do not return evil for evil or reviling for reviling; but on the contrary bless, for to this you have been called, that you may obtain a blessing. (1 Pet. 3:8–9)

Where there is order, there is also harmony; where there is harmony, there is also correct timing; where there is correct timing, there is also advantage. (St. Irenaeus)[140]

❖━━━━━━━❖

What is the best blueprint for building societal unity, order, harmony, and peace? Following God's commandments. Pope St. Clement I, in a letter to the Corinthians, expresses this truth well when he states, "Let the man truly possessed by the love of Christ keep his commandments.... Happy are we, beloved, if love enables us to live in harmony and in the observance of God's commandments, for then it will also gain for us the remission of our sins."[141] So love is the driving force in following God's commandments and leads to harmony and the remission of sins. St. Peter echoes this truth when teaches, "Above all hold unfailing your love for one another, since love covers a multitude of sins" (1 Pet. 4:8). Indeed, it is precisely sin (both personal and societal "structures of sin") that ushers in the opposites of unity, order, harmony, and peace: disunity, disorder, discord, and war. The Church's teaching is very clear on this: "Sin makes men accomplices of one another and causes concupiscence, violence, and injustice to reign among them. Sins give rise to social situations and institutions that are contrary to the divine goodness. 'Structures of sin'

---

[140] *Against Heresies*, bk. 4, chap. 20, in *Liturgy of the Hours*, vol. III, 1499.
[141] Quoted in *Liturgy of the Hours*, vol. III, 88–89.

are the expression and effect of personal sins. They lead their victims to do evil in their turn. In an analogous sense, they constitute a 'social sin'" (*CCC* 1869, quoting Pope St. John Paul II, *Reconciliatio et Paenitentia* 16). Strive to follow God's commandments so as to promote unity, order, harmony, and peace. As 2 Corinthians 13:11 exhorts you: "Live in peace, and the God of love and peace will be with you." (See days 8, 12, 14, 33, 37, 57, 118, 130, and 191.)

Day 123

Christ Died for Your Sins

For Christ also died for sins once for all, the righteous for the unrighteous, that he might bring us to God. (1 Pet. 3:18)

God's compassion for us is all the more wonderful because Christ died, not for the righteous or the holy but for the wicked and the sinful, and, though the divine nature could not be touched by the sting of death, he took to himself, through his birth as one of us, something he could offer on our behalf. (Pope St. Leo the Great)[142]

❖────────────❖

Jesus Christ died for your sins. He died for you. You probably have heard these words a lot throughout your life; for example, as a child or as an adolescent in your catechism classes, while at Mass during a homily, or during a retreat you attended. But have you ever really and truly let those words sink in? Say these words now: *Jesus Christ died for me and my sins.* Resounding this truth, 1 Corinthians 15:3 states that "Christ died for our sins," and Romans 5:8 teaches that "while we were yet sinners Christ died for us." John 3:16 tells us, "For God so loved the world that he gave his only Son, that whoever believes in him should not perish but have eternal life." As Mediator between God and man — and *through* His mediation — Jesus desires to lead you *to* the Father *in* the Holy Spirit. As 1 Timothy 2:5–6 teaches so perfectly: "For there is one God, and there is one mediator between God and men, the man Christ Jesus, who gave himself as a ransom for all, the testimony to which was borne at the proper time." Never forget this. Now, say those words again and *let them sink in*: *Jesus Christ died for me and my sins.* Repeat this truth often. (See days 15, 113, 114, and 200.)

---

[142] *Sermo 8 de passione Domini,* in *Liturgy of the Hours,* vol. II, 359–360.

Day 124

Conscience

For our boast is this, the testimony of our conscience. (2 Cor. 1:12)

This is our glory: the witness of our conscience [2 Cor. 1:12]. There are men who rashly judge, who slander, whisper and murmur, who are eager to suspect what they do not see, and eager to spread abroad things they have not even a suspicion of. Against men of this sort, what defense is there save the witness of our own conscience? (St. Augustine)[143]

The conscience is a glorious thing — literally. The *Catechism of the Catholic Church* defines conscience as "a judgment of reason whereby the human person recognizes the moral quality of a concrete act that he is going to perform, is in the process of performing, or has already completed" (1778). The *Catechism* also states that "moral conscience, present at the heart of the person, enjoins him at the appropriate moment to do good and to avoid evil. It also judges particular choices, approving those that are good and denouncing those that are evil" (1777; cf. Rom. 2:14–16; 1:32). Further, "a well-formed conscience is upright and truthful. It formulates its judgments according to reason, in conformity with the true good willed by the wisdom of the Creator. Everyone must avail himself of the means to form his conscience" (1798). You will form your conscience well if you avail yourself of the moral teachings of the Church, which are taught by way of Sacred Scripture, Tradition, and the Magisterium and are all part of the deposit of faith. The *Jerusalem Catecheses*, attributed to St. Cyril of Jerusalem, states the goal of a well-formed and "pure" conscience: transformation in Christ. This ancient

---

[143] *Sermo 47*, in *Liturgy of the Hours*, vol. III, 426.

document contains this beautiful prayer: "May purity of conscience remove the veil from the face of your soul so that by contemplating the glory of the Lord, as in a mirror, you may be transformed from glory to glory in Christ Jesus our Lord. To him be glory for ever and ever. Amen [cf. 2 Cor. 3:18]."[144] (See days 20, 21, 24, 39, 41, 43, 49, 80, 104, 111, 133, 140, 143, 156, 160, 165, 183, 185, and 188.)

---

[144] *Jerusalem Catecheses*, Cat. 22, *Mystagogica*, in *Liturgy of the Hours*, vol. II, 622.

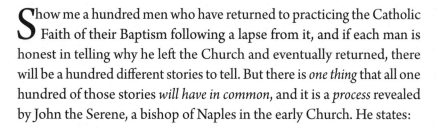

Day 125

Returning to the Lord and His Bride, the Church

And you, who once were estranged and hostile in mind, doing evil deeds, he has now reconciled in his body of flesh by his death, in order to present you holy and blameless and irreproachable before him, provided that you continue in the faith, stable and steadfast, not shifting from the hope of the gospel which you heard, which has been preached to every creature under heaven. (Col. 1:21–23)

[D]eath is acquired by sin but avoided by right living; life is lost through sin and preserved through good living. *The wages of sin is death; the gift of God is eternal life through Jesus Christ our Lord* [Rom. 6:23]. (St. Pacian)[145]

———————————

Show me a hundred men who have returned to practicing the Catholic Faith of their Baptism following a lapse from it, and if each man is honest in telling why he left the Church and eventually returned, there will be a hundred different stories to tell. But there is *one thing* that all one hundred of those stories *will have in common*, and it is a *process* revealed by John the Serene, a bishop of Naples in the early Church. He states:

> The Lord then is our light, the sun of justice and righteousness, who has shone on his Catholic Church spread throughout the world. The prophet [David] spoke as a figure of the Church when he cried: *The Lord is my light and my salvation; whom shall I fear?* [Ps. 27:1]....
>
> When this light begins to shine upon the man who sat *in darkness and the shadow of death* [Ps. 23:4; Matt. 4:16; Luke 1:79], in the darkness of evil and the shadow of sin, he is shocked, he calls

---

[145] Sermon on Baptism, in *Liturgy of the Hours*, vol. IV, 116.

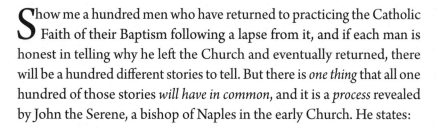

himself to account, repents of his misdeeds in shame, and says: *The Lord is my light and my salvation; whom shall I fear?* Great is this salvation, my brethren.[146]

The Lord lets His own light shine on His Bride, the Church, "the pillar and bulwark of the truth" (1 Tim. 3:15). May all who have fallen away from Christ and His Church return to Christ and His Church. (See days 47, 66, 88, 89, 100, 108, 121, 126, 179, and 182.)

---

[146] *Sermo* 7, in *Liturgy of the Hours*, vol. III, 130.

Quit Putting Off Conversion — or Reversion

And Jesus looking upon him loved him, and said to him, "You lack one thing; go, sell what you have, and give to the poor, and you will have treasure in heaven; and come, follow me." At that saying his countenance fell, and he went away sorrowful; for he had great possessions. And Jesus looked around and said to his disciples, "How hard it will be for those who have riches to enter the kingdom of God!" And the disciples were amazed at his words. But Jesus said to them again, "Children, how hard it is for those who trust in riches to enter the kingdom of God! It is easier for a camel to go through the eye of a needle than for a rich man to enter the kingdom of God." And they were exceedingly astonished, and said to him, "Then who can be saved?" Jesus looked at them and said, "With men it is impossible, but not with God; for all things are possible with God." (Mark 10:21–27)

Nothing makes God happier than a person's amendment of life, conversion, and salvation. This is why He sent His only Son to this earth. (St. Gregory Nazianzen)[147]

*C*onversion to the Catholic Faith happens when one who is not already Catholic officially joins the Church and receives the three Sacraments of Initiation: Baptism, Confirmation, and Eucharist. This could be a person who has never received the Sacrament of Baptism or a person who received a valid Baptism in a Protestant ecclesial community. In this latter case, the person would then receive the remaining two Sacraments of Initiation: Confirmation and Eucharist. *Reversion* happens when

---

[147] Schroeder, *Every Day Is a Gift*, 142.

one is already a Catholic but quits practicing the Faith—for whatever reason—but eventually returns to the Church and once again begins practicing the Catholic Faith of his Baptism. Regardless, Jesus states in Luke 15:7, "I tell you, there will be more joy in heaven over one sinner who repents than over ninety-nine righteous persons who need no repentance." What a beautiful teaching this is! And John the Serene gives spiritual guidance on the importance of *not* putting off conversion—or reversion. He says, "Though the blindness of concupiscence [the tugs toward temptation] assails us, again we say: *The Lord is my light* [Ps. 27:1]. For he is our strength; he gives himself to us and we give ourselves to him. Hasten to this physician while you can, or you may not be able to find him when you want him."[148] Echoing this, the Letter of James gives a somewhat haunting—but realistic—passage when it states: "You do not know about tomorrow. What is your life? For you are a mist that appears for a little time and then vanishes" (4:14). Indeed, you don't know about tomorrow. Remember, you could die today unexpectedly, such as through an accident. You should therefore live your daily life realistically in an "eternity minded" way—that is, free from sin, seeking God's grace *daily*, and looking ahead to the joy that God promises to those who are, and *remain*, faithful to Him. Do not delay your conversion—or reversion. (See days 45, 47, 80, 125, 134, 147, 156, and 187.)

---

[148] *Sermo 7*, in *Liturgy of the Hours*, vol. III, 130–131.

Love and Thanks Returned to the Creator

Thus says the LORD of hosts: Return to me, says the LORD of hosts, and I will return to you, says the LORD of hosts. (Zech. 1:3)

Of all the movements, sensations and feelings of the soul, love is the only one in which the creature can respond to the Creator and make some sort of similar return however unequal though it be. For when God loves, all he desires is to be loved in return; the sole purpose of his love is to be loved, in the knowledge that those who love him are made happy by their love of him. (St. Bernard of Clairvaux)[149]

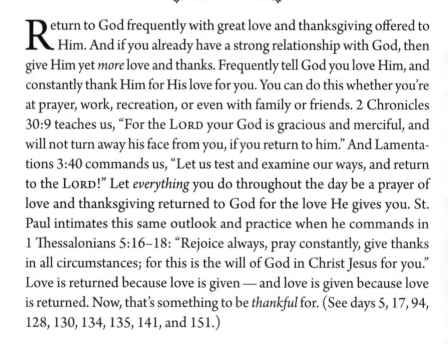

R eturn to God frequently with great love and thanksgiving offered to Him. And if you already have a strong relationship with God, then give Him yet *more* love and thanks. Frequently tell God you love Him, and constantly thank Him for His love for you. You can do this whether you're at prayer, work, recreation, or even with family or friends. 2 Chronicles 30:9 teaches us, "For the LORD your God is gracious and merciful, and will not turn away his face from you, if you return to him." And Lamentations 3:40 commands us, "Let us test and examine our ways, and return to the LORD!" Let *everything* you do throughout the day be a prayer of love and thanksgiving returned to God for the love He gives you. St. Paul intimates this same outlook and practice when he commands in 1 Thessalonians 5:16–18: "Rejoice always, pray constantly, give thanks in all circumstances; for this is the will of God in Christ Jesus for you." Love is returned because love is given — and love is given because love is returned. Now, that's something to be *thankful* for. (See days 5, 17, 94, 128, 130, 134, 135, 141, and 151.)

---

[149] *Sermo* 83, in *Liturgy of the Hours*, vol. IV, 1333.

Fight the Good Fight of Faith

But as for you, man of God, shun all this; aim at righteousness, godliness, faith, love, steadfastness, gentleness. Fight the good fight of the faith; take hold of the eternal life to which you were called. (1 Tim. 6:11–12)

No matter how fiercely the powers of this world oppress and oppose the Church, they will never bring it down. Ever since his ascension and from the time of the apostles to the present, the Lord Jesus has made his Church grow even in the midst of tribulation....

Hold fast, then, to the will of God and with all your heart fight the good fight under the leadership of Jesus; conquer again the diabolical power of this world that Christ has already vanquished.

I beg you not to fail in your love for one another, but to support one another and to stand fast until the Lord mercifully delivers us from our trials. (St. Andrew Kim Taegon)[150]

Faith is definitely something worth fighting for. The Church possesses a host of red martyrs who prove this fact. St. Paul teaches that "faith is the assurance of things hoped for, the conviction of things not seen" (Heb. 11:1). The Church fleshes out this teaching from St. Paul by going into greater detail. The *Catechism* teaches that faith is:

Both a gift of God and a human act by which the believer gives personal adherence to God who invites his response, and freely assents to the whole truth that God has revealed. It is this revelation of God which the Church proposes for our belief, and which we profess in the Creed, celebrate in the sacraments, live by right

[150] Final exhortation, *Pro Corea Documenta*, in *Liturgy of the Hours Supplement*, 19–20.

conduct that fulfills the twofold commandment of charity (as specified in the ten commandments [i.e., love of God and love of neighbor]), and respond to in our prayer of faith. Faith is both a theological virtue given by God as grace, and an obligation which flows from the first commandment of God" ["I am the Lord your God: You shall not have strange gods before me." (see Exod. 20:2–3; Deut. 5:6–7)]. (*CCC* glossary, s.v. "faith"; see *CCC* 26, 142, 150, 1814, 2087)

Indeed, these truths of faith are truths worth fighting for — even to the point of martyrdom. Fight the good fight of faith. (See days 20, 27, 36, 57, 76, 86, 89, 104, 109, 165, 173, and 194.)

Day 129

Vices Wreak Havoc on You and Your Relationships with Others

Put to death therefore what is earthly in you: immorality, impurity, passion, evil desire, and covetousness, which is idolatry. On account of these the wrath of God is coming. In these you once walked, when you lived in them. But now put them all away: anger, wrath, malice, slander, and foul talk from your mouth. Do not lie to one another, seeing that you have put off the old nature with its practices and have put on the new nature, which is being renewed in knowledge after the image of its creator. (Col. 3:5–10)

Vice is contrary to human nature, because it is against the order of reason. (St. Thomas Aquinas)[151]

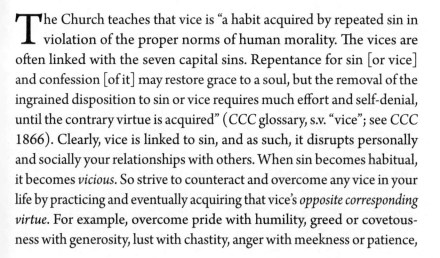

The Church teaches that vice is "a habit acquired by repeated sin in violation of the proper norms of human morality. The vices are often linked with the seven capital sins. Repentance for sin [or vice] and confession [of it] may restore grace to a soul, but the removal of the ingrained disposition to sin or vice requires much effort and self-denial, until the contrary virtue is acquired" (*CCC* glossary, s.v. "vice"; see *CCC* 1866). Clearly, vice is linked to sin, and as such, it disrupts personally and socially your relationships with others. When sin becomes habitual, it becomes *vicious*. So strive to counteract and overcome any vice in your life by practicing and eventually acquiring that vice's *opposite corresponding virtue*. For example, overcome pride with humility, greed or covetousness with generosity, lust with chastity, anger with meekness or patience,

---

[151] Thigpen, *A Dictionary of Quotes*, 242.

gluttony with temperance, envy with kindness or fraternal love, and sloth with diligence. In your daily life, practice concrete actions that promote these very virtues. By cooperating with God's grace, you *can* overcome vice. (See days 43, 106, 156, and 195.)

Virtues That Strengthen Your Relationships with Others

Put on then, as God's chosen ones, holy and beloved, compassion, kindness, lowliness, meekness, and patience, forbearing one another and, if one has a complaint against another, forgiving each other; as the Lord has forgiven you, so you also must forgive. And above all these put on love, which binds everything together in perfect harmony. And let the peace of Christ rule in your hearts, to which indeed you were called in the one body. And be thankful. Let the word of Christ dwell in you richly, as you teach and admonish one another in all wisdom, and as you sing psalms and hymns and spiritual songs with thankfulness in your hearts to God. And whatever you do, in word or deed, do everything in the name of the Lord Jesus, giving thanks to God the Father through him. (Col. 3:12–17)

Keep on making progress. This progress, however, must be in virtue; for there are some, the Apostle warns, whose only progress is in vice. If you make progress, you will be continuing your journey, but be sure that your progress is in virtue, true faith, and right living. (St. Augustine)[152]

※━━━━━━━━※

Church teaching identifies virtue as "a habitual and firm disposition to do the good. The moral virtues [prudence, justice, fortitude, and temperance — also called cardinal virtues] are acquired through human effort aided by God's grace; the theological virtues [faith, hope, and charity] are gifts of God" (*CCC* glossary, s.v. "virtue"; see *CCC* 1803). The *cardinal virtues* (from the Latin *cardo*, meaning "hinge," since the other virtues and thus the success of one's moral life "hinge" on them)

---

[152] *Sermo* 256, in *Liturgy of the Hours*, vol. IV, 610.

are "stable dispositions of the intellect and will that govern our acts, order our passions, and guide our conduct in accordance with reason and faith" (*CCC* glossary, s.v. "cardinal virtues"; see *CCC* 1805, 1834). The *theological virtues* are "gifts infused by God into the souls of the faithful to make them capable of acting as his children and of meriting eternal life" (*CCC* glossary, s.v. "virtues, theological"; see *CCC* 1813). What gems you have in these seven important virtues to guide your daily life in things both spiritual and temporal, personal and social. Practice them; attain them; live them. (See days 8, 9, 10, 14, 28, 30, 43, 44, 52, 53, 57, 69, 80, 90, 106, 109, 122, 164, and 191.)

God's Becoming Man: The Sacred Incarnation

That which was from the beginning, which we have *heard*, which we have *seen* with our eyes, which we have looked upon and *touched* with our hands, concerning the word of life — the *life was made manifest*, and we *saw* it, and testify to it, and proclaim to you the eternal life which was with the Father and was made *manifest* to us — that which we have *seen* and *heard* we proclaim also to you. (1 John 1:1–3, emphasis added)

Before the Son of God became man, his goodness was hidden.... It was promised, but it was not experienced, and as a result few believed in it....

... [But through the Sacred Incarnation of Jesus Christ,] [i]t is as if God the Father sent upon the earth a purse full of his mercy.... God's Son came in the flesh so that mortal men could see and recognize God's kindness. When God reveals his humanity, his goodness cannot possibly remain hidden. To show his kindness, what more could he do beyond taking my human form?...

How could he have shown his mercy more clearly than by taking on himself our condition?... The incarnation teaches us how much God cares for us and what he thinks and feels about us.... Let us think of all the Lord has done for us, and then we shall realize how his goodness appears through his humanity....

Truly great and manifest are the goodness and humanity of God. He has given us a most wonderful proof of his goodness by *adding humanity to his own divine nature*. (St. Bernard)[153]

❯───────────❮

B ecause He loves *you*, God became man for *you*, to save *you*. What a *gift*. Praise the *Giver* of that gift. (See days 103, 114, 158, 159, and 169.)

---

[153] *Sermo 1 in Epiphania Domini*, in *Liturgy of the Hours*, vol. I, 446–448, emphasis added.

Day 132

Finding Christ's Peace

On the evening of that day, the first day of the week, the doors being shut where the disciples were, for fear of the Jews, Jesus came and stood among them and said to them, "Peace be with you." When he had said this, he showed them his hands and his side. Then the disciples were glad when they saw the Lord. Jesus said to them again, "Peace be with you. As the Father has sent me, even so I send you." (John 20:19–21)

Once a man has been found worthy of Christ's peace, he can easily save his soul and guide his mind to carry out exactingly the demands of virtue....

... The results of these efforts will profit such men so that each will be able to gain his own salvation without difficulty. (St. Cyril of Alexandria)[154]

❧————————————❧

Notice that in the above Scripture passage from St. John's Gospel, the peace of Jesus Christ brings *gladness* to His disciples, even during a time of *fear*. This is a great lesson for you. When you are feeling fearful — maybe because of something to do with your marriage, your child's health, your finances, your job — do you strive to find Christ's peace during those moments of fear? Indeed, Christ's peace is a prominent theme given to you at every Mass you attend, just before the Rite of Communion, when you receive the Eucharist (cf. day 92). Remember: Christ wants to give you *His* peace. He doesn't want you to fall to pieces. The Eucharist is Christ truly present. The Eucharist, then, should bring you peace. (See days 21, 65, 92, 97, 99, 103, 114, 144, 145, 155, and 199.)

---

[154] *Commentary on Haggai*, chap. 14, in *Liturgy of the Hours*, vol. IV, 374–375.

Day 133

Happiness

Happy the people to whom such blessings fall! Happy the people whose God is the LORD! (Ps. 144:15)

We must search out the life of happiness, we must ask for it from the Lord our God. Many have discussed at great length the meaning of happiness, but surely we do not need to go to them and their long drawn out discussions. Holy Scripture says concisely and with truth: *Happy is the people whose God is the Lord* [Ps. 144:15]. We are meant to belong to that people, and to be able to see God and live with him for ever, and so *the object of this command is love from a pure heart, from a good conscience and a sincere faith* [1 Tim. 1:5]. (St. Augustine)[155]

Our Heavenly Father desires your happiness — not only during times of blessing but also during times of trial and tribulation. As to these latter, you are able to endure them because, with gladness of heart, you recognize any trial and tribulation as a share in the saving Cross of God's only-begotten Son. Such an attitude takes root and grows from three things: a pure heart, a clear conscience, and a sincere faith. Know this scriptural lesson: "A glad heart makes a cheerful countenance, but by sorrow of heart the spirit is broken" (Prov. 15:13). At any given time, may your heart be glad, not sorrowful; may your spirit be whole, not broken — even during times of trial or tribulation. (See days 19, 59, 77, 96, 106, 138, and 200.)

[155] *Letter to Proba, Epistle* 130, in *Liturgy of the Hours,* vol. IV, 422.

Day 134

Love for the Sacred Heart of Jesus

Come to me, all who labor and are heavy laden, and I will give you rest. Take my yoke upon you, and learn from me; for I am gentle and lowly in heart, and you will find rest for your souls. For my yoke is easy, and my burden is light. (Matt. 11:28–30)

What consoles me is the thought that the Sacred Heart of Our Lord Jesus Christ will do everything for me and make up for all my powerlessness and defects. (St. Margaret Mary Alacoque)[156]

If you let Him, Jesus Christ will *guide* you in every aspect of your life — not only through His divinity but also through His sacred humanity. He experienced life on earth in the modern world of His time just as you experience life on earth in the modern world of your time. Remember that as God incarnate, Jesus took on a human nature just like yours and was tempted in every way but never sinned (see Heb. 4:15). You live in a broken, wounded world because of the Fall of your first parents, which ushered in the Original Sin, two effects of which are a darkened intellect and a weakened will; thus, concupiscence — the tendency to sin, the tug toward sin — was also ushered in. So Jesus "gets" human nature; He understands it, and He wants to help you in your process of sanctification so that you, in turn, can help sanctify others by your example. To this end, St. Margaret Mary reminds you about the importance of always returning to Christ after each sinful fall and letting Him restore you, heal you, and strengthen you: "When you have committed faults, do not be

---

[156] Letter 130, to Rev. Fr. Jean Croiset, S.J., of the Society of Jesus at Lyons, April 14, 1689, in *Blessed Letters of Saint Margaret Mary Alacoque*, SaintWorks, https://www.saintsworks. net/books/St.%20Margaret%20Mary%20Alacoque%20-%20Letters.pdf.

anxious because anxiety, uneasiness and too much agitation withdraw the soul from God and cause Jesus Christ to withdraw from the soul. Let us, rather, ask pardon of Him and beg His Sacred Heart to restore us to favor."[157] Christ calls you to rest in Him always, especially during rough and tough times. Remember: He is gentle and lowly of heart, His yoke is easy, and His burden is light. (See days 5, 80, 91, 92, 96, 97, 116, 126, 135, 156, 188, 191, and 197.)

---

[157] *Vie et Oeuvres de Sainte Marguerite Marie* (Paris: J. de Gigord, 1920), 2:683, in Visitation Sisters, *Thoughts and Sayings of Saint Margaret Mary* (Charlotte, NC: TAN Books, 1986), "April: Peace — Trust — Abandonment."

Day 135

Love for the Immaculate Heart of Mary

Mary kept all these things, pondering them in her heart. (Luke 2:19)

The man who burns with the fire of divine love is a son of the Immaculate Heart of Mary, and wherever he goes, he enkindles that flame; he desires and works with all this strength to inflame all men with the fire of God's love. Nothing deters him: he rejoices in poverty; he labors strenuously; he welcomes hardships; he laughs off false accusations; he rejoices in anguish. He thinks only of how he might follow Jesus Christ and imitate him by his prayers, his labors, his sufferings, and by caring always and only for the glory of God and the salvation of souls. (St. Anthony Mary Claret)[158]

The Immaculate Heart of Mary is closely aligned with the Sacred Heart of Jesus. The Sacred Heart of Jesus was *formed* by the Immaculate Heart of Mary — physiologically, literally. Both of these hearts are important for the formation of your *own heart* as a true man of God. Poetically speaking, across cultures and across times, the human heart has been seen as a vessel of love. Form your heart as a vessel of love — to love yourself, your parents, your spouse, your children, your family, your friends, strangers, and yes — even your enemies. A statement attributed to St. Catherine Labouré, the visionary to whom Mary entrusted the Miraculous Medal of her Immaculate Conception, teaches quite plainly, "One must see God in everyone." This can be difficult to do, but the message is clear: you must form your heart so that, in good times and in bad, you love *all.* When Simeon greeted Joseph and Mary at the Presentation of the Child Jesus in the Temple, he prophesied to Mary, "And a sword will

---

[158] *L'Egoismo vinto,* in *Liturgy of the Hours,* vol. IV, 1511.

pierce through your own soul also, that thoughts out of many hearts may be revealed" (see Luke 2:35). The word *soul* here is sometimes translated "heart," meaning Mary's heart. Life wasn't always easy for Mary as the Mother of God (*Theotokos* — "God bearer"), nor will it be for you. Let Mary's Immaculate Heart guide your heart to have a greater love for her divine Son and His Sacred Heart. (See days 5, 92, 116, and 134.)

Day 136

The Best Version of Yourself

Therefore, if any one is in Christ, he is a new creation; the old has passed away, behold, the new has come. (2 Cor. 5:17)

The time is now at hand when we enter on a new beginning. (St. Athanasius)[159]

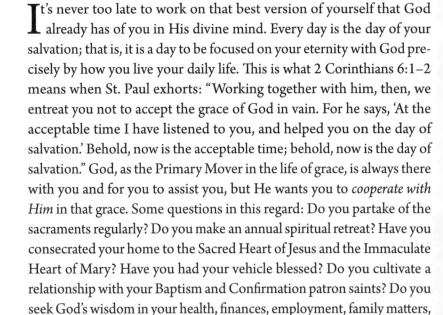

It's never too late to work on that best version of yourself that God already has of you in His divine mind. Every day is the day of your salvation; that is, it is a day to be focused on your eternity with God precisely by how you live your daily life. This is what 2 Corinthians 6:1–2 means when St. Paul exhorts: "Working together with him, then, we entreat you not to accept the grace of God in vain. For he says, 'At the acceptable time I have listened to you, and helped you on the day of salvation.' Behold, now is the acceptable time; behold, now is the day of salvation." God, as the Primary Mover in the life of grace, is always there with you and for you to assist you, but He wants you to *cooperate with Him* in that grace. Some questions in this regard: Do you partake of the sacraments regularly? Do you make an annual spiritual retreat? Have you consecrated your home to the Sacred Heart of Jesus and the Immaculate Heart of Mary? Have you had your vehicle blessed? Do you cultivate a relationship with your Baptism and Confirmation patron saints? Do you seek God's wisdom in your health, finances, employment, family matters, and even recreation and leisure? Every day is the day on which to work on your best version of self. Indeed, *now* is the acceptable time; behold, *now* is the day of salvation. (See days 2, 9, 47, 185, 193, and 200.)

---

[159] *Easter letter*, Epistle 5, in *Liturgy of the Hours*, vol. II, 322.

Day 137

Leading a Worthy Life

And so ... we have not ceased to pray for you, asking that you may be filled with the knowledge of his will in all spiritual wisdom and understanding, to lead a life worthy of the Lord, fully pleasing to him, bearing fruit in every good work and increasing in the knowledge of God. May you be strengthened with all power, according to his glorious might, for all endurance and patience with joy. (Col. 1:9–11)

What is man that you are mindful of him? [Ps. 8:4] What is this new mystery surrounding me? I am both small and great, both lowly and exalted, mortal and immortal, earthly and heavenly. I am to be buried with Christ and to rise again with him, to become a coheir with him, a son of God, and indeed God himself.

This is what the great mystery means for us; this is why God became man and became poor for our sake: it was to raise up our flesh, to recover the divine image, to re-create mankind, so that all of us might become one in Christ who perfectly became in us everything that he is himself. ... We are to be so formed and molded by him that we are recognized as belonging to his one family. ...

... In a spirit of hope and out of love for him, let us then *bear and endure all things* [1 Cor. 13:7] and give thanks for everything that befalls us, since even reason can often recognize these things as weapons to win salvation. (St. Gregory Nazianzen)[160]

No circumstance — good or bad — should ever disrupt your leading a life worthy of the Lord and *fully* pleasing to Him. No good

---

[160] *Oratio 7 in laudem Caesarii fratris*, in *Liturgy of the Hours*, vol. IV, 493.

circumstance should ever lead you to become pompous and self-serving; no bad circumstance should ever lead you to discouragement or despair. God lowered Himself to you to *raise you up to Himself.* Live a life worthy of *that* fact. (See days 3, 7, 30, 52, 80, 120, 175, and 200.)

Day 138

Attaining the Crown

I have fought the good fight, I have finished the race, I have kept the faith. Henceforth there is laid up for me the crown of righteousness, which the Lord, the righteous judge, will award to me on that Day, and not only to me but also to all who have loved his appearing. (2 Tim. 4:7–8)

Remember how the crown was attained by those whose sufferings gave new radiance to their faith. The whole company of Saints bears witness to the unfailing truth that without genuine effort, no one wins the crown. (St. Thomas Becket)[161]

In ancient times, winning athletes were "crowned" with an olive wreath that would eventually wilt, as there was no way to preserve it. This is why 1 Corinthians 9:24–25 states, "Do you not know that in a race all the runners compete, but only one receives the prize? So run that you may obtain it. Every athlete exercises self-control in all things. They do it to receive a perishable wreath, but we an imperishable." As a faithful Catholic Christian, you do not strive for a crown that soon becomes a wilting, perishable wreath. No. Rather, you strive for the crown that does not wither and so remains imperishable: eternal beatitude, the Beatific Vision, eternal life with the Blessed Trinity in Heaven. (See days 19, 95, 110, 198, and 200.)

---

[161] Schroeder, *Every Day Is a Gift*, 188.

You Are a True Adopted Son of God

But when the time had fully come, God sent forth his Son, born of woman, born under the law, to redeem those who were under the law, so that we might receive adoption as sons. And because you are sons, God has sent the Spirit of his Son into our hearts, crying, "Abba! Father!" So through God you are no longer a slave but a son, and if a son then an heir. (Gal. 4:4–7)

He [Christ] became man, finally, to make our sufferings his own and thus prepare us for adoption as sons, to win for us that kingdom, into which, I pray, we may all be made worthy to enter by the grace and mercy of the Lord Jesus Christ, who with the Father and the Holy Spirit has glory, honor and power, now and for ever. Amen. (St. Proclus of Constantinople)[162]

St. Fulgentius of Ruspe, in a book addressed to Monimus of Syracuse, states that "[t]he holy Trinity, the one true God, is of its nature unity, equality and love, and by one divine activity sanctifies its adopted sons."[163] Almighty God — the Father, the Son, and the Holy Spirit — wants to sanctify you; that is, God wants to make you precious and holy in His sight as a true adopted son. Keep in mind that Monimus was a Cynic philosopher who endorsed philosophical skepticism, thus denying that there is a criterion for truth. This is why St. Fulgentius was witnessing to Monimus, sharing with him the spiritual heights to which God was calling both men. But Monimus was a skeptic. Are you a skeptic? Do you believe that you *are* the Father's true adopted Son *through* Jesus Christ *in* the Holy Spirit? Don't be skeptical about this awesome revealed truth. Believe it. Don't be a skeptic. (See days 39, 140, 147, 152, and 172.)

---

[162] *De Nativitate Domini*, in *Liturgy of the Hours*, vol. III, 1643.
[163] From a book addressed to Monimus, bk. 2, *Liturgy of the Hours*, vol. II, 652.

Day 140

Unity in True Righteousness and Holiness

Put off your old nature which belongs to your former manner of life and is corrupt through deceitful lusts, and be renewed in the spirit of your minds, and put on the new nature, created after the likeness of God in true righteousness and holiness. (Eph. 4:22–24)

The Holy Spirit, who is the one Spirit of the Father and the Son, produces in those to whom he gives the grace of divine adoption the same effect as he produced among those whom the Acts of the Apostles describes as having received the Holy Spirit. We are told that *the company of those who believed were of one heart and soul* [Acts 4:32], because the one Spirit of the Father and the Son, who with the Father and the Son is one God, had created a single heart and soul in all those who believed. (St. Fulgentius of Ruspe)[164]

A big part of authentic conversion from being more worldly minded to becoming more spiritually minded is the Holy Spirit's gift of unity. For example, you may begin to experience a greater unity with God by way of a more peaceful conscience after making several good confessions. If you're married, you will probably discover, too, a greater unity with your wife, with your children, with other family members, and even with coworkers whom you might not have cared for earlier. Be on guard that the "deceitful lusts" mentioned in the above passage from Ephesians do not disrupt unity in your life. The vice of lust makes you turn in on yourself and away from others; lust makes you more self-centered and less other-centered. Pray to God for an increase in righteousness and holiness that leads to unity — the same unity experienced by the earliest Christians among whom the Holy Spirit moved and breathed. (See days 8, 99, 100, 139, 143, 144, and 145.)

[164] From a book addressed to Monimus, bk. 2, in *Liturgy of the Hours*, vol. II, 653.

Day 141

Disciplining in Love

Have you forgotten the exhortation which addresses you as sons? — "My son, do not regard lightly the discipline of the Lord, nor lose courage when you are punished by him. For the Lord disciplines him whom he loves, and chastises every son whom he receives." It is for discipline that you have to endure. God is treating you as sons; for what son is there whom his father does not discipline? (Heb. 12:5–7)

Where there is justice as well as fear, adversity will surely test the spirit. But it is not the torment of a slave. Rather it is the discipline of a child by its parent. (St. Peter Damien)[165]

❧────────────❧

God desires from you not *servile* fear but *filial* fear (see day 22). In other words, He wants you to experience the fear of not wanting to disappoint Him as a loving parent, precisely because you know full well that He loves you and that you love Him. Pope St. Leo the Great hints at this truth in his sermon on the Beatitudes when he says, "[The giving of the Beatitudes by Christ] was a tranquil discourse which clearly reached the ears of all who stood nearby so that the harshness of the [L]aw [the Ten Commandments] might be softened by the gentleness of grace, and the spirit of adoption might dispel the terror of slavery."[166] Whereas the Ten Commandments are all imperatives that are still valid, the Beatitudes (see Matt. 5:1–12) are statements of faith showing you certain dispositions in living out the demands of the Ten Commandments as a true follower of Jesus Christ. Jesus came not to abolish the Old Law but to bring it to perfection — that is, to fulfill it. Indeed, Christ Himself

---

[165] Letter, in *Liturgy of the Hours*, vol. II, 1682.
[166] *Sermo* 95, in *Liturgy of the Hours*, vol. IV, 206.

teaches, "Think not that I have come to abolish the law and the prophets; I have come not to abolish them but to fulfil them" (Matt. 5:17). You have a visual of this truth when you see on a parish's grounds a beautiful granite display of the Ten Commandments *and* the Beatitudes side by side. Look at it this way: whereas the Ten Commandments make up the *letter of the Law*, the Beatitudes constitute the *spirit of the Law*. The Beatitudes can be said to go hand in hand with the Ten Commandments. Build your life on the truths offered by *both* the Ten Commandments and the Beatitudes. (See days 22, 36, 57, 73, 76, 86, 128, 147, 188, and 200.)

Day 142

The True Conqueror

Who is it that overcomes the world but he who believes that Jesus is the Son of God? This is he who came by water and blood, Jesus Christ, not with the water only but with the water and the blood. (1 John 5:5–6)

There is no evil to be faced that Christ does not face with us. There is no enemy that Christ has not already conquered. There is no cross to bear that Christ has not already borne for us, and does not now bear with us. And on the far side of every cross we find the newness of life in the Holy Spirit, that new life which will reach its fulfillment in the resurrection. This is our *faith*. This is our *witness* before the world. (Pope St. John Paul II)[167]

In the second account of creation, Eve (Adam's bride) is fashioned from the side of Adam (see Gen. 2:18–23). The Church, too, is fashioned from the side of her Bridegroom, Jesus Christ, and both Christ and the Church give you the sacraments. In Catholic theology, the blood and water that flowed from Christ's pierced side while He hung on the Cross on that first Good Friday are symbolic, respectively, of the Sacraments of the Eucharist and Baptism. In fact, the entire *sacramental economy* of the Church was born on that day from the Cross, and so Baptism is referred to as the "gateway" sacrament, meaning that it is ordinarily the first to be received before the other six sacraments can be received; indeed, it "opens the gateway" to the other six sacraments. And the Eucharist is the "source and summit" of the Christian life. As both Vatican II and the *Catechism* teach: "The Eucharist is 'the source and summit of the Christian life.' 'The other sacraments, and indeed all ecclesiastical

---

[167] Homily during the Eucharistic Celebration at Oriole Park at Camden Yards, Baltimore, October 8, 1995 during his apostolic journey to the United States, no. 5.

ministries and works of the apostolate, are bound up with the Eucharist and are oriented toward it. For in the blessed Eucharist is contained the whole spiritual good of the Church, namely Christ himself, our Pasch'" (*CCC* 1324, quoting *Lumen Gentium*, 11 and *Presbyterorum Ordinis*, 5). Here, then, is a quick summary of that wonderful sacramental economy of the Church that was born from Christ's wounded side when blood and water flowed out — a sacramental economy to last until the end of time. There are: three Sacraments of Initiation (Baptism, Eucharist, and Confirmation); two Sacraments of Service, also known as Sacraments of Vocation and Mission (Matrimony and Holy Orders); and two Sacraments of Healing (Reconciliation [Confession] and Anointing of the Sick). The seven sacraments are the gifts that conquer! (See days 60, 65, 108, 114, 155, and 199.)

Day 143

The Heavenly and Holy Sacrifice of the Mass

And he took bread, and when he had given thanks he broke it and gave it to them, saying, "This is my body which is given for you. Do this in remembrance of me." And likewise the cup after supper, saying, "This cup which is poured out for you is the new covenant in my blood." (Luke 22:19–20)

The heavenly sacrifice, instituted by Christ, is the most gracious legacy of his new covenant. On the night he was delivered up to be crucified he left us this gift as a pledge of his abiding presence.

This sacrifice is our sustenance on life's journey; by it we are nourished and supported along the road of life until we depart from this world and make our way to the Lord. For this reason he addressed these words to us: *Unless you eat my flesh and drink my blood, you will not have life in you* [John 6:53].

It was the Lord's will that his gifts should remain with us, and that we who have been redeemed by his precious blood should constantly be sanctified according to the pattern of his own passion. And so he commanded those faithful disciples of his whom he made the first priests of his Church to enact these mysteries of eternal life continuously. All priests throughout the churches of the world must celebrate these mysteries until Christ comes again from heaven. Therefore let us all, priests and people alike, be faithful to this everlasting memorial of our redemption. Daily it is before our eyes as a representation of the passion of Christ. We hold it in our hands, we receive it in our mouths, and we accept it in our hearts.

It is appropriate that we should receive the body of Christ in the form of bread, because, as there are many grains of wheat in the flour from which bread is made by mixing it with water and baking it with fire, so also we know that many members make up the one body of Christ which is brought to maturity by the fire of the Holy Spirit....

Similarly, the wine of Christ's blood, drawn from the many grapes of the vineyard that he had planted, is extracted in the winepress of the cross. When men receive it with believing hearts, like capacious wineskins, it ferments within them by its own power. (St. Gaudentius of Brescia)[168]

The Catholic doctrine of the Eucharist is one that lends itself to absolutely no "in between" stance; that is, you either believe it *is* the Body and Blood of Christ, or you don't. Again, there is no in-between. The Church's teaching is very clear that the Eucharist *is* the Body and Blood of Christ. Do you believe this? If so, what can you do to strengthen that belief? Here's a game plan: begin to make a weekly Eucharistic Holy Hour at your local church. Start to share with others about this wonderful doctrine by distributing pamphlets and holy cards from a reputable Catholic publisher that express it well. If you don't believe in the Eucharist, why not? What can you do to overcome your doubt? Become a better student of your Catholic Faith and read more about the Eucharistic doctrine by way of what Sacred Scripture, Tradition, and the Magisterium teach about it. Share your doubt with a trusted Catholic priest-confessor, mentor, or friend. Do not be unbelieving any longer, but believe (see John 20:27). *Believe in the Eucharist.* (See days 2, 20, 41, 65, 72, 82, 97, 104, 111, 124, 144, 145, 147, 160, 165, 181, 186, 188, and 199.)

---

[168] *Tract.* 2, in *Liturgy of the Hours*, vol. II, 669–670.

The Reality of the Eucharist

"This is the bread which comes down from heaven, that a man may eat of it and not die. I am the living bread which came down from heaven; if any one eats of this bread, he will live for ever; and the bread which I shall give for the life of the world is my flesh." The Jews then disputed among themselves, saying, "How can this man give us his flesh to eat?" So Jesus said to them, "Truly, truly, I say to you, unless you eat the flesh of the Son of man and drink his blood, you have no life in you; he who eats my flesh and drinks my blood has eternal life, and I will raise him up at the last day. For my flesh is food indeed, and my blood is drink indeed. He who eats my flesh and drinks my blood abides in me, and I in him. As the living Father sent me, and I live because of the Father, so he who eats me will live because of me. This is the bread which came down from heaven, not such as the fathers ate and died; he who eats this bread will live for ever." This he said in the synagogue, as he taught at Capernaum. (John 6:50–59)

Since Christ himself has declared the bread to be his body, who can have any further doubt? Since he himself has said quite categorically, *This is my blood*, who would dare to question it and say that it is not his blood?

Therefore, it is with complete assurance that we receive the bread and wine as the body and blood of Christ. His body is given to us under the symbol of bread, and his blood is given to us under the symbol of wine, in order to make us by receiving them one body and blood with him. Having his body and blood in our members, we become bearers of Christ and sharers, as Saint Peter says, in the divine nature [2 Pet. 1:4].

Once, when speaking to the Jews, Christ said: *Unless you eat my flesh and drink my blood you shall have no life in you* [John 6:53]. This horrified them and they left him. Not understanding his words in a spiritual way, they thought the Savior wished them to practice cannibalism.

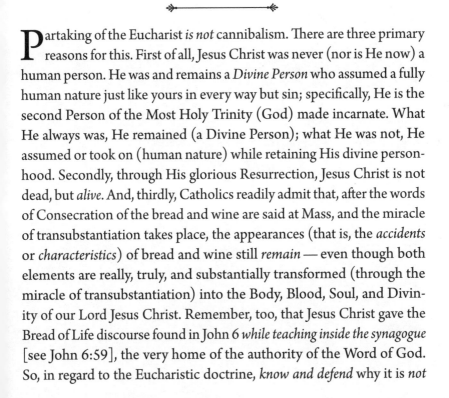

Under the old covenant there was showbread, but it came to an end with the old dispensation to which it belonged. Under the new covenant there is bread from heaven and the cup of salvation. These sanctify both soul and body....

Do not, then, regard the eucharistic elements as ordinary bread and wine: they are in fact the body and blood of the Lord, as he himself has declared. Whatever your senses may tell you, be strong in faith.

You have been taught and you are firmly convinced that what looks and tastes like bread and wine is not bread and wine but the body and the blood of Christ. (attributed to St. Cyril of Jerusalem)[169]

P artaking of the Eucharist *is not* cannibalism. There are three primary reasons for this. First of all, Jesus Christ was never (nor is He now) a human person. He was and remains a *Divine Person* who assumed a fully human nature just like yours in every way but sin; specifically, He is the second Person of the Most Holy Trinity (God) made incarnate. What He always was, He remained (a Divine Person); what He was not, He assumed or took on (human nature) while retaining His divine person-hood. Secondly, through His glorious Resurrection, Jesus Christ is not dead, but *alive*. And, thirdly, Catholics readily admit that, after the words of Consecration of the bread and wine are said at Mass, and the miracle of transubstantiation takes place, the appearances (that is, the *accidents* or *characteristics*) of bread and wine still *remain* — even though both elements are really, truly, and substantially transformed (through the miracle of transubstantiation) into the Body, Blood, Soul, and Divin-ity of our Lord Jesus Christ. Remember, too, that Jesus Christ gave the Bread of Life discourse found in John 6 *while teaching inside the synagogue* [see John 6:59], the very home of the authority of the Word of God. So, in regard to the Eucharistic doctrine, *know and defend* why it is *not*

---

[169] *Jerusalem Catecheses*, Cat. 22, *Mystagogica*, in *Liturgy of the Hours*, vol. II, 621–622.

cannibalism: (1) Jesus is not a human person; He's a Divine Person; (2) He's not dead; He's alive through the power of His Resurrection; and (3) Catholics admit that the appearances of bread and wine remain the same after the words of Consecration are said over the elements and after the miracle of transubstantiation takes place. Know your Faith; defend your Faith; share your Faith; love your Faith. (See days 14, 21, 26, 43, 62, 65, 72, 82, 92, 97, 99, 103, 114, 132, 143, 145, 152, 155, 168, 197, and 199.)

The Effects of the Eucharist

The cup of blessing which we bless, is it not a participation in the blood of Christ? The bread which we break, is it not a participation in the body of Christ? Because there is one bread, we who are many are one body, for we all partake of the one bread.... You cannot drink the cup of the Lord and the cup of demons. You cannot partake of the table of the Lord and the table of demons. (1 Cor. 10:16–17, 21)

[T]he effect of our sharing in the body and blood of Christ is to change us into what we receive. As we have died with him, and have been buried and raised to life with him, so we bear him within us, both in body and in spirit, in everything we do. (Pope St. Leo the Great)[170]

According to the *Catechism*, the Eucharist has a multiplicity of primary effects (or fruits) when it is received worthily (CCC 1391–1405). A summation of these are as follows: the Eucharist unites one intimately with Christ; it unites one with the Heavenly liturgy; through the celebration of the Eucharist we participate in Christ's one sacrifice on the Cross; the Eucharist cleanses and separates us from venial sins; it preserves us from committing future mortal sins; it is true spiritual food wherein we receive the very Author of grace Himself; the Eucharist communicates the mystery of the communion of the Most Holy Trinity; it establishes the community of believers; it provides a foretaste of the future life in Heaven; it provides growth in the Christian life; it preserves, increases, and renews the life of grace received at Baptism; it is a source aiding one in conversion; it helps transform the person through Christ; it commits

---

[170] *Sermo 12 de Passione*, in *Liturgy of the Hours*, vol. II, 661.

us to the poor; the Eucharist is meant to be the preeminent sign of unity among Christians as well as its bond of charity. All of these are spiritual effects worth receiving to strengthen *your* spiritual life, individually, and to strengthen it with other Catholic Christians as well, socially. Be sure to receive the Eucharist *worthily* and *regularly*. Let the Eucharist transform you into the man God is calling you to be, and, with others who do the same, help to transform the world. (See days 1, 2, 3, 21, 65, 72, 82, 92, 97, 99, 103, 114, 132, 143, 144, 155, and 199.)

Devotion to St. Joseph

Now when they had departed, behold, an angel of the Lord appeared to Joseph in a dream and said, "Rise, take the child and his mother, and flee to Egypt, and remain there till I tell you; for Herod is about to search for the child, to destroy him." And he rose and took the child and his mother by night, and departed to Egypt, and remained there until the death of Herod. This was to fulfil what the Lord had spoken by the prophet, "Out of Egypt have I called my son" [Hos. 11:1]. Then Herod, when he saw that he had been tricked by the wise men, was in a furious rage, and he sent and killed all the male children in Bethlehem and in all that region who were two years old or under, according to the time which he had ascertained from the wise men. Then was fulfilled what was spoken by the prophet Jeremiah: "A voice was heard in Ramah, / wailing and loud lamentation, / Rachel weeping for her children; / she refused to be consoled, because they were no more." (Matt. 2:13–18)

I took for my advocate and lord the glorious Saint Joseph and commended myself earnestly to him; and I found that this my father and lord delivered me both from this trouble and also from other and greater troubles concerning my honor and the loss of my soul, and that he gave me greater blessings than I could ask of him. I do not remember even now that I have ever asked anything of him which he has failed to grant.

I am astonished at the great favors which God has bestowed on me through this blessed saint, and at the perils from which He has freed me, both in body and in soul. To other saints the Lord seems to have given grace to succor us in some of our necessities but of this glorious saint my experience is that he succors us in them all and that the Lord wishes to teach us that as He was Himself subject to him on earth (for, being His guardian and being called His father, he could command Him), just so in Heaven He still does all that he asks. This has also been the experience of other persons whom I have advised to commend themselves to him; and even today there are many who have great devotion to him through having newly experienced this truth.

I wish I could persuade everyone to be devoted to this glorious saint, for I have great experience of the blessings which he can obtain from God. I have never known anyone to be truly devoted to him and render him particular services who did not notably advance in virtue, for he gives very real help to souls who commend themselves to him. For some years now, I think, I have made some request of him every year on his festival and I have always had it granted. If my petition is in any way ill directed, he directs it aright for my greater good.

I only beg, for the love of God, that anyone who does not believe me will put what I say to the test, and he will see by experience what great advantages come from his commending himself to this glorious patriarch and having devotion to him. Those who practice prayer should have a special affection for him always. I do not know how anyone can think of the Queen of the Angels, during the time that she suffered so much with the Child Jesus, without giving thanks to Saint Joseph for the way he helped them. If anyone cannot find a master to teach him how to pray, let him take this glorious saint as his master and he will not go astray. (St. Teresa of Ávila)[171]

✦————————✦

St. Joseph speaks not one word in the Bible. Not one word. Let that sink in. Yet, as the chosen earthly foster father of the God-Man, Jesus Christ, he helped to fulfill a prophecy (see Matt. 2:15) and successfully protected his family from a furiously raging and jealous king who practiced infanticide. This is one of the reasons the Litany of St. Joseph calls Joseph "terror of demons": he protected the Infant Christ from the

---

[171] *The Autobiography of St. Teresa of Avila*, chap. 6.

demonic murder plot instigated by Herod and carried out by his army. As a man of God, you need to know more about St. Joseph; that is, you need to know those things about him of which Scripture does not speak. How do you do this? Look to his thirty-two titles in the Church-approved Litany of St. Joseph found in the back of this book (see the appendix of selected prayers). The Catholic Church has given these various titles to St. Joseph because of what She has discovered about him throughout the centuries from scriptural exegeses, the writings of the Church Fathers and saints, Her doctrines concerning the sanctification of marriage and family life, the dignity of the human person, and what could be called the *theology of masculinity* or *masculine genius* (to complement Pope St. John Paul II's writings on the theology of femininity or feminine genius). The world today needs more men like St. Joseph — in all vocations and states in life. So begin to pray regularly the Litany of St. Joseph with great fervor and become devoted to this great saint. Even pray frequently the Litany of St. Joseph; contemplate his thirty-two titles and turn to him often with great confidence, just as the great Carmelite and Doctor of the Church St. Teresa of Ávila did. (See days 40, 71, 76, 79, 148, 149, 160, 167, 175, and 176.)

Your Particular Judgment and the General Judgment

Again, the kingdom of heaven is like a net which was thrown into the sea and gathered fish of every kind; when it was full, men drew it ashore and sat down and sorted the good into vessels but threw away the bad. So it will be at the close of the age. The angels will come out and separate the evil from the righteous, and throw them into the furnace of fire; there men will weep and gnash their teeth. (Matt. 13:47–50)

When harvest time comes, the day of judgment, those who have grown to maturity in the grace of God will find the joy of adopted children in the kingdom of heaven; those who have not grown to maturity will become God's enemies and, even though they were once his children, they will be punished according to their deeds for all eternity. (St. Andrew Kim Taegon)[172]

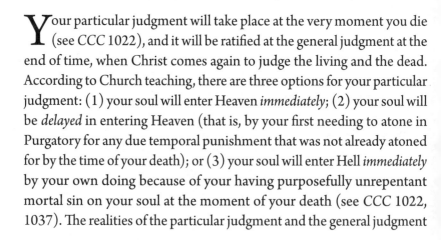

Your particular judgment will take place at the very moment you die (see CCC 1022), and it will be ratified at the general judgment at the end of time, when Christ comes again to judge the living and the dead. According to Church teaching, there are three options for your particular judgment: (1) your soul will enter Heaven *immediately*; (2) your soul will be *delayed* in entering Heaven (that is, by your first needing to atone in Purgatory for any due temporal punishment that was not already atoned for by the time of your death); or (3) your soul will enter Hell *immediately* by your own doing because of your having purposefully unrepentant mortal sin on your soul at the moment of your death (see CCC 1022, 1037). The realities of the particular judgment and the general judgment

---

[172] Final exhortation, *Pro Corea Documenta*, in *Liturgy of the Hours Supplement*, 19.

should lead you to live "eternity minded" — in joyful hope for the coming of your Savior, Jesus Christ; these judgments should *not* cause you to live in servile fear. Indeed, the public prayer of the Church is replete with references to the joy and peace you should have when contemplating both of these judgments and their realities, which are forthcoming. For example, in Eucharistic Prayer I (the Roman Canon) during the celebration of the Eucharist (Holy Mass), we ask God to "order our days in your peace, and command that we be delivered from eternal damnation and counted among the flock of those you have chosen" (*Roman Missal*, 490). Pray daily for your salvation. A great way to do this is to be faithful to your Morning Offering prayer each day upon rising. Pray daily, too, for the grace to follow *joyfully* God's will for you and to grow in that grace, so as to "work out your salvation" with a humble and filial fear (see Phil. 2:12). (See days 2, 22, 47, 73, 126, 141, 143, 155, 181, 186, and 187.)

Day 148

Christ's Soldiers and Truth

Jesus answered, "My kingship is not of this world; if my kingship were of this world, my servants would fight, that I might not be handed over to the Jews; but my kingship is not from the world." Pilate said to him, "So you are a king?" Jesus answered, "You say that I am a king. For this I was born, and for this I have come into the world, to bear witness to the truth. Every one who is of the truth hears my voice." Pilate said to him, "What is truth?" (John 18:36–38)

Against Christ's army the world arrays a twofold battleline. It offers temptation to lead us astray; it strikes terror into us to break our spirit. Hence if our personal pleasures do not hold us captive, and if we are not frightened by brutality, then the world is overcome. At both of these approaches Christ rushes to our aid, and the Christian is not conquered. (St. Augustine)[173]

Do you remember learning that the Sacrament of Confirmation makes you a "soldier of Christ"? Why is this? According to the *Catechism*, the Sacrament of Confirmation "completes the grace of Baptism by a special outpouring of the gifts of the Holy Spirit, which seal or 'confirm' the baptized in union with Christ and equip them for active participation in the worship and apostolic life of the Church" (*CCC* glossary, s.v. "confirmation"; see *CCC* 1285). Think about it: your being a soldier of Christ is part and parcel with your "active participation in the worship and the apostolic life of the Church." The Sacrament of Confirmation, too, is one of the three Sacraments of Initiation, which lead one to his

---

[173] *Sermo* 276, in *Liturgy of the Hours*, vol. III, 1316.

or her optimal membership in the Church (that is, one becomes "fully initiated" into the Catholic Church once he or she has received all three of the Sacraments of Baptism, Eucharist, and Confirmation). That's the good news. The bad is that there are *a lot* of baptized Catholics today (of all ages) who have received the Sacraments of Baptism and Eucharist but have *not* received the Sacrament of Confirmation. If *you* have not yet received the Sacrament of Confirmation, make an appointment immediately with your pastor at your local parish, or with his director of religious education, so that you can be formed and prepared to receive the Sacrament of Confirmation — indeed, so that you can become a *strengthened* "soldier of Christ." (See days 79, 149, 160, 161, 163, 164, and 176.)

Day 149

Soldier of Christ

Put on the whole armor of God, that you may be able to stand against the wiles of the devil. For we are not contending against flesh and blood, but against the principalities, against the powers, against the world rulers of this present darkness, against the spiritual hosts of wickedness in the heavenly places. Therefore take the whole armor of God, that you may be able to withstand in the evil day, and having done all, to stand. Stand therefore, having girded your loins with truth, and having put on the breastplate of righteousness, and having shod your feet with the equipment of the gospel of peace; above all taking the shield of faith, with which you can quench all the flaming darts of the evil one. And take the helmet of salvation, and the sword of the Spirit, which is the word of God. Pray at all times in the Spirit, with all prayer and supplication. To that end keep alert with all perseverance, making supplication for all the saints. (Eph. 6:11–18)

As we do battle and fight in the contest of faith, God, his angels and Christ himself watch us. How exalted is the glory, how great the joy of engaging in a contest with God presiding, of receiving a crown with Christ as judge.

Dear brethren, let us arm ourselves with all our might, let us prepare ourselves for the struggle by innocence of heart, integrity of faith, dedication to virtue....

Let us take this armor and defend ourselves with these spiritual defenses from heaven, so that we may be able to resist the threats of the devil, and fight back on the evil day.

Let us put on the breastplate of righteousness so that our hearts may be safeguarded, proof against the arrows of the enemy. Let our feet be protected by the shoes of the teaching of the Gospel so that when we begin to trample on the serpent and crush it, we may not be bitten and tripped up by it.

Let us with fortitude bear the shield of faith to protect us by extinguishing all the burning arrows that the enemy may launch against us....

Let us arm our right hand with the sword of the spirit ... and like the hand — mindful of the eucharist — that receives the body of the Lord, stretch out to embrace him, and so gain from the Lord the future prize of a heavenly crown.

Dear brethren, have all this firmly fixed in your hearts. If the day of persecution finds us thinking on these things and meditating upon them, the soldier of Christ, trained by Christ's commands and instructions, does not begin to panic at the thought of battle, but is ready for the crown of victory. (St. Cyprian)[174]

You are called to be a soldier of Christ while being a member of the Church Militant living on earth. This teaching is part of the doctrines of the three states of the Church and the Communion of Saints. The souls already in Heaven awaiting reunification with their bodies at the end of time (the general judgment) are members of the Church Triumphant. Those persons living on earth are members of the Church Militant, fighting the good fight of faith (see 1 Tim. 6:12). And the Holy Souls in Purgatory (who are assured entrance into Heaven following their purgation of temporal punishment) are members of the Church Suffering (sometimes also referred to as the Church Penitent or the Church Purgative). The *Catechism* beautifully sums up this teaching by stating the following:

> *The three states of the Church.* "When the Lord comes in glory, and all his angels with him, death will be no more and all things will be subject to him. But at the present time some of his disciples are pilgrims on earth. Others have died and are being purified, while

---

[174] Epistle 58, in *Liturgy of the Hours*, vol. II, 1768–1769.

still others are in glory, contemplating 'in full light, God himself triune and one, exactly as he is.'" (*CCC* 954, quoting *LG* 49; cf. Matt. 25:31; 1 Cor. 15:26–27; Council of Florence (1439): DS 1305)

The term "communion of saints" refers also to the communion of "holy persons" (*sancti*) in Christ who "died for all," so that what each one does or suffers in and for Christ bears fruit for all. (*CCC* 961)

We believe in the communion of all the faithful of Christ, those who are pilgrims on earth, the dead who are being purified, and the blessed in heaven, all together forming one Church; and we believe that in this communion, the merciful love of God and his saints is always [attentive] to our prayers." (*CCC* 962, quoting Paul VI, *Credo of the People of God*, § 30)

Indeed, as a member of the Church Militant on earth, you are called to be a ready, fit, and proud soldier of Christ united with the Church Triumphant in Heaven and with the Church Suffering in Purgatory. You are called into battle. As Ephesians 6:12 teaches: "We are not contending against flesh and blood, but against the principalities, against the powers, against the world rulers of this present darkness, against the spiritual hosts of wickedness in the heavenly places." Be combat-ready. Don't miss your deployment. (See days 3, 79, 85, 90, 148, 157, 160, and 176.)

More on Your Baptismal Priesthood

And they sang a new song, saying, "Worthy art thou to take the scroll and to open its seals, for thou wast slain and by thy blood didst ransom men for God from every tribe and tongue and people and nation, and hast made them a kingdom and priests to our God, and they shall reign on earth." (Rev. 5:9–10)

You are a chosen race, a royal priesthood [1 Pet. 2:9]. This praise was given long ago by Moses to the ancient people of God, and now the apostle Peter rightly gives it to the Gentiles, since they have come to believe in Christ who, as the cornerstone, has brought the nations together in the salvation that belonged to Israel.

Peter calls them *a chosen race* because of their faith, to distinguish them from those who by refusing to accept the living stone have themselves been rejected. They are *a royal priesthood* because they are united to the body of Christ, the supreme king and true priest. As sovereign he grants them his kingdom, and as high priest he washes away their sins by the offering of his blood. Peter says they are *a royal priesthood;* they must always remember to hope for an everlasting kingdom and to offer to God the sacrifice of a blameless life.

They are also called *a consecrated nation, a people claimed by God as his own,* in accordance with the apostle Paul's explanation of the prophet's teaching.... Thus, through the blood of our Redeemer, we have become *a people claimed by God as his own,* as in ancient times the people of Israel were ransomed from Egypt by the blood of a lamb. (St. Bede the Venerable)[175]

---

[175] *Commentary on the First Letter of Peter,* chap. 2, in *Liturgy of the Hours,* vol. II, 704–705.

Under the term *priesthood* in the glossary of the *Catechism of the Catholic Church*, you can find a nice summation of both the priesthood of the faithful (that is, the baptismal priesthood or common priesthood of all the baptized) and the ministerial priesthood, which is received in the Sacrament of Holy Orders. The priesthood of the faithful is "the priestly people of God. Christ has made of his Church a 'kingdom of priests,' and gives the faithful a share in his priesthood through the Sacraments of Baptism and Confirmation." The ministerial priesthood received in the Sacrament of Holy Orders differs in essence from this common priesthood of all the faithful. It has as its purpose to serve the priesthood of all the faithful by building up and guiding the Church in the name of Christ, who is Head of the Body" (*CCC* glossary, s.v. "priesthood"; see *CCC* 784, 1119, 1546, 1547). Although different in *kind*, both priesthoods serve the entire Body of Christ, and both take part in Christ's threefold office as Priest, Prophet, and King (see *CCC* 783–786). Never forget the dignity of your baptismal priesthood. And for you ordained priests, never forget the dignity of your ministerial priesthood. (See days 23, 67, 72, 105, and 200.)

Day 151

Don't Fall Prey to the Godless

Now the Spirit expressly says that in later times some will depart from the faith by giving heed to deceitful spirits and doctrines of demons, through the pretensions of liars whose consciences are seared. (1 Tim. 4:1–2)

For the people who live in this region are all pagans, and Christians who are known to live in the area have taken on pagan ways, showing none of that charity which human beings, even barbarians, regularly display in numerous compassionate deeds. (Pope St. Martin I)[176]

The Second Letter to Timothy has a haunting yet telling passage that speaks specifically of the godless and their ways near the time of Christ's Second Coming. It reads:

> Understand this, that in the last days there will come times of stress. For men will be lovers of self, lovers of money, proud, arrogant, abusive, disobedient to their parents, ungrateful, unholy, inhuman, implacable, slanderers, profligates, fierce, haters of good, treacherous, reckless, swollen with conceit, lovers of pleasure rather than lovers of God, holding the form of religion but denying the power of it. Avoid such people. (3:1–5)

Yet the sad truth is, even Christians can fall under the spell of the godless — that is, their way of life and their way of thought. Those who deny the authentic teachings of Jesus Christ, the only-begotten Son of God come in the flesh — teachings that are part of the deposit of faith and are promulgated by the Church's Magisterium and meant to be embraced — can

---

[176] Epistle 17, in *Liturgy of the Hours*, vol. II, 1771.

easily fall prey to godless ways. Evidence of this is the veritable culture of death raging in the world right now whose tenets many self-proclaimed baptized Christians follow, even though they denigrate the innate dignity of the human person when it comes to human life issues, such as denying the immorality of contraception and promoting abortion, euthanasia, unnatural marriage, immoral lifestyles, and transgender ideology. These are just a few examples; there are others. But you will not fall prey to godless ways if you stand firm in your divinely revealed Catholic Faith. So be sure to *be on guard* and *stand your ground*. Be vigilant for the truth and be vigilant for attacks against the truth as 1 Peter 5:8–9 exhorts you: "Be sober, be watchful. Your adversary the devil prowls around like a roaring lion, seeking some one to devour. Resist him, firm in your faith, knowing that the same experience of suffering is required of your brotherhood throughout the world." (See days 23, 73, 89, 94, 123, and 180.)

Partaking in God's Divine Nature

His divine power has granted to us all things that pertain to life and godliness, through the knowledge of him who called us to his own glory and excellence, by which he has granted to us his precious and very great promises, that through these you may escape from the corruption that is in the world because of passion, and become partakers of the divine nature. (2 Pet. 1:3–4)

God made us so that we might become "partakers of the divine nature" (2 Pet. 1:4) and sharers in His eternity, and so that we might come to be like Him (cf. 1 John 3:2) through deification by grace. It is through deification that all things are reconstituted and achieve their permanence; and it is for its sake that what is not is brought into being and given existence. (St. Maximus the Confessor)[177]

There are many passages in Sacred Scripture and in the writings of the Church Fathers and saints that imply very clearly that the human person is meant to "partake" or "share in" the divine nature of God; that is, that the human person is meant to partake in "deification by [God's own] grace" and in *that sense* becomes "deified." Does such theology or wording mean that one *literally becomes God*? No, not at all; that would be heresy. In fact, both pantheism (which states that everything is God) and polytheism (which states that there are many gods) are condemned by the Church as heresies. So what does such wording mean? In short,

---

[177] "Maximus the Confessor: Various Texts on Theology, the Divine Economy, and Virtue and Vice," no. 42, Orthodox Church Fathers, https://orthodoxchurchfathers.com/fathers/philokalia/maximus-the-confessor-various-texts-on-theology-the-divine-economy-and-virtue-an.html.

it means that man is meant to partake in God's divine life *through grace*. What the Church teaches in this regard is the very biblical concept of *theosis*; that is, *divinization*, which states that man — through his divine, adopted sonship by Almighty God made possible through the Sacrament of Baptism — is called by grace to *partake* or *share in* the divine nature of God precisely through God's divine life granted to the individual (see *CCC* 460), even beyond Baptism and through the other sacraments as well. Some of the Church Fathers, when providing exegesis on Genesis 1:26, for example, teach that for humans, being made in the "image" of God refers to intellective and rational abilities or faculties, and being made after God's "likeness" refers to the *ability to partake* in a life of His divine grace. In other words, we become *like* God, but we *don't become* Him. The latter, again, would clearly be a heresy. Rest in the truth that Almighty God loves you so much that He not only *created* you but also desires for you to *share in His likeness through grace*! As Colossians 2:9–10 teaches: "For in him the whole *fulness of deity* dwells bodily, and *you have come to fulness of life in him*, who is the head of all rule and authority" (emphasis added). (See days 14, 26, 43, 62, 144, 168, and 197.)

Day 153

Walking Blamelessly

O LORD, who shall sojourn in thy tent? Who shall dwell on thy holy hill? He who walks blamelessly, and does what is right, and speaks truth from his heart; who does not slander with his tongue, and does no evil to his friend, nor takes up a reproach against his neighbor. (Ps. 15:1–3)

O Jesus, I adore the thoroughly holy and divine dispositions which characterized Thy activity among men. With what dignity, charity, meekness, patience, modesty, detachment from creatures and attention to God didst Thou move and act in the world of men! O my Saviour, I desire that such dispositions may henceforth characterize all my relations with my neighbor. Alas! How far I am from such perfection and how many faults I have committed in the days gone by. For all these I beg Thy forgiveness, imploring Thee to implant in me all the dispositions I have requested. (St. John Eudes)[178]

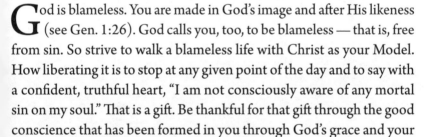

God is blameless. You are made in God's image and after His likeness (see Gen. 1:26). God calls you, too, to be blameless — that is, free from sin. So strive to walk a blameless life with Christ as your Model. How liberating it is to stop at any given point of the day and to say with a confident, truthful heart, "I am not consciously aware of any mortal sin on my soul." That is a gift. Be thankful for that gift through the good conscience that has been formed in you through God's grace and your faithfulness to that grace. You should strive to be free not only from mortal sin but also from any venial sin — especially those habitual

---

[178] *Meditation on Various Subjects*, trans. Reverend Charles Lebrun (New York: P. J. Kenedy and Sons, 1947), 26, http://www.liberius.net/livres/Meditations_on_various_subjects_000000345.pdf.

ones. Be attentive, too, to your daily faults and weaknesses, which, while maybe not venial sins in and of themselves, do act as flaws on your masculine Christian character. (See days 8, 14, 35, 57, 122, 154, 176, 177, and 191.)

Watch Your Tongue

So the tongue is a little member and boasts of great things. How great a forest is set ablaze by a small fire! And the tongue is a fire. The tongue is an unrighteous world among our members, staining the whole body, setting on fire the cycle of nature, and set on fire by hell. For every kind of beast and bird, of reptile and sea creature, can be tamed and has been tamed by humankind, but no human being can tame the tongue — a restless evil, full of deadly poison. With it we bless the Lord and Father, and with it we curse men, who are made in the likeness of God. From the same mouth come blessing and cursing. My brethren, this ought not to be so. Does a spring pour forth from the same opening fresh water and brackish? Can a fig tree, my brethren, yield olives, or a grapevine figs? No more can salt water yield fresh. (James 3:5–12)

At those times when I suffer much, I try to remain silent, as I do not trust my tongue which, at such moments, is inclined to talk for itself, while its duty is to help me praise God for all the blessings and gifts which He has given me. When I receive Jesus in Holy Communion, I ask Him fervently to deign to heal my tongue so that I would offend neither God nor neighbor by it. I want my tongue to praise God without cease. Great are the faults committed by the tongue. The soul will not attain sanctity if it does not keep watch over its tongue. (St. Faustina Kowalska)[179]

* * *

While you may not be able literally to watch your tongue while speaking, you can surely exercise watchful care over it in regard to what it says. The human tongue is indeed a little, yet powerful, member of

[179] *Diary*, no. 92.

the body, as the Letter of James clearly tells you. For example, the tongue reveals temperaments and personalities — the favorable and unfavorable traits of each of these. James cautions, "Know this, my beloved brethren. Let every man be quick to hear, slow to speak, slow to anger.... If any one thinks he is religious, and does not bridle his tongue but deceives his heart, this man's religion is vain" (1:19, 26). Point well made. Watch your words. Watch your tongue. (See days 101, 150, 153, and 166.)

Day 155

The Eucharist and Your Salvation

Truly, truly, I say to you, he who believes has eternal life. I am the bread of life. Your fathers ate the manna in the wilderness, and they died. This is the bread which comes down from heaven, that a man may eat of it and not die. I am the living bread which came down from heaven; if any one eats of this bread, he will live for ever; and the bread which I shall give for the life of the world is my flesh. (John 6:47–51)

If our flesh is not saved, then the Lord has not redeemed us with his blood, the eucharistic chalice does not make us sharers in his blood, and the bread we break does not make us sharers in his body. There can be no blood without veins, flesh and the rest of the human substance, and this the Word of God actually became: it was with his own blood that he redeemed us. As the Apostle says: *In him, through his blood, we have been redeemed, our sins have been forgiven* [see Eph. 1:7; Col. 1:14].

We are his members and we are nourished by creation, which is his gift to us, for it is he who causes the sun to rise and the rain to fall. He declared that the chalice, which comes from his creation, was his blood, and he makes it the nourishment of our blood. He affirmed that the bread, which comes from his creation, was his body, and he makes it the nourishment of our body. When the chalice we mix and the bread we bake receive the word of God, the eucharistic elements become the body and blood of Christ, by which our bodies live and grow. How then can it be said that flesh belonging to the Lord's own body and nourished by his body and blood is incapable of receiving God's gift of eternal life? Saint Paul says in his letter to the Ephesians that *we are members of his body* [Eph. 5:30], of his flesh and bones. He is not speaking of some spiritual and incorporeal kind of man, *for spirits do not have flesh and bones* [Luke 24:39]. He is speaking of a real human body composed of flesh, sinews and bones, nourished by the chalice of Christ's blood and receiving growth from the bread which is his body.

... The Wisdom of God places these things at the service of man and when they receive God's word they become the eucharist, which is the body and blood of Christ. (St. Irenaeus)[180]

❧————————❧

Whenever you receive the Eucharist, you must do so *worthily* — that is, you must not be morally aware of any mortal sin on your soul. If you are morally aware of mortal sin on your soul (see *CCC* 1854–1864), then you must first be reconciled to God and the Church by receiving the Sacrament of Reconciliation — holy Confession. By following this important path in the spiritual life that concerns the "source and summit" of the Christian life (*LG* 11; *CCC* 1324), you will be cooperating with God to *work out your salvation* with a filial fear (see Phil. 2:12). Also, make frequent visits to the Most Blessed Sacrament to enrich your life and vocation. As Pope St. John Paul II instructs:

> The visit to the Blessed Sacrament ... is a great treasure of the Catholic faith. It nourishes social love and gives us opportunities for adoration and thanksgiving, for reparation and supplication. Benediction of the Blessed Sacrament, Exposition and Adoration of the Blessed Sacrament, Holy Hours and Eucharistic processions are likewise precious elements ... in full accord with the teaching of the Second Vatican Council. (homily, Phoenix Park, Dublin, Ireland, September 29, 1979).

(See days 21, 60, 65, 92, 97, 99, 103, 114, 132, 142, 144, 145, 147, 185, and 199.)

---

[180] *Against Heresies,* bk. 5, chap. 2, in *Liturgy of the Hours,* vol. II, 727–728.

Day 156

The Reality of Sin, Vice, and Disorder

I do not understand my own actions. For I do not do what I want, but I do the very thing I hate. Now if I do what I do not want, I agree that the law is good. So then it is no longer I that do it, but sin which dwells within me. For I know that nothing good dwells within me, that is, in my flesh. I can will what is right, but I cannot do it. For I do not do the good I want, but the evil I do not want is what I do. Now if I do what I do not want, it is no longer I that do it, but sin which dwells within me. So I find it to be a law that when I want to do right, evil lies close at hand. For I delight in the law of God, in my inmost self, but I see in my members another law at war with the law of my mind and making me captive to the law of sin which dwells in my members. Wretched man that I am! Who will deliver me from this body of death? Thanks be to God through Jesus Christ our Lord! So then, I of myself serve the law of God with my mind, but with my flesh I serve the law of sin. (Rom. 7:15–25)

This is the definition of sin: the misuse of powers given us by God for doing good, a use contrary to God's commandments. On the other hand, the virtue that God asks of us is the use of the same powers based on a good conscience in accordance with God's command. (St. Basil the Great)[181]

❧────────────❧

In the above Scripture passage from the Letter to the Romans, St. Paul is implying that *concupiscence* is real. Remember that the Church defines *concupiscence* as "human appetites or desires which remain disordered due to the temporal consequences of original sin, which remain even after Baptism, and which produce an inclination to sin" (*CCC* glossary,

---

[181] *Detailed Rules for Monks*, Resp. 2, in *Liturgy of the Hours*, vol. III, 59.

s.v. "concupiscence"; see *CCC* 1264, 1426, 2515). Although Christ never sinned, He fully understands your weakness and what it is you struggle with. Two effects of the Fall of our first parents (i.e., their disobedience, which ushered in the Original Sin) are a darkened intellect and a weakened will. Because of this, you might often misuse the bodily and spiritual powers that God gave you, powers that are part of human nature and are good in and of themselves; for example, the bodily powers (or senses) of sight, smell, taste, touch, and hearing *and* the spiritual powers (or faculties) of the soul: intellect, will, memory, and imagination. You need to use these powers virtuously, in an ordered way, not in an inordinate or disordered way (see *CCC* 1803). Each day, you can pray for virtue and order in your life and even offer Holy Communions for this intention. Virtue and order are much better than vice and disorder. (See days 34, 37, 43, 80, 118, 126, 129, 134, 164, and 195.)

Day 157

Persevering to the End

Let us also lay aside every weight, and sin which clings so closely, and let us run with perseverance the race that is set before us, looking to Jesus the pioneer and perfecter of our faith, who for the joy that was set before him endured the cross, despising the shame, and is seated at the right hand of the throne of God. (Heb. 12:1–2)

This is the glory of man: to persevere and remain in the service of God. (St. Irenaeus)[182]

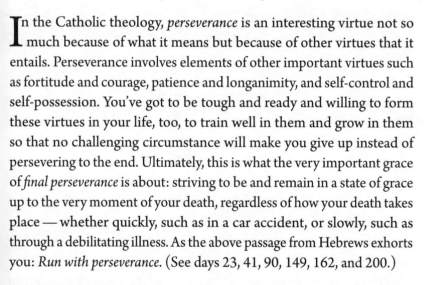

In the Catholic theology, *perseverance* is an interesting virtue not so much because of what it means but because of other virtues that it entails. Perseverance involves elements of other important virtues such as fortitude and courage, patience and longanimity, and self-control and self-possession. You've got to be tough and ready and willing to form these virtues in your life, too, to train well in them and grow in them so that no challenging circumstance will make you give up instead of persevering to the end. Ultimately, this is what the very important grace of *final perseverance* is about: striving to be and remain in a state of grace up to the very moment of your death, regardless of how your death takes place — whether quickly, such as in a car accident, or slowly, such as through a debilitating illness. As the above passage from Hebrews exhorts you: *Run with perseverance.* (See days 23, 41, 90, 149, 162, and 200.)

---

[182] *Against Heresies*, bk. 4, chap. 13, in *Liturgy of the Hours*, vol. II, 78.

Day 158

God's Time and Man's Time

For everything there is a season, and a time for every matter under heaven: a time to be born, and a time to die; a time to plant, and a time to pluck up what is planted; a time to kill, and a time to heal; a time to break down, and a time to build up; a time to weep, and a time to laugh; a time to mourn, and a time to dance; a time to cast away stones, and a time to gather stones together; a time to embrace, and a time to refrain from embracing; a time to seek, and a time to lose; a time to keep, and a time to cast away; a time to rend, and a time to sew; a time to keep silence, and a time to speak; a time to love, and a time to hate; a time for war, and a time for peace. (Eccles. 3:1–8)

By the Incarnation of the Word, human time is called to share in the eternity of God. (Pope St. John Paul II)[183]

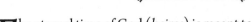

The eternal time of God (*kairos*) is meant to "collide" with the created and chronological time of man (*chronos*). These two enter into one another. God entered into your time so that you might enter into His. Through His Sacred Incarnation in the womb of His Blessed Mother (*Theotokos* — "God bearer"), God, Who is eternal, entered into the created and chronological time of man — a time that He Himself *created for man*. Since Almighty God offers you so much of His time, be sure to offer Him much of your time. You can do this while in prayer (whether personal or familial, communal or congregational, such as when participating in the Holy Sacrifice and Sacred Banquet of the Mass) and while partaking in acts of charity (whether through volunteering or financial contributions).

---

[183] Homily, *Te Deum* Vespers, December 31, 1996.

Also, *consecrate* to God your prayer, family life, friendships, employment, recreation, leisure, and the "time" it takes to be faithful to all of these areas for a life of virtuous "balance." You can do this through the Morning Offering that you make each day (see the appendix of prayers). In your balanced, well-lived life, be sure to sanctify — that is, make holy — *every moment* of time. (See days 103, 114, 131, 159, and 169.)

The Unfathomable Incarnation of God

And Mary said to the angel, "How can this be, since I have no husband?" And the angel said to her, "The Holy Spirit will come upon you, and the power of the Most High will overshadow you; therefore the child to be born will be called holy, the Son of God." (Luke 1:34–35)

Since our weak minds cannot comprehend the Father or the Son, we have been given the Holy Spirit as our intermediary and advocate, to shed light on that hard doctrine of our faith, the incarnation of God. (St. Hilary of Poitiers)[184]

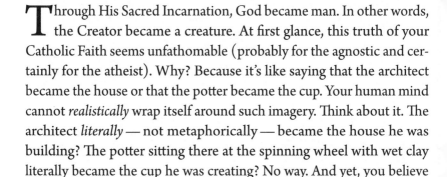

Through His Sacred Incarnation, God became man. In other words, the Creator became a creature. At first glance, this truth of your Catholic Faith seems unfathomable (probably for the agnostic and certainly for the atheist). Why? Because it's like saying that the architect became the house or that the potter became the cup. Your human mind cannot *realistically* wrap itself around such imagery. Think about it. The architect *literally* — not metaphorically — became the house he was building? The potter sitting there at the spinning wheel with wet clay literally became the cup he was creating? No way. And yet, you believe in the Sacred Incarnation of the Son of God. Why? This can be answered in only one word: *love* — the love that He has for you and the love that you have for Him. (See days 103, 114, 131, 158, and 169.)

---

[184] *On the Trinity*, bk. 2, in *Liturgy of the Hours*, vol. II, 998–999.

Seeking God

Seek the LORD while he may be found, call upon him while he is near. (Isa. 55:6)

My soul, have you found what you are looking for? You were looking for God, and you have discovered that he is the supreme being, and that you could not possibly imagine anything more perfect. You have discovered that this supreme being is life itself, light, wisdom, goodness, eternal blessedness and blessed eternity. He is everywhere, and he is timeless. (St. Anselm)[185]

———✦———

St. Catherine of Siena wrote, "Eternal God, eternal Trinity ... you are a mystery as deep as the sea; the more I search, the more I find, and the more I find the more I search for you. But I can never be satisfied; what I receive will ever leave me desiring more. When you fill my soul I have an even greater hunger, and I grow more famished for your light. I desire above all to see you, the true light, as you really are."[186] The saints have a special way of communicating the truth that the mystery of Almighty God — the Most Holy Trinity — is an inexhaustible mystery. And yet God is a *knowable* God because of what He has revealed about Himself in Sacred Scripture and Tradition, which is taught by the Magisterium of the Church and safeguarded in the deposit of faith. You, too, are called to search for Almighty God in the many ways the saints searched for Him, to discover Him in the many ways the saints discovered Him, and to keep on pondering and entering into His mystery just as the saints — in many ways — pondered and entered into it. Become a great saint. (See days 20, 41, 104, 111, 124, 143, 165, and 188.)

[185] *Proslogion*, chap. 14, in *Liturgy of the Hours*, vol. II, 1774.
[186] Dialogue *On Divine Providence*, chap. 167, in *Liturgy of the Hours*, vol. II, 1794.

Day 161

Standing Up for Truth

Jesus then said to the Jews who had believed in him, "If you continue in my word, you are truly my disciples, and you will know the truth, and the truth will make you free." (John 8:31–32)

Anyone who does not love the truth has not yet come to know it. (Pope St. Gregory the Great)[187]

The great Carmelite and Auschwitz martyr St. Teresa Benedicta of the Cross (St. Edith Stein) teaches that "God is truth. All who seek truth seek God, whether this is clear to them or not."[188] And St. Paulinus states, "Our love for truth must be very great. So great in fact that all our words must possess the value of oaths."[189] The Most Holy Trinity is the God of truth (see Isa. 65:16). The devil, on the other hand, is the father of lies. Jesus makes this clear when He states that the devil "was a murderer from the beginning, and has nothing to do with the truth, because there is no truth in him. When he lies, he speaks according to his own nature, for he is a liar and the father of lies" (John 8:44). Hopefully, you are always a man of truth. Or are you a liar? Sometimes? Often? For example, by fudging on your tax returns? By calling in sick to work when you're not sick? By lying to your spouse about — whatever? Become *fully committed* to the truth. Be a man of truth, not a man of lies. (See days 12, 107, 148, 151, 163, 164, 168, 169, 174, 175, and 182.)

[187] Homily 14 on the Gospels, in *Liturgy of the Hours*, vol. II, 753.
[188] Letter 259, to Sr. Adelgundis Jaegerschmid, OSB, March 23, 1938, Carmelite Quotes, March 23, https://carmelitequotes.blog/2023/03/22/edith-godistruth/.
[189] Schroeder, *Every Day Is a Gift*, 37.

Purity of Intention

Create in me a clean heart, O God, and put a new and right spirit within me. (Ps. 51:10)

O inexhaustible treasure of purity of intention which makes all our actions perfect and so pleasing to God!

O Jesus, You know how weak I am; be then ever with me; guide my actions and my whole being, You who are my very best Teacher! Truly, Jesus, I become frightened when I look at my own misery, but at the same time I am reassured by Your unfathomable mercy, which exceeds my misery by the measure of all eternity. This disposition of soul clothes me in Your power. O joy that flows from the knowledge of one's self! O unchanging Truth, Your constancy is everlasting! (St. Faustina Kowalska)[190]

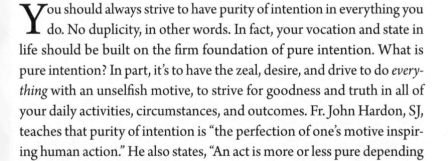

You should always strive to have purity of intention in everything you do. No duplicity, in other words. In fact, your vocation and state in life should be built on the firm foundation of pure intention. What is pure intention? In part, it's to have the zeal, desire, and drive to do *everything* with an unselfish motive, to strive for goodness and truth in all of your daily activities, circumstances, and outcomes. Fr. John Hardon, SJ, teaches that purity of intention is "the perfection of one's motive inspiring human action." He also states, "An act is more or less pure depending on the degree of selfless love of God with which it is performed."[191] Your goal, then, is to strive for a perfect motive in all that inspires your actions throughout any given day — and build that motive on the foundation of

---

[190] *Diary*, no. 66.
[191] Hardon, *Modern Catholic Dictionary*, s.v. "purity of intention," 452.

selfless love of God and neighbor. Notice, too, that St. Faustina implies in the above quote that an added benefit of living with purity of intention is that it helps one to grow in self-knowledge, to "know yourself" better; in other words, to identify your virtues in order to advance them in your life and to identify your vices in order to begin to uproot them out of your life. The lesson here? Purity of intention is pretty powerful. (See days 4, 7, 19, 25, 52, 115, 184, 185, and 200.)

The Way, the Truth, the Life

Jesus said to him, "I am the way, and the truth, and the life; no one comes to the Father, but by me." (John 14:6)

There is no doubt that blessed John [the Baptist] suffered imprisonment and chains as a witness to our Redeemer, whose forerunner he was, and gave his life for him. His persecutor [King Herod] had demanded not that he should deny Christ, but only that he should keep silent about the truth. Nevertheless, he died for Christ. Does Christ not say: *I am the truth*? Therefore, because John shed his blood for the truth, he surely died for Christ. (St. Bede the Venerable)[192]

❖───────────❖

Jesus Christ is the truth. And when the Second Person of the Trinity — the Word, the Divine Logos (see John 1:1) — became the *incarnate* Son of God in the womb of the Blessed Virgin Mary, you know that "the Word became flesh and dwelt among us, full of grace and truth" (John 1:14). Proverbs 8:6–7 states, "Hear, for I will speak noble things, and from my lips will come what is right; for my mouth will utter truth." And James 3:14 commands you, "If you have bitter jealousy and selfish ambition in your hearts, do not boast and be false to the truth." So, when it comes to living, breathing, speaking, and professing the truth, take Jesus Christ as your Model. Jesus Christ is God, and God is truth. (See days 148, 151, 161, 164, 168, 175, and 182.)

---

[192] Homily 23, in *Liturgy of the Hours*, vol. IV, 1359.

Day 164

Faith and Reason

"Come now, let us reason together," says the LORD. (Isa. 1:18)

Faith and reason are like two wings on which the human spirit rises to the contemplation of truth; and God has placed in the human heart a desire to know the truth — in a word, to know himself — so that, by knowing and loving God, men and women may also come to the fullness of truth about themselves (cf. Ex 33:18; Ps 27:8–9; 63:2–3; Jn 14:8; 1 Jn 3:2). (Pope St. John Paul II)[193]

Psalms 8:4–6 speaks beautifully about the greatness that the human person — because of the dignity of human nature — is called to and, by default, the greatness *you* are called to precisely because you share in that same human nature: "What is man that thou art mindful of him, and the son of man that thou dost care for him? Yet thou hast made him little less than God, and dost crown him with glory and honor. Thou hast given him dominion over the works of thy hands; thou hast put all things under his feet." This greatness that you are called to as a human person — as a man — is built on the foundation of truth, truth that is both *sought after* and *grounded in* human faith and reason. The human intellect and will are great gifts indeed: the intellect as the driving force *to seek and to know*, and the will as the driving force *to choose and to do*, all that is in accord with God's holy will for you. Employ your intellect and will to engage your faith and reason to seek, know, choose, and do all that is good, true, and beautiful (see *CCC* 1803). Human persons are set apart for awesome tasks, as only human persons are made in God's

---

[193] Encyclical letter *Fides et Ratio* (September 14, 1998), opening paragraph.

image and after His likeness (see Gen. 1:26). The nonrational brute animals, on the other hand, act according to their instincts. Pursue truth with your faith and with your reason. Seek after it and become grounded in it, and immerse yourself in all that is good, true, and beautiful — just as God wills for you to do. (See days 28, 30, 43, 80, 106, 130, and 156.)

Day 165

Wanting to Know God

And this is eternal life, that they know thee the only true God, and Jesus Christ whom thou hast sent. (John 17:3)

O God, let me know you and love you so that I may find my joy in you; and if I cannot do so fully in this life, let me at least make some progress every day, until at last that knowledge, love and joy come to me in all their plenitude. While I am here on earth let me learn to know you better, so that in heaven I may know you fully; let my love for you grow deeper here, so that there I may love you fully. On earth then I shall have great joy in hope, and in heaven complete joy in the fulfilment of my hope. (St. Anselm)[194]

St. Anselm of Canterbury had an interesting take on faith and reason (i.e., understanding). He famously wrote, "I do not seek to understand in order that I may believe, but rather, I believe in order that I may understand" (*Proslogion*). In other words, St. Anselm believed that human faith is the foundation upon which human reason (or understanding) is built, and not vice versa. The Latin phrase that sums up St. Anselm's thought here is *fides quaerens intellectum* — "faith seeking understanding." This illustrates the preeminence that faith should have in your life. Almighty God — the Blessed Trinity — is a God of truth "who can neither deceive nor be deceived" (words from the Act of Faith; see the appendix of prayers). Remember that faith is "both a gift of God and a human act by which the believer gives personal adherence to God who invites his response, and freely assents to the whole truth that God has revealed" by

[194] *Proslogion*, chap. 14, in *Liturgy of the Hours*, vol. II, 1775.

way of Sacred Scripture, Tradition, and the Magisterium (the teaching office of the Church which itself is *rooted* or *grounded* in the Apostolic College) (*CCC* glossary, s.v. "faith"; *CCC* 26, 142, 150, 1814, 2087). In short, St. Anselm believed — and so should you — that God will not lead one into error in his understanding by way of embracing revealed, true, grounded faith. Remain grounded, then, in your Catholic Faith. (See days 20, 41, 104, 111, 124, 128, 143, 160, and 188.)

Speaking about Christ

Therefore God has highly exalted him and bestowed on him the name which is above every name, that at the name of Jesus every knee should bow, in heaven and on earth and under the earth, and every tongue confess that Jesus Christ is Lord, to the glory of God the Father. (Phil. 2:9–11)

When we speak about wisdom, we are speaking of Christ. When we speak about virtue, we are speaking of Christ. When we speak about justice, we are speaking of Christ. When we speak about peace, we are speaking of Christ. When we speak about truth and life and redemption, we are speaking of Christ. (St. Ambrose)[195]

B e eloquent, charitable, and courageous when speaking to others about Jesus Christ as your Lord and Savior. To do this effectively, you must ground yourself in everything the Old Testament foretold of Him. You must ground yourself in everything the New Testament teaches about Him. You must ground yourself in everything He Himself says and teaches in the four Gospels. And you must ground yourself in how the Church — Christ's Bride — upholds all of it. (See days 98, 107, 182, and 200.)

---

[195] *Explanations of the Psalms*, Ps. 36, in *Liturgy of the Hours*, vol. III, 216.

Speaking about Bridegroom and Bride

Be subject to one another out of reverence for Christ. Wives, be subject to your husbands, as to the Lord. For the husband is the head of the wife as Christ is the head of the church, his body, and is himself its Savior. As the church is subject to Christ, so let wives also be subject in everything to their husbands. Husbands, love your wives, as Christ loved the church and gave himself up for her, that he might sanctify her, having cleansed her by the washing of water with the word, that he might present the church to himself in splendor, without spot or wrinkle or any such thing, that she might be holy and without blemish. Even so husbands should love their wives as their own bodies. He who loves his wife loves himself. For no man ever hates his own flesh, but nourishes and cherishes it, as Christ does the church, because we are members of his body. "For this reason a man shall leave his father and mother and be joined to his wife, and the two shall become one flesh" [Gen. 2:24]. This is a great mystery, and I mean in reference to Christ and the church; however, let each one of you love his wife as himself, and let the wife see that she respects her husband. (Eph. 5:21–33)

When he entrusted his sheep to Peter as one person to another, Christ chose to make Peter one with himself. He wanted to entrust him with the sheep in such a way that he himself might be the head and Peter might represent the body, that is, the Church. As bridegroom and bride, Christ and the Church were to be two in one flesh. (St. Augustine)[196]

There are a lot of people — both men and women — who feel uncomfortable whenever they come across the above passage from

---

[196] *Sermo* 46 on pastors, in *Liturgy of the Hours*, vol. IV, 307.

St. Paul's Letter to the Ephesians. But this should not be the case. Jesus Christ clearly came to serve, not to be served (see Matt. 20:28; Mark 10:45). As St. Cyril of Alexandria echoes this: "[Jesus Christ] came into this world in human flesh not to be served, but, as he himself said, to serve and to give his life as a ransom for many."[197] So, husbands — and men in general — take heed. Your leadership is about sacrificial love and serving. Men are meant to be leaders, yes. After all, their skilled leadership in both spiritual and temporal affairs is part of their *masculine genius* as providers, protectors, and defenders. But the authentic and true leadership of men is not about their being served. No. Rather, it's about *their serving*, and sacrificially so, just as Christ Himself did throughout the four Gospels. Let Christ and His example form you into the true leader you are meant to be as a man: a loving leader in serving and a loving leader of service. (See days 1, 71, 146, and 175.)

---

[197] *Commentary on the letter to the Romans*, chap. 15, in *Liturgy of the Hours*, vol. II, 807.

Man's Greatness

Have this mind among yourselves, which was in Christ Jesus, who, though he was in the form of God, did not count equality with God a thing to be grasped, but emptied himself, taking the form of a servant, being born in the likeness of men. And being found in human form he humbled himself and became obedient unto death, even death on a cross. (Phil. 2:5–8)

[Jesus Christ] took the nature of a servant without stain of sin, enlarging our humanity without diminishing his divinity. He emptied himself; though invisible he made himself visible, though Creator and Lord of all things he chose to be one of us mortal men. Yet this was the condescension of compassion, not the loss of omnipotence. So he who in the nature of God had created man, became in the nature of a servant, man himself.

Thus the Son of God enters this lowly world. He comes down from the throne of heaven, yet does not separate himself from the Father's glory. (Pope St. Leo the Great)[198]

Stop and think about this: it is *precisely* in God's condescension in becoming man and taking on your human nature that you are elevated and called to partake in *His* divine life (see 2 Pet. 1:4). Be thankful for these great truths: God wants you to share in His glory one day in Heaven, *and* He wants you to share in His own divine life even now by receiving and partaking in His sanctifying grace. This is your greatness, O man, now and in the future. St. Basil the Great echoes

---

[198] Epistle 28, *ad Flavianum*, in *Liturgy of the Hours*, vol. II, 1746.

all of this when he states, "Here is man's greatness, here is man's glory and majesty: to know in truth what is great, to hold fast to it, and to seek glory from the Lord of glory."[199] (See days 14, 20, 26, 43, 144, 152, 161, 163, and 197.)

[199] Homily 20 *De humilitate*, 3, in *Liturgy of the Hours*, vol. II, 223.

Day 169

A True Child of God

Jesus said, "Let the children come to me, and do not hinder them; for to such belongs the kingdom of heaven." (Matt. 19:14)

To be a child of God means to walk at the hand of God, to do God's will, to put all worries and all hopes in God's hands.... God in us, and we in Him, that is our portion in the divine realm for which the Incarnation laid the foundation. (St. Teresa Benedicta of the Cross [St. Edith Stein])[200]

><

To be a child of God does not mean to be childish (see 1 Cor. 13:11). Rather, to be a child of God means to be humble, trusting, and ever attentive and ready to hear and learn from Him and to do His will — indeed, to conform your will to His. For grown men, such characteristics are *not* signs of weakness. No, not at all. Your Heavenly Father wants you to be humble and trusting toward Him. He wants you to be ever attentive and ready to hear Him and learn from Him. Because He knows what's best for you, He desires that you freely do His will and freely conform your will to His. Just as a loving child would be humble and trusting toward his parent, who knows what's best for him, that same child desires to be ever attentive and ready to hear and learn from that parent. So should be your relationship with God. St. John Chrysostom says, "There are no artists more divine than those who know how to fashion a child's soul within themselves. Such artists know how to draw forth the greatest divine radiance into their souls."[201] As a true man of God, be a true child of God. (See days 12, 42, 51, 61, 107, 161, 177, and 181.)

[200] *Daybook*, 118, in María Ruiz Scaperlanda, *Edith Stein: The Life and Legacy of St. Teresa Benedicta of the Cross* (Manchester, NH: Sophia Institute Press, 2017), 197.
[201] Schroeder, *Every Day Is a Gift*, 61.

Conquer Evil with Good

Repay no one evil for evil, but take thought for what is noble in the sight of all. If possible, so far as it depends upon you, live peaceably with all. Beloved, never avenge yourselves, but leave it to the wrath of God; for it is written, "Vengeance is mine, I will repay, says the Lord." No, "if your enemy is hungry, feed him; if he is thirsty, give him drink; for by so doing you will heap burning coals upon his head." Do not be overcome by evil, but overcome evil with good. (Rom. 12:17–21)

We should love and feel compassion for those who oppose us, rather than abhor and despise them, since they harm themselves and do us good, and adorn us with crowns of everlasting glory while they incite God's anger against themselves. And even more than this, we should pray for them and not be overcome by evil, but overcome evil by goodness. We should heap good works *like red-hot coals* of burning love *upon their heads*, as our Apostle [Paul] urges us to do [see Rom. 12:20], so that when they become aware of our tolerance and gentleness they may undergo a change of heart and be prompted to turn in love to God.

In his mercy, God has chosen us, unworthy as we are, out of this world, to serve him and thus to advance in goodness and to bear the greatest possible fruit of love in patience. (St. Anthony Zaccaria)[202]

Sometimes, it is rather easy to conquer evil with good; sometimes, it is rather hard — for example, when trying to overcome an ingrained vice. Regardless, you must *always* strive to conquer evil with good. It is your Christian calling to do so. And there are many helps to assist you

---

[202] Sermon to fellow members of his society, J. A. Gabutio, in *Liturgy of the Hours*, vol. III, 1523–1524.

in this noble effort: the daily meditative reading of Scripture (*Lectio Divina*), the daily praying of the Rosary and the Divine Mercy Chaplet, frequent reception of Confession and the Eucharist, and even good, sound spiritual direction. The devil loves evil, and he wants to conquer. Don't let him. With God's grace and your cooperation with it, you've got this. (See days 5, 13, 63, 179, 180, 185, 190, 195, and 196.)

Day 171

Never Be Deterred from Your Ultimate Goal

Enter by the narrow gate; for the gate is wide and the way is easy, that leads to destruction, and those who enter by it are many. For the gate is narrow and the way is hard, that leads to life, and those who find it are few. (Matt. 7:13–14)

Anyone who is determined to reach his destination is not deterred by the roughness of the road that leads to it. Nor must we allow the charm of success to seduce us, or we shall be like a foolish traveler who is so distracted by the pleasant meadows through which he is passing that he forgets where he is going. (Pope St. Gregory the Great)[203]

Your ultimate goal is Heaven. Never forget this. The average human life expectancy is about eighty years. This is merely an instant when you think of the eternity that awaits you. Getting to Heaven may be a rougher road for you than for others (or vice versa), given the fact that humans live in a broken, wounded world because of Original Sin and given the fact, too, that the world is seemingly becoming more inimical to Christianity. Nevertheless, as Pope St. Gregory the Great advises above, you must never become deterred by the roughness of that road nor become so enamored with your successes that you forget that God made you to share an eternity with Him. Know this: regardless of the bad and the good you endure throughout life, God — along with His angels and saints — is there to guide you and assist you toward your ultimate goal: Heaven. (See days 1, 3, 14, 16, 43, 101, 120, 124, 162, 186, 187, and 200.)

---

[203] Homily 14 on the Gospels, in *Liturgy of the Hours*, vol. II, 754.

The Call of Baptism

And the eunuch said to Philip, "About whom, pray, does the prophet say this, about himself or about some one else?" Then Philip opened his mouth, and beginning with this scripture he told him the good news of Jesus. And as they went along the road they came to some water, and the eunuch said, "See, here is water! What is to prevent my being baptized?" And he commanded the chariot to stop, and they both went down into the water, Philip and the eunuch, and he baptized him. And when they came up out of the water, the Spirit of the Lord caught up Philip; and the eunuch saw him no more, and went on his way rejoicing. (Acts 8:34–39)

Our Lord made a covenant with us through baptism in order to give us eternal life. There is in baptism an image both of death and of life, the water being the symbol of death, the Spirit giving the pledge of life. The association of water and the Spirit is explained by the twofold purpose for which baptism was instituted, namely, to destroy the sin in us so that it could never again give birth to death, and to enable us to live by the Spirit and so win the reward of holiness. The water into which the body enters as into a tomb symbolizes death; the Spirit instills into us his life-giving power, awakening our souls from the death of sin to the life that they had in the beginning. This then is what it means to be born again of water and the Spirit: we die in the water, and we come to life again through the Spirit.

To signify this death and to enlighten the baptized by transmitting to them knowledge of God, the great sacrament of baptism is administered by means of a triple immersion and the invocation of each of the three divine Persons. Whatever grace there is in the water comes not from its own nature but from the presence of the Spirit, since *baptism is not a cleansing of the body, but a pledge made to God from a clear conscience* [1 Pet. 3:21]. (St. Basil the Great)[204]

———————◆———————

By way of adopted sonship, you are called to be *fully* a child of God the Father, *through* Jesus Christ, His Son, *in* the Holy Spirit. The Sacrament of Baptism achieves this. This is why a valid Baptism requires a valid Trinitarian formula. St. Peter Damian teaches that "anyone who wishes to offer himself to God in the tent of Christ, which is the Church, must first bathe in the spring of holy baptism; then he must put on the various garments of the virtues."[205] If you are not yet baptized, know that you are invited to be baptized. So, make an appointment with your local parish to meet its pastor and inquire about the Sacrament of Baptism. If you are already baptized (whether as an infant, adolescent, or adult), ask yourself this question: "Do I know my baptismal anniversary day?" That is, do you know the very calendar day (and year) on which you were baptized in the name of the Father, and of the Son, and of the Holy Spirit? If not, why not? Your baptismal day is the most important day in your life's history, along with your actual conception day and birthday. So if you don't know the day and year of your Baptism, contact the church where you were baptized to find out that important date — and celebrate it each year committedly and joyfully. (See days 1, 3, 23, 72, 99, 105, 108, 114, 126, 136, 142, 145, 148, 150, 152, 186, and 187.)

---

[204] *On the Holy Spirit*, chap. 15, in *Liturgy of the Hours*, vol. II, 762–763.
[205] Sermon 3 on St. George, Martyr, in *Liturgy of the Hours*, vol. II, 1778.

Day 173

To Love Your Neighbor Is to Love God

And he said to him, "You shall love the Lord your God with all your heart, and with all your soul, and with all your mind. This is the great and first commandment. And a second is like it, You shall love your neighbor as yourself. On these two commandments depend all the law and the prophets." (Matt. 22:37–40)

If we love our neighbor, we automatically love God as well. For it is in the unity of this twofold love that God has constituted the fullness of the Law and the Prophets. (Pope St. Leo the Great)[206]

Think about this: ideally, to love God is to love your neighbor, and to love your neighbor is to love God. While this is intimated by analogy, the strength of the link is definitely known through Christian revelation. St. Anthony Zaccaria describes the link this way: "Let us run like fools not only to God but also to our neighbor, who is the intermediary to whom we give what we cannot give to God."[207] So, run like a fool — every day — to both Almighty God and to your neighbor, and show *both* that you really love them. (See days 27, 36, 57, 76, 128, 141, and 188.)

[206] Schroeder, *Every Day Is a Gift*, 163.
[207] Quoted in Robert Ellsberg, *Blessed Among Us: Day by Day with Saintly Witnesses* (Collegeville, MN: Liturgical Press, 2016), 384.

Day 174

Do Not Be Led Astray

Although they knew God they did not honor him as God or give thanks to him, but they became futile in their thinking and their senseless minds were darkened. Claiming to be wise, they became fools, and exchanged the glory of the immortal God for images resembling mortal man or birds or animals or reptiles. Therefore God gave them up in the lusts of their hearts to impurity, to the dishonoring of their bodies among themselves, because they exchanged the truth about God for a lie and worshiped and served the creature rather than the Creator, who is blessed for ever! Amen. For this reason God gave them up to dishonorable passions. Their women exchanged natural relations for unnatural, and the men likewise gave up natural relations with women and were consumed with passion for one another, men committing shameless acts with men and receiving in their own persons the due penalty for their error. And since they did not see fit to acknowledge God, God gave them up to a base mind and to improper conduct. (Rom. 1:21–28)

Do not be led astray by false doctrines or by old and idle tales.... The holy prophets lived according to Jesus Christ, and that is why they were persecuted. They were inspired by his grace to bring full conviction to an unbelieving world that there is one God, manifested now through Jesus Christ his Son, his Word, who came forth from the Father and was in all things pleasing to the one who sent him. (St. Ignatius of Antioch)[208]

O ne topic or theme that the Church Fathers, early ecclesiastical writers (such as Origen and Tertullian), Doctors of the Church, and the

---

[208] *Letter to the Magnesians*, in *Liturgy of the Hours*, vol. III, 521.

blesseds and saints of the Catholic Church seem to return to often is the reality that it is possible to fall away from the truth. But what does this mean, exactly? To many of them, it means to fall away from the *Church*. Why is this? To fall away from truth is to fall away from Christ, Who is "the way, and the truth, and the life" (John 14:6). And remember this, too: "Wherever Jesus Christ is, there is the Catholic Church" (St. Ignatius, *Epistle to the Smyrnaeans*, chap. 8). Many of these holy men and women, then, equate falling away from truth with falling away from the Church established by Jesus Christ, which is "the pillar and bulwark of the truth" (1 Tim. 3:15). In this regard, St. John Chrysostom states, "Never separate yourself from the Church. No institution has the power of the Church. The Church is your hope. The Church is your salvation. The Church is your refuge."[209] And then there is St. Athanasius, who exhorts you *never* to fall away from the Church when he teaches, "It will not be out of place to consider the ancient tradition, teaching and faith of the Catholic Church, which was revealed by the Lord, proclaimed by the apostles and guarded by the fathers. For upon this faith the Church is built, and if anyone were to lapse from it, he would no longer be a Christian either in fact or in name."[210] In short, to *fall away* from the Church is to fall away from Christ, and to fall away from Christ is to fall away from truth. To fall away from truth is to *fall into* lies, error, and falsehood. Guard yourself in the truth (see 2 Tim. 2:15); stay in the Church. (See days 12, 24, 43, 58, 129, 156, 157, 175, and 195.)

---

[209] Schroeder, *Every Day Is a Gift*, 134.
[210] *First letter to Serapion*, in *Liturgy of the Hours*, vol. III, 584.

Day 175

Unity in Things Spiritual and Temporal

I hope to come to you soon, but I am writing these instructions to you so that, if I am delayed, you may know how one ought to behave in the household of God, which is the church of the living God, the pillar and bulwark of the truth. Great indeed, we confess, is the mystery of our religion: He was manifested in the flesh, vindicated in the Spirit, seen by angels, preached among the nations, believed on in the world, taken up in glory. (1 Tim. 3:14–16)

I would have you all guard against falling into the snares of false doctrine. Have a firm faith in the reality of the Lord's birth, and passion and resurrection which took place when Pontius Pilate was Procurator. All these deeds were truly and certainly accomplished by Jesus Christ, who is our hope; may none of you ever be turned away from Him!...

... Take care, then, to be firmly grounded in the teachings of the Lord and his apostles so that *you may prosper in all your doings* [1 Kings 2:3] both in body and in soul, in faith and in love, in the Son, and in the Father and in the Spirit, in the beginning and in the end, along with your most worthy bishop and his spiritual crown, your presbyters, and with the deacons, who are men of God. Be obedient to the bishop and to one another, as Jesus Christ was in the flesh to the Father, and the apostles to Christ and to the Father and to the Spirit, so that there may be unity in flesh and in spirit. (St. Ignatius of Antioch)[211]

P art of the masculine genius is the "theology of settlement"; that is, of a man's "being settled." In other words, of his *not* being flighty. Of

---

[211] *Letter to the Magnesians*, in *Liturgy of the Hours*, vol. III, 524–525.

his *not* being tossed here and there by every whim and fancy, never getting his act together, and acting childish (see Eph. 4:14). This is true for things both spiritual and temporal in your life. Men — males — are, *per se*, are called to be grounded, rooted, and anchored. Why is this? Because part of the masculine genius, too, is providing, protecting, and defending such realities as women, family, faith, virtue, and culture. You need to be grounded, rooted, and anchored in things both spiritual and temporal. For example, besides faithfully fulfilling your Sunday Mass obligation, along with weekly reception of the Eucharist and monthly Confession, and arriving at work on time each day and helping to set a diligent example for your coworkers, be sure to remain grounded in *all* those daily activities that help you prosper and advance in virtue and virtuous living. All of these are founded — and *grounded* — in your being a true man of Jesus Christ and a true man of Jesus Christ's Bride, the Church. (See days 1, 35, 55, 71, 146, 167, 169, 174, 181, and 185.)

Detachment: On Not Putting Too Much Stock in Material Goods

And behold, one came up to him, saying, "Teacher, what good deed must I do, to have eternal life?" And he said to him, "Why do you ask me about what is good? One there is who is good. If you would enter life, keep the commandments." He said to him, "Which?" And Jesus said, "You shall not kill, You shall not commit adultery, You shall not steal, You shall not bear false witness, Honor your father and mother, and, You shall love your neighbor as yourself." The young man said to him, "All these I have observed; what do I still lack?" Jesus said to him, "If you would be perfect, go, sell what you possess and give to the poor, and you will have treasure in heaven; and come, follow me." When the young man heard this he went away sorrowful; for he had great possessions. (Matt. 19:16–22)

Saint George was a man who abandoned one army for another: he gave up the rank of tribune to enlist as a soldier for Christ. Eager to encounter the enemy, he first stripped away his worldly wealth by giving all he had to the poor. Then, free and unencumbered, bearing the shield of faith, he plunged into the thick of the battle, an ardent soldier for Christ.

Clearly, what he did serves to teach us a valuable lesson: if we are afraid to strip ourselves of our worldly possessions, then we are unfit to make a strong defense of the faith. (St. Peter Damian)[212]

The virtue of detachment is about loving persons, places, and things in the way they are meant to be loved; that is, in an *ordered* way. In other words, you are not to become too attached to persons, places, and

---

[212] Sermon 3 on St. George, Martyr, in *Liturgy of the Hours*, vol. II, 1777.

things in an *inordinate*, that is, excessive, way. So the virtue of detachment is about *ordered* love. If you love persons, places, and things in the right way (that is, in the way they're supposed to be loved), you end up fostering an *ordered* love toward them and so you remain in control of the proper love you're called to have toward them. But if you love persons, places, and things in a *disordered* way, you foster an *inordinate* love of them, and the inordinate love ends up *controlling you*. For example, if you are married and are the boss in your place of business, do you love your secretary in a proper way? That is, do you love your secretary in the proper way that a boss is called to love his secretary — and, indeed, love all of his employees? I certainly hope you do. After all, we are all called to love. Or do you love your secretary in a disordered way that leads to a subsequent adulterous and sinful relationship? Do you love in an ordered way that bar that you and your friends go to only occasionally during the playoff season? Or do you go to that bar too often, even without your buddies, and so love that bar inordinately? Do you love and use the Internet in an ordered way for work and family business? The Internet is a wonderful invention, after all. Or do you use the Internet in a disordered way that leads, for example, to pornographic addiction? You get the point. Almighty God has given you an intellect (to *know*) and a will (to *choose*) so that you can love persons, places, and things in a proper and ordered way, not in an improper and disordered way. Work on fostering the virtue of detachment in your life. Love persons, places, and things in the way they're meant to be loved. (See days 35, 153, 177, 185, and 199.)

Day 177

The Utmost Importance of Love

Love is patient and kind; love is not jealous or boastful; it is not arrogant or rude. Love does not insist on its own way; it is not irritable or resentful; it does not rejoice at wrong, but rejoices in the right. Love bears all things, believes all things, hopes all things, endures all things. (1 Cor. 13:4–7)

God makes the Church itself a sacrifice pleasing in his sight by preserving within it the love which his Holy Spirit has poured out. Thus the grace of that spiritual love is always available to us, enabling us continually to offer ourselves to God as a living sacrifice, holy and pleasing to him for ever. (St. Fulgentius of Ruspe)[213]

True, authentic love rooted in the moral law of God is a powerful thing. True, authentic love brings order to your life. False, inauthentic love brings chaos. True love is built upon virtue; false love is built upon vice. Know the difference and live a life of true, authentic love and virtue. (See days 101, 153, 176, 178, 185, and 187.)

[213] From a book addressed to Monimus, bk. 2, in *Liturgy of the Hours*, vol. II, 653.

Day 178

Zeal for and Defense of the Church

[Jesus] said to them, "But who do you say that I am?" Simon Peter replied, "You are the Christ, the Son of the living God." And Jesus answered him, "Blessed are you, Simon Bar-Jona! For flesh and blood has not revealed this to you, but my Father who is in heaven. And I tell you, you are Peter, and on this rock I will build my church, and the powers of death shall not prevail against it." (Matt. 16:15–18)

O Catholic faith, how solid, how strong you are! How deeply rooted, *how firmly founded on a solid rock!* [see Matt. 7:24; 16:18; Luke 6:48]. Heaven and earth will pass away, but you can never pass away. From the beginning the whole world opposed you, but you mightily triumphed over everything. *This is the victory that overcomes the world, our faith* [1 John 5:4]. (St. Fidelis of Sigmaringen)[214]

St. Peter had a deep conviction of who Jesus was — indeed, that Jesus was the Christ. Yet Peter was a weak man, who, on the night of the arrest of Jesus, would deny Jesus three times out of fear. Then Peter would weep bitterly because of that triple denial (see Luke 22:54–62). And later, Peter would have a chance to make up for that threefold denial by offering a faith-filled threefold affirmation of his love for Jesus (John 21:15–17). St. Augustine describes the drama this way: "Therefore do not be disheartened, Peter; reply once, reply twice, reply a third time. The triple confession of your love is to regain what was lost three times by your fear. You must loose three times what you bound three times; untie by love that which your fear bound. Once, and again, and a third

---

[214] Words from his last sermon before his martyrdom, as quoted in a eulogy for Saint Fidelis of Sigmaringen, in *Liturgy of the Hours*, vol. II, 1780–1781.

time did the Lord entrust his sheep to Peter."[215] The main point is this: although a weak man, Peter had faith in Christ and love for Christ. So whenever you feel yourself getting weak in the spiritual life or moral life, turn immediately to the Heavenly intercession of St. Peter. He will assist you and help you grow in your faith in Christ and love for Christ and in your zeal for and defense of Christ's Bride, the Church. (See days 96, 108, 166, 175, 179, 182, and 188.)

[215] *Sermo* 295, in *Liturgy of the Hours*, vol. III, 1506.

The Power of the Keys to Forgive

[Jesus said to Peter,] "I will give you the keys of the kingdom of heaven, and whatever you bind on earth shall be bound in heaven, and whatever you loose on earth shall be loosed in heaven." (Matt. 16:19)

Now the apostle Peter, because of the primacy of his apostleship, stood as a symbol of the entire Church.

In himself he was by nature one man, by grace one Christian, by a more abundant grace an apostle and the chief of the apostles. But Christ said to him: *To you I shall give the keys of the kingdom of heaven and whatever you will bind upon the earth will be bound also in heaven and whatever you will forgive upon the earth will be forgiven also in heaven* [Matt. 16:19]. Now these words applied to the entire Church. In this life it [the Church] is shaken by various trials, as if by rains, floods and tempests, but it does not fall because it is founded upon the rock from which Peter received his name....

The Church, which is founded upon Christ, received from him the keys of the kingdom of heaven, that is, the power of binding and forgiving sins, in the person of Peter. Therefore this Church, by loving and following Christ, is set free from evil. But this is even more the case with those who fight in behalf of truth even to the death. (St. Augustine)[216]

❧───────❧

Sin is real, but so is forgiveness through the great gift of the Sacrament of Reconciliation (Confession). The Church, through Jesus Christ, has the power to forgive sin — both mortal and venial. Christ gave this power to the Church in the person of St. Peter, who, by his primacy among

---

[216] *Treatise on John, Tract.* 124, in *Liturgy of the Hours*, vol. II, 1797–1798.

the apostles, leads the Church. This reality is seen even today in the office of the pope, who leads the Church with the Catholic bishops of the world in union with him. All of these truths, too, are gifts bestowed by Christ on His Bride, the Church. The forgiveness of sins leads to holiness. Do not miss out on such wonderful gifts granted by Christ Himself to the entire Church, which He founded and established on solid rock. (See days 66, 88, 89, 96, 100, 108, 121, 125, 166, 175, 178, 182, and 188.)

Vigilance

Keep your heart with all vigilance; for from it flow the springs of life. Put away from you crooked speech, and put devious talk far from you. Let your eyes look directly forward, and your gaze be straight before you. Take heed to the path of your feet, then all your ways will be sure. Do not swerve to the right or to the left; turn your foot away from evil. (Prov. 4:23–27)

Be watchful and vigilant. It is by design that Jesus concealed the last day from us. [This is because] He wants us to be on the lookout for Him every day of our lives. (St. Augustine)[217]

Vigilance is important in daily living and it's tied to your will — that is, your *will to be vigilant* in wanting and seeking to do what is right, just, true, and good. St. John Chrysostom states, "We must live in constant vigilance.... Does this mean we must give up the possibility of sleeping? Not at all. We cannot do without bodily sleep. What we must avoid is the sleep of the will."[218] And you are not alone in this call to vigilance, as 1 Peter 5:8–9 makes clear when it states to all, "Be sober, be watchful. Your adversary the devil prowls around like a roaring lion, seeking some one to devour. Resist him, firm in your faith, knowing that the same experience of suffering is required of your brotherhood throughout the world." Daily vigilance should also extend to your faith and love of Almighty God, thus helping to form your will always to choose wisely in every action of every day that which is true, good, and beautiful. St. Elizabeth of the Trinity shows this link when she prays, "O my God, Trinity whom I adore ... grant

---

[217] Schroeder, *Every Day Is a Gift*, 189.
[218] Schroeder, *Every Day Is a Gift*, 89.

my soul peace. Make it your heaven, your beloved dwelling, and the place of your rest. May I never abandon you there, but may I be there, whole and entire, completely vigilant in my faith, entirely adoring, and wholly given over to your creative action" (*Compendium of the Catechism of the Catholic Church*, q. 49, 20). (See days 3, 19, 28, 30, 80, 149, 151, and 200.)

From Childhood to Manhood

Attain to the unity of the faith and of the knowledge of the Son of God, to mature manhood, to the measure of the stature of the fulness of Christ; so that we may no longer be children, tossed to and fro and carried about with every wind of doctrine, by the cunning of men, by their craftiness in deceitful wiles. Rather, speaking the truth in love, we are to grow up in every way into him who is the head, into Christ, from whom the whole body, joined and knit together by every joint with which it is supplied, when each part is working properly, makes bodily growth and upbuilds itself in love. Now this I affirm and testify in the Lord, that you must no longer live as the Gentiles do, in the futility of their minds; they are darkened in their understanding, alienated from the life of God because of the ignorance that is in them, due to their hardness of heart; they have become callous and have given themselves up to licentiousness, greedy to practice every kind of uncleanness. (Eph. 4:13–19)

The man of God must reach maturity. (St. Gregory of Nyssa)[219]

⊱————————⊰

There are at least two reasons why it is important for a man to grow into psychological, intellectual, and social maturity: (1) to protect himself *from himself* — that is, so that he does not fall victim to his own immature ways and experience stunted growth in multiple areas, such as faith and finances; and (2) so that he does not fall victim to *others' taking advantage of him* precisely because of his immaturity. St. Paul himself witnesses to this growth in maturity when he says in 1 Corinthians 13:11, "When I was a child, I spoke like a child, I thought like a child,

---

[219] Homily 6 on Ecclesiastes, in *Liturgy of the Hours*, vol. III, 238.

I reasoned like a child; when I became a man, I gave up childish ways." Remember: though one is called to be *childlike*, one is not called to be *childish*. Whether in spiritual things (such as fostering the virtue of faith and receiving the sacraments) or in temporal things (such as being responsible in your job and finances and the protection of your loved ones), you are called to the fullness of Christian maturity in your manhood. Look to Jesus Himself — to His life as described in the four Gospels — to be your own Model and Guide in this process of growing "to mature manhood, to the measure of the stature of the fulness of Christ" (Eph. 4:13). (See days 2, 143, 147, 169, 177, and 186.)

The Church Spreads and Grows

And Peter said to them, "Repent, and be baptized every one of you in the name of Jesus Christ for the forgiveness of your sins; and you shall receive the gift of the Holy Spirit. For the promise is to you and to your children and to all that are far off, every one whom the Lord our God calls to him." And he testified with many other words and exhorted them, saying, "Save yourselves from this crooked generation." So those who received his word were baptized, and there were added that day about three thousand souls. And they devoted themselves to the apostles' teaching and fellowship, to the breaking of bread and the prayers. (Acts 2:38–42)

The Church, which has spread everywhere, even to the ends of the earth, received the faith from the apostles and their disciples....

The Church, spread throughout the whole world, received this preaching and this faith and now preserves it carefully, dwelling as it were in one house. Having one soul and one heart, the Church holds this faith, preaches and teaches it consistently as though by a single voice. For though there are different languages, there is but one tradition.

The faith and the tradition of the churches founded in Germany are no different from those founded among the Spanish and the Celts, in the East, in Egypt, in Libya and elsewhere in the Mediterranean world. Just as God's creature, the sun, is one and the same the world over, so also does the Church's preaching shine everywhere to enlighten all men who want to come to a knowledge of the truth. (St. Irenaeus)[220]

---

[220] *Against Heresies*, bk. 1, chap. 10, in *Liturgy of the Hours*, vol. II, 1784–1785.

Rejoice in the growth of the Church, because it means that Christ's truth is being proclaimed and embraced. Are you one to freely express to others — for example, to other men specifically — the truth and beauty of your one, holy, catholic, and apostolic Faith? If not, why not? What is preventing you from valiantly sharing your Catholic Faith with others? What is keeping you from more proactively sharing the truth of Jesus Christ and His Bride, the Church? What is keeping you from telling others about the Church's teachings regarding the Most Holy Trinity, the seven sacraments, the Blessed Virgin Mary, and the angels and saints? Scripture scholars say that the phrase "Be not afraid" (or a variant thereof, such as "Fear not"; e.g., Luke 2:10) appears in the Bible some 365 times — in other words, one for each day of the year. That's a comforting thought. So, *be not afraid* to share your Catholic Faith with others. (See days 12, 66, 88, 89, 98, 100, 107, 108, 121, 125, 166, 178, 179, and 188.)

Conscience versus Reputation

I always take pains to have a clear conscience toward God and toward men. (Acts 24:16)

Conscience and reputation are two different things. Your conscience depends on you, whereas your reputation depends on your neighbor's estimation of you. (St. Augustine)[221]

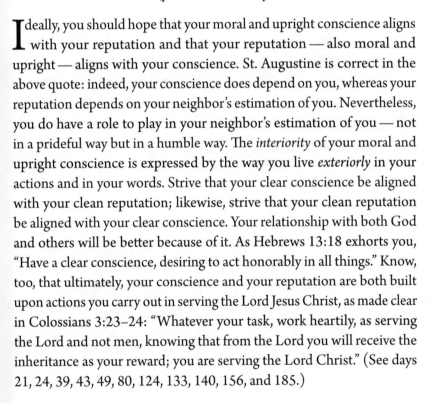

Ideally, you should hope that your moral and upright conscience aligns with your reputation and that your reputation — also moral and upright — aligns with your conscience. St. Augustine is correct in the above quote: indeed, your conscience does depend on you, whereas your reputation depends on your neighbor's estimation of you. Nevertheless, you do have a role to play in your neighbor's estimation of you — not in a prideful way but in a humble way. The *interiority* of your moral and upright conscience is expressed by the way you live *exteriorly* in your actions and in your words. Strive that your clear conscience be aligned with your clean reputation; likewise, strive that your clean reputation be aligned with your clear conscience. Your relationship with both God and others will be better because of it. As Hebrews 13:18 exhorts you, "Have a clear conscience, desiring to act honorably in all things." Know, too, that ultimately, your conscience and your reputation are both built upon actions you carry out in serving the Lord Jesus Christ, as made clear in Colossians 3:23–24: "Whatever your task, work heartily, as serving the Lord and not men, knowing that from the Lord you will receive the inheritance as your reward; you are serving the Lord Christ." (See days 21, 24, 39, 43, 49, 80, 124, 133, 140, 156, and 185.)

[221] Schroeder, *Every Day Is a Gift*, 162.

Day 184

Let Christ Transform You

I am sure that he who began a good work in you will bring it to completion at the day of Jesus Christ. (Phil. 1:6)

Beloved, Jesus Christ is our salvation, he is the high priest through whom we present our offerings and the helper who supports us in our weakness. Through him our gaze penetrates the heights of heaven and we see, as in a mirror, the most holy face of God. Through Christ the eyes of our hearts are opened, and our weak and clouded understanding reaches up toward the light. Through him the Lord God willed that we should taste eternal knowledge. (Pope St. Clement I)[222]

Speak often to your Heavenly Father about how much you wish to be transformed into the likeness of His only-begotten Son, Jesus Christ, and to grow in holiness. Jesus, too, wants you to communicate with Him as one dear friend communicates with another dear friend. Welcome Jesus into every aspect of your life: your thoughts, your words, your deeds. Invite also the Holy Spirit to guide you in the areas of your life that you know need transformation in Christ. As Psalm 139:23–24 cries out, "Search me, O God, and know my heart! Try me and know my thoughts! And see if there be any wicked way in me, and lead me in the way everlasting!" (See days 4, 7, 18, 19, 40, 51, 52, 162, and 200.)

---

[222] *Letter to the Corinthians*, chap. 36, in *Liturgy of the Hours*, vol. II, 796–797.

Good Fruit and Bad Fruit

[Jesus said,] "For no good tree bears bad fruit, nor again does a bad tree bear good fruit; for each tree is known by its own fruit. For figs are not gathered from thorns, nor are grapes picked from a bramble bush. The good man out of the good treasure of his heart produces good, and the evil man out of his evil treasure produces evil; for out of the abundance of the heart his mouth speaks." (Luke 6:43–45)

As our Saviour says: *A good tree is not able to produce bad fruit* [Luke 6:43].

He says: A good tree, that is, a good heart as well as a soul inflamed with charity, can do nothing but good and holy works. For this reason St. Augustine said: *Love, and do what you will* [see *Sermon* on 1 John 4:4–12], namely, possess love and charity and then do what you will. It is as if he had said: Charity is not able to sin. (St. Angela Merici)[223]

Have you ever produced bad fruit in your life? If so, fear not. God desires you to produce good fruit, and He will help you to do so. But you need to cooperate with Him. As St. Augustine says, "God created us without us: but he did not will to save us without us" (*Sermo* 169; *CCC* 1847). In other words, while it is true that God is always the Primary Mover in the life of grace, He does will that you *actively cooperate with Him* in moving yourself closer to *partake in* that life of sanctifying grace. You have an intellect *to know* and a will *to choose*. Employ these in your daily spiritual and temporal life to draw closer to God so that you may, indeed, bear good fruit in your life as lived and expressed within your vocation and state in life, whatever that might be. As for the bad fruit

---

[223] *Spiritual Testament*, in *Liturgy of the Hours*, vol. III, 1332–1333.

you've produced? Have faith that Almighty God indeed wants to forgive you of your sinful past; make a good examination of your conscience, then, go to a priest and make a good, holy, reverent Confession. Confess, especially, any mortal sins you might have on your soul. You are also welcome to confess any venial sins during Confession. The Sacrament of Penance will cleanse you of your guilt and allow you to make a fresh start to move forward and produce good fruit. God will forgive you. (See days 1, 5, 13, 17, 24, 33, 34, 39, 49, 66, 87, 93, 109, 116, 136, 155, 170, 175, 176, 186, 188, and 193.)

Moving Forward from Your Sinful Past

Brethren, I do not consider that I have made it my own; but one thing I do, forgetting what lies behind and straining forward to what lies ahead, I press on toward the goal for the prize of the upward call of God in Christ Jesus. (Phil. 3:13–14)

Christ is risen! He has burst open the gates of hell and let the dead go free; he has renewed the earth through the members of his Church now born again in baptism, and has made it blossom afresh with men brought back to life. His Holy Spirit has unlocked the doors of heaven, which stand wide open to receive those who rise up from the earth. Because of Christ's resurrection the thief ascends to paradise....

And so, my brothers, each of us ought surely to rejoice on this holy day. Let no one, conscious of his sinfulness, withdraw from our common celebration, nor let anyone be kept away from our public prayer by the burden of his guilt. Sinner he may indeed be, but he must not despair of pardon on this day which is so highly privileged; for if a thief could receive the grace of paradise, how could a Christian be refused forgiveness? (St. Maximus of Turin)[224]

❖────────────❖

Your Heavenly Father never wants you to despair over your sinful past. His Son, Jesus Christ, never wants you to despair over your sinful past. The Holy Spirit, too, never wants you to despair over your sinful past. A big part of understanding these truths is always to strive to move forward from your maybe not-too-virtuous and sinful past. There's an old saying that, just as the names of the three archangels are *Michael*,

---

[224] *Sermo* 53, in *Liturgy of the Hours*, vol. II, 815–817.

Gabriel, and *Raphael,* the names of the three so-called archdemons are *Woulda, Coulda,* and *Shoulda.* Simply put, give up the hope of a better past because it isn't going to happen. The past is the past: accept this fact. Now, should you strive to learn from your bad past so as not to repeat it? Of course. But don't dwell on your past *inordinately;* if you do, it can lead you to depression and despair. Here are four wonderful passages from Sacred Scripture to help you *not* stay focused on your less-than-stellar past and thus to *move forward:* St. Peter teaches in 2 Peter 2:22, "The dog turns back to his own vomit, and the sow is washed only to wallow in the mire." Also, Jesus Himself counsels in Luke 9:62, "No one who puts his hand to the plow and looks back is fit for the kingdom of God." Jesus, in John 8:11, also instructs the woman who was "caught in the act of adultery" to move forward when he tells her, "Go, and do not sin again." Isaiah 12:2 states: "Behold, God is my salvation; I will trust, and will not be afraid; for the LORD GOD is my strength and my song, and he has become my salvation." And don't forget, too, that the above quote from St. Paul in Philippians 3:13–14 is another good one to defend the truth that you are not meant to stay inordinately focused on your past. So move forward from your sinful past; this is part of growing in Christian maturity. (See days 2, 143, 147, 181, and 185.)

Living in God and He in You

By this we know that we abide in him and he in us, because he has given us of his own Spirit. And we have seen and testify that the Father has sent his Son as the Savior of the world. Whoever confesses that Jesus is the Son of God, God abides in him, and he in God. So we know and believe the love God has for us. God is love, and he who abides in love abides in God, and God abides in him. In this is love perfected with us, that we may have confidence for the day of judgment, because as he is so are we in this world. (1 John 4:13–17)

Let the wisdom of John teach us how we live in Christ and Christ lives in us: *The proof that we are living in him and he is living in us is that he has given us a share in his Spirit* [1 John 4:13]. Just as the trunk of the vine gives its own natural properties to each of its branches, so, by bestowing on them the Holy Spirit, the Word of God, the only-begotten Son of the Father, gives Christians a certain kinship with himself and with God the Father because they have been united to him by faith and determination to do his will in all things. He helps them to grow in love and reverence for God, and teaches them to discern right from wrong and to act with integrity. (St. Cyril of Alexandria)[225]

❖━━━━━━━━❖

To truly be living in God — Father, Son, and Holy Spirit — and He living in you means living in a state of His sanctifying grace with no known mortal sin on your soul. This is a daily goal to strive constantly for — and you'll become a better man because of it. At the same time, do your best to shun even venial sin. Such an attitude will help you to

---

[225] *Commentary on the Gospel of John*, bk. 10, in *Liturgy of the Hours*, vol. II, 834.

live in a way that is *eternity minded*, always looking forward to that eternity with God in Heaven. Along with being eternity minded, foster an intentional *Trinitarian spirituality* wherein you offer all things daily *to* the Father, *through* the Son, *in* the Holy Spirit. After all, if you want to spend an eternity with Almighty God in Heaven, then it makes sense that you should be doing everything in your power *now* — while still living on earth — to foster an intimacy with Him *today*. Be certain of this: Almighty God — the Blessed Trinity — wants to live in you, and you were created to live *in* Him and *with* Him forever. (See days 29, 38, 47, 114, 126, 147, 172, and 200.)

Do Not Be Ashamed of Jesus Christ

For God did not give us a spirit of timidity but a spirit of power and love and self-control. Do not be ashamed then of testifying to our Lord ... but take your share of suffering for the gospel in the power of God, who saved us and called us with a holy calling, not in virtue of our works but in virtue of his own purpose and the grace which he gave us in Christ Jesus ages ago and now has manifested through the appearing of our Savior Christ Jesus, who abolished death and brought life and immortality to light through the gospel. (2 Tim. 1:7–10)

In the preaching of the holy Gospel, all should receive a strengthening of their faith. No one should be ashamed of the cross of Christ, through which the world has been redeemed.

No one should fear to suffer for the sake of justice; no one should lose confidence in the reward that has been promised. The way to rest is through toil; the way to life is through death. Christ has taken on himself the whole weakness of our lowly human nature. If then we are steadfast in our faith in him and in our love for him, we win the victory that he has won, we receive what he has promised. (Pope St. Leo the Great)[226]

Are you shy, bashful, or — worse yet — ashamed of Jesus Christ, His truth, and His Church? If so, what exactly makes you so? Make a list of those things that are preventing you from being the most effective disciple of Christ that you can be. Address these things and overcome them. According to 2 Timothy 1:8, you should not be afraid of "testifying to our Lord." And 1 Timothy 3:15 reminds all that the Church is "the

---

[226] *Sermo* 51, in *Liturgy of the Hours*, vol. II, 150–151.

pillar and bulwark of the truth." God did not give you a spirit of timidity but a spirit of power to carry out such testifying. Such testifying brings with it a share in suffering for the sake of the gospel of Jesus Christ, but that's okay. Through such a process, your faith is strengthened, your confidence is renewed, justice is proclaimed, and your love for Christ remains steadfast. So, whether regarding Sacred Scripture, Tradition, or the Magisterium — or anything else involving these, such as the benefits of partaking of regular Confession and the Eucharist, the obligatory reality of Sunday Mass, the importance of *Lectio Divina*, spiritual reading, why you should familiarize yourself with the saints of the Church, the importance of charitable acts, the Ten Commandments, the precepts of the Church, the Beatitudes, virtue ethics and morality, or any other teaching of Jesus Christ and His Church — *do not be ashamed.* (See days 20, 36, 41, 57, 76, 86, 96, 97, 104, 111, 124, 128, 134, 141, 143, 160, 165, 178, 179, 182, 185, 191, and 197.)

Day 189

Striving to Please God, Not Men

But though we had already suffered and been shamefully treated ... as you know, we had courage in our God to declare to you the gospel of God in the face of great opposition. For our appeal does not spring from error or uncleanness, nor is it made with guile; but just as we have been approved by God to be entrusted with the gospel, so we speak, not to please men, but to please God who tests our hearts. (1 Thess. 2:2–4)

If you, Christian soul, desire to become holy and enjoy uninterrupted peace, strive as often as you can to mortify your will. Do nothing for your own satisfaction, but everything to please God. To this end renounce all vain desires and inordinate inclinations. Worldly-minded people are intent upon following their own will as much as they possibly can; it is the constant aim of the Saints to mortify their will, and they seek opportunities for doing so. (St. Alphonsus Liguori)[227]

In all things, you are to strive to please and obey God, not man. Now, it's great if a situation is such that you happen to please *both* God and man (such as accepting a job that God indeed wills for you and which your family members and future employer are thrilled you accepted), but this will *not* always be the case. Own this truth. For example, you may be asked to do something unethical at work that your coworkers see no problem with but that you know is morally unacceptable. In such an instance, you should take Acts 5:29 as your guide; this Scripture passage has St. Peter and the other apostles answering the high priest: "We

---

[227] *The School of Perfection*, trans. Cornelius J. Warren (Boston: Mission Church Press, 1910), chap. 9, e-Catholic 2000, https://www.ecatholic2000.com/liguori/school/perfect.shtml.

must obey God rather than men." The desire always to please and obey God over your fellow man is depicted, too, in the life of St. Joan of Arc, the great French soldier saint who put God front and center in her life. According to the *Catechism*, in "a question posed as a trap by her ecclesiastical judges," St. Joan was asked if she knew whether she was in a state of God's sanctifying grace. She replied to them, "If I am not, may it please God to put me in it; if I am, may it please God to keep me there" (Acts of the trial of St. Joan of Arc; CCC 2005). The apostles, after Pentecost, and St. Joan of Arc were known to be fearless. You, too, must be fearless in your striving to please and obey God over men. (See days 3, 7, 14, 30, 52, 61, 80, 120, and 175.)

Day 190

Trust God, Don't Test Him

Think of the Lord with uprightness, and seek him with sincerity of heart; because he is found by those who do not put him to the test, and manifests himself to those who do not distrust him. (Wisd. 1:1–2)

O my Jesus, despite the deep night that is all around me and the dark clouds which hide the horizon, I know that the sun never goes out. O Lord, though I cannot comprehend You and do not understand Your ways, I nonetheless trust in Your mercy. If it is Your will, Lord, that I live always in such darkness, may You be blessed. I ask You only one thing, Jesus: do not allow me to offend You in any way. O my Jesus, You alone know the longings and the sufferings of my heart. I am glad I can suffer for You, however little. When I feel that the suffering is more than I can bear, I take refuge in the Lord in the Blessed Sacrament, and I speak to Him with profound silence. (St. Faustina Kowalska)[228]

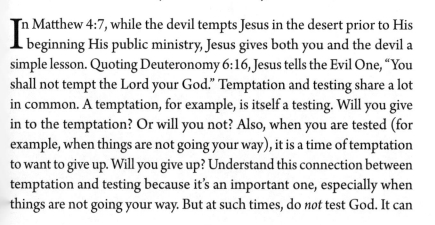

In Matthew 4:7, while the devil tempts Jesus in the desert prior to His beginning His public ministry, Jesus gives both you and the devil a simple lesson. Quoting Deuteronomy 6:16, Jesus tells the Evil One, "You shall not tempt the Lord your God." Temptation and testing share a lot in common. A temptation, for example, is itself a testing. Will you give in to the temptation? Or will you not? Also, when you are tested (for example, when things are not going your way), it is a time of temptation to want to give up. Will you give up? Understand this connection between temptation and testing because it's an important one, especially when things are not going your way. But at such times, do *not* test God. It can

---

[228] *Diary*, no. 73.

be a temptation to do so; for example, when you want to tell God, "God, if You do [such and such] for me, then I will do [such and such] for You." Don't test God; rather, *trust* Him, "so that the genuineness of your faith, more precious than gold which though perishable is tested by fire, may redound to praise and glory and honor" (1 Pet. 1:7). Some helpful advice in this regard? Get to know St. Faustina, her *Diary*, and the Divine Mercy devotion. These will teach you to trust in God and *not* test Him. Jesus, I trust in You. (See days 13, 32, 107, and 192.)

Harmony in Jesus Christ

May the God of steadfastness and encouragement grant you to live in such harmony with one another, in accord with Christ Jesus, that together you may with one voice glorify the God and Father of our Lord Jesus Christ. Welcome one another, therefore, as Christ has welcomed you, for the glory of God. (Rom. 15:5–7)

I urge you to strive to do all things in the harmony of God. The bishop is to preside as God's representative, the presbyters are to perform the rule of the apostolic council, and the deacons, who are so dear to me, are to be entrusted with the service of Jesus Christ, who was with the Father before time began and has now at last manifested himself to us. (St. Ignatius of Antioch)[229]

Harmony is a beautiful thing, and Jesus Christ desires you to live a harmonious life within His Bride, the Church, in all things spiritual and temporal. In everyday living, even amid trial and suffering, God desires for you to have concord and peace. These, in turn, can lead to fellowship, amicability, and greater understanding and empathy toward others who may be suffering or experiencing trials themselves. Always stay active in the Church and receive the sacraments — especially weekly Eucharist and monthly Confession. Know that, despite the wounded world that you live in and are a part of, you *can* strive for harmony in all aspects of your life, even amid moments of discord. In your daily prayer, ask God to lead you into all things that will increase the harmony in your life that He so desires for you. As Philippians 4:13 instructs you, "I can do all things in him who strengthens me." (See days 8, 14, 57, 96, 97, 122, 130, 134, 188, and 197.)

[229] *Letter to the Magnesians*, in *Liturgy of the Hours*, vol. III, 520.

Fear Not, Be Strong

And he said, "O man greatly beloved, fear not, peace be with you; be strong and of good courage." And when he spoke to me, I was strengthened and said, "Let my lord speak, for you have strengthened me." (Dan. 10:19)

Do not look forward in fear to the changes in life; rather, look to them with full hope that as they arise, God, whose very own you are, will lead you safely through all things; and when you cannot stand it, God will carry you in His arms. Do not fear what may happen tomorrow; the same understanding Father who cares for you today will take care of you then and every day. He will either shield you from suffering or will give you unfailing strength to bear it. Be at peace, and put aside all anxious thoughts and imaginations. (attributed to St. Francis de Sales)

❦──────────❦

Have you ever read the poem "Footprints," also known as "Footprints in the Sand"? If not, look it up and read it. Even if you have read it, look it up and read it again to refresh your memory about it. Let it speak to you. This poem aligns well with Deuteronomy 1:31: "In the wilderness ... you have seen *how the LORD your God bore you, as a man bears his son*, in all the way that you went until you came to this place" (emphasis added). It also aligns well with the above quotes from the book of Daniel and St. Francis de Sales and echoes the Divine Mercy devotion's "Jesus, I trust in You." Remember what Jesus teaches you in Matthew 10:29–31: "Are not two sparrows sold for a penny? And not one of them will fall to the ground without your Father's will. But even the hairs of your head are all numbered. Fear not, therefore; you are of more value than many sparrows." Indeed, God cares for you. So, fear not and be strong. (See days 13, 32, 107, and 190.)

Let God Lead You

Thus says the LORD, your Redeemer… "I am the LORD your God, who teaches you to profit, who leads you in the way you should go." (Isa. 48:17)

For man and woman thus created and commissioned by God, the ordinary working day has great and wonderful significance. People's ideas, activities and undertakings — however commonplace they may be — are used by the Creator to renew the world, to lead it to salvation, to make it a more perfect instrument of divine glory. (Pope John Paul II)[230]

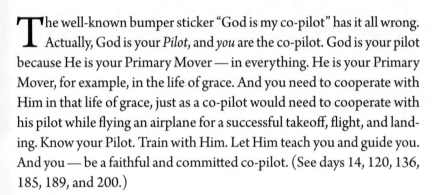

The well-known bumper sticker "God is my co-pilot" has it all wrong. Actually, God is your *Pilot,* and *you* are the co-pilot. God is your pilot because He is your Primary Mover — in everything. He is your Primary Mover, for example, in the life of grace. And you need to cooperate with Him in that life of grace, just as a co-pilot would need to cooperate with his pilot while flying an airplane for a successful takeoff, flight, and landing. Know your Pilot. Train with Him. Let Him teach you and guide you. And you — be a faithful and committed co-pilot. (See days 14, 120, 136, 185, 189, and 200.)

[230] "The Christian Message in a Computer Culture," message for the Twenty-Fourth World Communications Day, May 27, 1990, second paragraph.

Day 194

Belief

And Jesus said to him, "If you can! All things are possible to him who believes." Immediately the father of the child cried out and said, "I believe; help my unbelief!" (Mark 9:23–24)

The Father's purpose in revealing the Son was to make himself known to us all and so to welcome into eternal rest those who believe in him, establishing them in justice, preserving them from death. To believe in him means to do his will. (St. Irenaeus)[231]

❧————————————❧

Belief in God leads to strengthened faith, and strengthened faith leads to wanting to seek and do God's will in *all* things in your life. That said, maybe you are suffering from unbelief. If so, why is that? And what are you going to do about it? When was the last time you practiced *Lectio Divina*? That is, when was the last time you read a passage of Sacred Scripture and then seriously meditated on it in silence and allowed God to speak to you through it? When was the last time you prayed the Rosary and truly contemplated the mysteries of your salvation recalled therein? When was the last time you prayed the Divine Mercy Chaplet and so focused and sincerely meditated on the Passion of Christ? When was the last time you went to Confession? When was the last time you received the Eucharist worthily? Get back on track — and believe. (See days 104, 128, 143, and 200.)

[231] *Against Heresies*, bk. 4, chap. 6, in *Liturgy of the Hours*, vol. III, 63.

Day 195

Avoiding Sin and Vice

Now the works of the flesh are plain: immorality, impurity, licentiousness, idolatry, sorcery, enmity, strife, jealousy, anger, selfishness, dissension, party spirit, envy, drunkenness, carousing, and the like. I warn you, as I warned you before, that those who do such things shall not inherit the kingdom of God. (Gal. 5:19–21)

My dearest son, my first instruction is that you should love the Lord your God with all your heart and all your strength. Without this there is no salvation. Keep yourself, my son, from everything that you know displeases God, that is to say, from every mortal sin. You should permit yourself to be tormented by every kind of martyrdom before you would allow yourself to commit a mortal sin. (King St. Louis IX of France)[232]

In Sacred Scripture, both Jesus and St. Paul give you ample examples of sin and vice. For instance, in addition to what he teaches in the above quote from Galatians, St. Paul also admonishes you in Colossians 3:5–10:

Put to death therefore what is earthly in you: immorality, impurity, passion, evil desire, and covetousness, which is idolatry. On account of these the wrath of God is coming. In these you once walked, when you lived in them. But now put them all away: anger, wrath, malice, slander, and foul talk from your mouth. Do not lie to one another, seeing that you have put off the old nature with its practices and have put on the new nature, which is being renewed in knowledge after the image of its creator.

---

[232] Spiritual testament to his son, in *Liturgy of the Hours*, vol. IV, 1347.

And in Mark 7:20–23, Jesus teaches you that "what comes out of a man is what defiles a man. For from within, out of the heart of man, come evil thoughts, fornication, theft, murder, adultery, coveting, wickedness, deceit, licentiousness, envy, slander, pride, foolishness. All these evil things come from within, and they defile a man." You get the point: Sin is real, and vice is real. St. Basil the Great gives you this definition of vice: "It is the wrong use — in violation of the Lord's command — of what has been given us by God for a good purpose."[233] And Galatians 5:24 states, "Those who belong to Christ Jesus have crucified the flesh with its [inordinate] passions and desires." As an added lesson, remember what Romans 6:23 teaches you: "The wages of sin is death, but the free gift of God is eternal life in Christ Jesus our Lord." (See days 5, 24, 39, 43, 58, 129, 156, and 198.)

---

[233] Schroeder, *Every Day Is a Gift*, 30.

Undermining Satan's Works

Then Jesus said to him, "Begone, Satan! for it is written, 'You shall worship the Lord your God and him only shall you serve.'" Then the devil left him, and behold, angels came and ministered to him. (Matt. 4:10–11)

Try to gather together more frequently to give thanks to God and to praise him. For when you come together frequently, Satan's powers are undermined, and the destruction that he threatens is done away with in the unanimity of your faith. Nothing is better than peace, in which all warfare between heaven and earth is brought to an end.

None of this will escape you if you have perfect faith and love toward Jesus Christ. These are the beginning and the end of life: faith the beginning, love the end. When these two are found together, there is God, and everything else concerning right living follows from them....

... Why do we perish in our stupidity, not knowing the gift the Lord has truly sent us? (St. Ignatius of Antioch)[234]

❖─────────❖

As a Catholic, you know full well that there are certain things that the devil absolutely hates and cannot stand: for example, the Most Holy Trinity — Father, Son, and Holy Spirit — the Blessed Virgin Mary, the saints, the Most Holy Eucharist, and Confession, to name a few. So it is, then, that the man who builds his life upon these very truths and realities that God has given him and which the devil hates is sure to simultaneously build a "fortress of faith" around his life that will make it much more difficult for the devil to penetrate or infiltrate. Believe this, and live it. *Live* your Catholic Faith. (See days 7, 28, 58, 103, and 106.)

---

[234] *Letter to the Ephesians*, in *Liturgy of the Hours*, vol. III, 84–85.

Growing in the Knowledge of God through Jesus Christ

Grow in the grace and knowledge of our Lord and Savior Jesus Christ. To him be the glory both now and to the day of eternity. Amen. (2 Pet. 3:18)

When we have come to know the true God, both our bodies and our souls will be immortal and incorruptible. We shall enter the kingdom of heaven, because while we lived on earth we acknowledged heaven's King. Friends of God and coheirs with Christ, we shall be subject to no evil desires or inclinations, or to any affliction of body or soul, for we shall have become divine. It was because of our human condition that God allowed us to endure these things, but when we have been deified and made immortal, God has promised us a share in his own attributes.

The saying "Know yourself" means therefore that we should recognize and acknowledge in ourselves the God who made us in his own image, for if we do this, we in turn will be recognized and acknowledged by our Maker.... In the beginning God made man in his image and so gave proof of his love for us. If we obey his holy commands and learn to imitate his goodness, we shall be like him and he will honor us. God is not beggarly, and for the sake of his own glory he has given us a share in his divinity. (St. Hippolytus)[235]

Growing in the knowledge of God is part of your human dignity, of your being made in God's image and after His likeness (see Gen 1:26). In fact, your growing in the knowledge of God *actually gives glory* to God. This is because God made you to *know* Him, *love* Him, and *serve*

---

[235] *On the Refutation of All Heresies*, chap. 10, in *Liturgy of the Hours*, vol. I, 460–461.

Him in *this life* so as to be forever happy with Him in the *next life*. But God desires that you have *more* than just knowledge about Him. Proof of this is that, while you're still living on earth, God wants you to partake in His own divine life — and intimately so — through His sanctifying grace working in your soul. And you become an actual *partaker* in the divine nature of God by doing so (see 2 Pet. 1:4). Look at it this way: Several scripture passages mention the concept of having friendship with God, as St. Hippolytus also mentions in the above quote. For example, Wisdom 7:14 states that those who possess the wealth of the gift of wisdom (one of the seven gifts of the Holy Spirit) "obtain friendship with God." And James 2:23 teaches that " 'Abraham believed God, and it was reckoned to him as righteousness'; and he was called the friend of God [Gen. 15:6; Isa. 41:8; 2 Chron. 20:7]." But partaking in God's own divine life — His divine nature — through His sanctifying grace is the highest form of "friendship with God." Growing in the knowledge of God through all that Jesus Christ has revealed about Himself, the Father, and the Holy Spirit — including about Christ's own Real Presence in the Eucharist — will also help you to acquire the *self-knowledge* needed to grow in holiness and which St. Hippolytus mentions above as well. Know God and know yourself — *in* Him. (See days 14, 26, 40, 43, 62, 96, 97, 134, 144, 152, 168, 188, and 191.)

Teach Well, Learn Well

All scripture is inspired by God and profitable for teaching, for reproof, for correction, and for training in righteousness, that the man of God may be complete, equipped for every good work. (2 Tim. 3:16–17)

My dearest son, if you desire to honor the royal crown, I advise, I counsel, I urge you above all things to maintain the Catholic and apostolic faith with such diligence and care that you may be an example for all those placed under you by God and that the clergy may rightly call you a man of true Christian profession. Failing to do this, you may be sure that you will not be called a Christian or a son of the Church. Indeed, in the royal palace after the faith itself, the Church holds second place, first propagated as she was by our Head, [Jesus] Christ; then transplanted, firmly constituted and spread through the whole world by his members, the apostles and holy fathers. And though she always produced fresh offspring, nevertheless in certain places she is regarded as ancient....

... Be merciful to all who are suffering violence, keeping always in your heart the example of the Lord who said: *I desire mercy and not sacrifice* [Matt. 9:13, quoting Hos. 6:6]. Be patient with everyone, not only with the powerful, but also with the weak.

... Be humble in this life, that God may raise you up in the next... Be chaste so that you may avoid all the foulness of lust like the pangs of death. (St. Stephen of Hungary)[236]

It is clear from the above quote from St. Stephen of Hungary that he loved his son so much in *this life* that he actively desired his son's

---

[236] Admonitions to his son, chap. 1, in *Liturgy of the Hours*, vol. IV, 1328–1329.

salvation in Jesus Christ in the *next life*. As stated in the meditation in day 95, above, the greatest love that you can have for another person in *this life* — that is, while still living on earth — is to be willing to lay down your life for them (see John 15:13). But the greatest love that you can have for another person even *beyond* this earthly life is to want to see that person one day in Heaven for all eternity. So here are a couple of questions for you: Do you pray *daily* — truly and sincerely — for the salvation of your loved ones? Do you pray daily for the salvation of your enemies? Let all of Sacred Scripture and the writings of the saints teach you well in this regard. And you, on your part, make an effort to learn well. (See days 3, 7, 30, 52, 53, 80, 95, 120, 175, and 195.)

Day 199

Following Christ and Drawing Closer to God

And he said to all, "If any man would come after me, let him deny himself and take up his cross daily and follow me. For whoever would save his life will lose it; and whoever loses his life for my sake, he will save it. For what does it profit a man if he gains the whole world and loses or forfeits himself? For whoever is ashamed of me and of my words, of him will the Son of man be ashamed when he comes in his glory and the glory of the Father and of the holy angels." (Luke 9:23–26)

Urged to reflect upon myself, I entered under your guidance into the inmost depth of my soul. I was able to do so because *you were my helper* [see Ps. 28:7; 54:4]. On entering into myself I saw, as it were with the eye of the soul, what was beyond the eye of the soul, beyond my spirit: your immutable light.... He who has come to know the truth knows this light.

O eternal truth, true love and beloved eternity. You are my God. To you do I sigh day and night. When I first came to know you, you drew me to yourself so that I might see that there were things for me to see, but that I myself was not yet ready to see them. Meanwhile, you overcame the weakness of my vision, sending forth most strongly the beams of your light, and I trembled at once with love and dread. I learned that I was in a region unlike yours and far distant from you, and I thought I heard your voice from on high: "I am the food of grown men; grow then, and you will feed on me. Nor will you change me into yourself like bodily food, but you will be changed into me." (St. Augustine)[237]

---

[237] *Confessions*, bk. 7, in *Liturgy of the Hours*, vol. IV, 1355–1356.

The greatest gift that Jesus Christ has given you to continue to follow Him and become more like Him in this life is the Eucharist: His true and abiding Real Presence in the Eucharistic Host you receive at Mass each time you receive Holy Communion. Do not forsake such a great gift — indeed, the greatest gift: Christ Himself — the God-Man — truly present in His Body, Blood, Soul, and Divinity in the most holy Eucharist. This truth likewise draws you into a deeper communion with the Father and the Holy Spirit. Receive the Eucharist *worthily*, and draw closer to God — *literally*. Remember the important words of Our Lord to St. Augustine above: "I am the food of grown men; grow then, and you will feed on me. Nor will you change me into yourself like bodily food, but you will be changed into me." (See days 21, 65, 92, 97, 99, 101, 103, 114, 132, 142, 143, 144, 145, and 155.)

Day 200

In Thanksgiving to God—for You

We always thank God, the Father of our Lord Jesus Christ, when we pray for you, because we have heard of your faith in Christ Jesus and of the love which you have for all the saints, because of the hope laid up for you in heaven. Of this you have heard before in the word of the truth, the gospel which has come to you, as indeed in the whole world it is bearing fruit and growing—so among yourselves, from the day you heard and understood the grace of God in truth. (Col. 1:3–6)

I offer then all the powers of my soul in praise and thanksgiving. As I contemplate his [God's] greatness, which knows no limits, I joyfully surrender my whole life, my senses. (St. Bede the Venerable)[238]

In your daily prayers, be sure to thank Almighty God for the *great gift of your life*. Yes, be thankful for *your life*. Love your life. Improve your life. Strive for the best version of your life. You are a son of Almighty God. You know this through the great gift of your faith. So, despite any trials or sufferings you may undergo throughout your life, you know that such trials and sufferings can be *salvific*—that is, *saving*—for your own soul and for others, known and unknown to you, when they are offered to Almighty God as a pleasing sacrifice *to* the Father, *through* His Son, the Lord Jesus Christ, *in* the Holy Spirit. This is made possible through the merits of Christ's Paschal Mystery—that is, His Passion, Death, Resurrection, and Ascension into Heaven.[239] The same goes for your life's contentments, joys, and pleasures. Even these can be offered

---

[238] *Commentary on Luke*, bk. 1, in *Liturgy of the Hours*, vol. I, 362.

[239] See Pope St. John Paul II, apostolic letter *Salvifici Doloris*, on the Christian Meaning of Human Suffering (February 11, 1984).

to Almighty God as a salvific sacrifice pleasing to Him. Live these truths through your baptismal priesthood (and ministerial priesthood, if you are a priest) by making frequent offerings to God. And know this: having such a faith-filled vision — while living your Catholic Faith devotedly and committedly — serves in itself as a form of *prayer of thanksgiving* to Almighty God for the great gift of your life. (See days 4, 7, 19, 23, 41, 52, 62, 72, 114, 150, and 187.)

O Most Holy Trinity — Father, Son, and Holy Spirit — my God,
how I love Thee and thank Thee! Amen.

Appendix

Selected Prayers

DAILY PRAYERS

Morning Offering to the Most Holy Trinity

O Most Holy Trinity, Father, Son, and Holy Spirit: In union with every
Mass that is celebrated this day throughout the whole world, I want to
offer to You all of my prayers, sufferings, sorrows, joys, and good works. I
do so to praise You, O Blessed Trinity, and for all the desires of the Most
Sacred Heart of Jesus and the Immaculate Heart of Mary. I do so also in
union with all the angels and saints in reparation for all sin and for the
conversion of poor sinners — especially those who have no one to pray
for them — and for our finally being united with You in Heaven for all
eternity. Give me the graces necessary, O Most Holy Trinity, while still
living on earth, to endure heroically any temporal punishment needed so
as to atone fully for my already-forgiven mortal and venial sins, thereby
avoiding Purgatory and attaining the great grace of immediately entering
Heaven upon my death to be with You for all eternity. Amen.

Glory Be

Glory be to the Father, and to the Son, and to the Holy Spirit. As it was
in the beginning, is now, and ever shall be, world without end. Amen.

Our Father

Our Father, Who art in Heaven, hallowed be Thy name. Thy Kingdom come. Thy will be done, on earth as it is in Heaven. Give us this day our daily bread; and forgive us our trespasses, as we forgive those who trespass against us; and lead us not into temptation, but deliver us from evil. Amen.

Hail Mary

Hail Mary, full of grace, the Lord is with thee. Blessed art thou among women, and blessed is the fruit of thy womb, Jesus. Holy Mary, Mother of God, pray for us sinners now, and at the hour of our death. Amen.

Sub Tuum Praesidium

We fly to thy protection, O Holy Mother of God; despise not our petitions in our necessities, but deliver us always from all dangers, O glorious and Blessed Virgin.

Memorare

Remember, O most gracious Virgin Mary, that never was it known that anyone who fled to thy protection, implored thy help, or sought thy intercession was left unaided. Inspired by this confidence, I fly unto thee, O Virgin of virgins, my Mother; to thee do I come, before thee I stand, sinful and sorrowful. O Mother of the Word Incarnate, despise not my petitions, but in thy mercy hear and answer me. Amen.

St. Michael the Archangel

St. Michael the Archangel, defend us in battle. Be our protection against the wickedness and snares of the devil. May God rebuke him, we humbly pray, and do thou, O Prince of the Heavenly hosts, by the power of God, thrust into Hell Satan, and all evil spirits, who wander through the world for the ruin of souls. Amen.

Act of Faith

O my God, I firmly believe that You are one God in three Divine Persons, Father, Son, and Holy Spirit. And I believe that Your Divine Son, Jesus, became man and died for our sins, and that He will come again to judge the living and the dead. I believe these and all the truths that the holy Catholic Church teaches, because You have revealed them, O God, Who can neither deceive nor be deceived. Amen.

Act of Hope

O my God, relying on Your almighty power and infinite mercy and promises, I hope to obtain pardon of my sins, the help of Your grace, and life everlasting, through the merits of Jesus Christ, my Lord and Redeemer. Amen.

Act of Charity

O my God, I love You above all things, with my whole heart and soul, because You are all good and deserving of all my love. I love my neighbor as myself for the love of You. I forgive all those who have injured me, and I ask pardon of all those whom I have injured. Amen.

Act of Contrition

O my God, I am heartily sorry for having offended You, and I detest all my sins because I dread the loss of Heaven and the pains of Hell; but most of all, because they have offended You, my God, Who are all good and deserving of all my love. I firmly resolve, with the help of Your grace, to confess my sins, to do penance, and to amend my life. Amen.

Prayer to the Holy Spirit

Come, Holy Spirit, fill the hearts of Your faithful and kindle in them the fire of Your love. Send forth Your Spirit and they shall be created, and You shall renew the face of the earth.

Let us pray: O God, Who did instruct the hearts of the faithful by the Light of the Holy Spirit, grant us in the same Spirit to be truly wise and ever to rejoice in His consolation. Through Christ our Lord. Amen.

Prayer to the Holy Spirit before Confession

Come, Holy Spirit, enlighten my mind that I may clearly know my sins. Move my heart that I may be sincerely sorry for them, honestly confess them, and firmly resolve to amend my life. Holy Spirit of Wisdom, grant me to see the malice of sin and my ingratitude toward You, the all-loving God together with the Father and the Son. Holy Spirit of Fortitude, help me to make whatever sacrifice is needed to avoid sin in the future. Amen.

LITANIES

Litany of the Holy Eucharist

V. Lord, have mercy.
R. Lord, have mercy.
V. Christ, have mercy.
R. Christ, have mercy.
V. Lord, have mercy.
R. Lord, have mercy.

Jesus, the Most High, *have mercy on us.*
Jesus, the Holy One, *have mercy on us.*
Jesus, Word of God, *have mercy on us.*
Jesus, only Son of the Father, *have mercy on us.*
Jesus, Son of Mary, *have mercy on us.*
Jesus, crucified for us, *have mercy on us.*
Jesus, risen from the dead, *have mercy on us.*
Jesus, reigning in glory, *have mercy on us.*
Jesus, coming in glory, *have mercy on us.*
Jesus, our Lord, *have mercy on us.*

Jesus, our hope, *have mercy on us.*
Jesus, our peace, *have mercy on us.*
Jesus, our Savior, *have mercy on us.*
Jesus, our salvation, *have mercy on us.*
Jesus, our resurrection, *have mercy on us.*
Jesus, Judge of all, *have mercy on us.*
Jesus, Lord of the Church, *have mercy on us.*
Jesus, Lord of creation, *have mercy on us.*
Jesus, Lover of all, *have mercy on us.*
Jesus, Life of the world, *have mercy on us.*
Jesus, freedom for the imprisoned, *have mercy on us.*
Jesus, joy of the sorrowing, *have mercy on us.*
Jesus, giver of the Spirit, *have mercy on us.*
Jesus, giver of good gifts, *have mercy on us.*
Jesus, source of new life, *have mercy on us.*
Jesus, Lord of life, *have mercy on us.*
Jesus, Eternal High Priest, *have mercy on us.*
Jesus, Priest and Victim, *have mercy on us.*
Jesus, true Shepherd, *have mercy on us.*
Jesus, true Light, *have mercy on us.*
Jesus, Bread of Heaven, *have mercy on us.*
Jesus, Bread of Life, *have mercy on us.*
Jesus, Bread of Thanksgiving, *have mercy on us.*
Jesus, Life-Giving Bread, *have mercy on us.*
Jesus, Holy Manna, *have mercy on us.*
Jesus, new covenant, *have mercy on us.*
Jesus, Food for everlasting life, *have mercy on us.*
Jesus, Food for our journey, *have mercy on us.*
Jesus, holy Banquet, *have mercy on us.*
Jesus, true Sacrifice, *have mercy on us.*
Jesus, perfect Sacrifice, *have mercy on us.*
Jesus, eternal Sacrifice, *have mercy on us.*

Jesus, divine Victim, *have mercy on us.*

Jesus, Mediator of the new covenant, *have mercy on us.*

Jesus, mystery of the altar, *have mercy on us.*

Jesus, mystery of faith, *have mercy on us.*

Jesus, medicine of immortality, *have mercy on us.*

Jesus, pledge of eternal glory, *have mercy on us.*

Jesus, Lamb of God, You take away the sins of the world,
    have mercy on us.

Jesus, Bearer of our sins, You take away the sins of the world,
    have mercy on us.

Jesus, Redeemer of the world, You take away the sins of the world,
    have mercy on us.

V. Christ, hear us.

R. Christ, hear us.

V. Christ, graciously hear us.

R. Christ, graciously hear us.

V. Lord Jesus, hear our prayer.

R. Lord Jesus, hear our prayer.

Let us pray: Lord our God, in this great sacrament, we come into the presence of Jesus Christ, Your Son, born of the Virgin Mary and crucified for our salvation. May we who declare our faith in this fountain of love and mercy drink from it the water of everlasting life. Amen.[240]

---

[240] Closing prayer: United States Conference of Catholic Bishops, *Order for the Solemn Exposition of the Holy Eucharist* (1992).

Litany of the Sacred Heart of Jesus

V. Lord, have mercy.

R. Lord, have mercy.

V. Christ, have mercy.

R. Christ, have mercy.

V. Lord, have mercy.

R. Lord, have mercy.

V. Christ, hear us.

R. Christ, hear us.

V. Christ, graciously hear us.

R. Christ, graciously hear us.

God, the Father of Heaven, *have mercy on us.*

God, the Son, Redeemer of the world, *have mercy on us.*

God, the Holy Spirit, *have mercy on us.*

Holy Trinity, One God, *have mercy on us.*

Heart of Jesus, Son of the Eternal Father, *have mercy on us.*

Heart of Jesus, formed by the Holy Spirit in the womb
of the Virgin Mother, *have mercy on us.*

Heart of Jesus, substantially united to the Word of God,
have mercy on us.

Heart of Jesus, of Infinite Majesty, *have mercy on us.*

Heart of Jesus, Sacred Temple of God, *have mercy on us.*

Heart of Jesus, Tabernacle of the Most High, *have mercy on us.*

Heart of Jesus, House of God and Gate of Heaven,
have mercy on us.

Heart of Jesus, burning furnace of charity, *have mercy on us.*

Heart of Jesus, abode of justice and love, *have mercy on us.*

Heart of Jesus, full of goodness and love, *have mercy on us.*

Heart of Jesus, abyss of all virtues, *have mercy on us.*

Heart of Jesus, most worthy of all praise, *have mercy on us.*

Heart of Jesus, King and center of all hearts, *have mercy on us.*

Heart of Jesus, in Whom are all treasures of wisdom
and knowledge, *have mercy on us.*
Heart of Jesus, in Whom dwells the fullness of divinity,
have mercy on us.
Heart of Jesus, in Whom the Father is well pleased,
have mercy on us.
Heart of Jesus, of Whose fullness we have all received,
have mercy on us.
Heart of Jesus, desire of the everlasting hills, *have mercy on us.*
Heart of Jesus, patient and rich in mercy, *have mercy on us.*
Heart of Jesus, enriching all who invoke Thee, *have mercy on us.*
Heart of Jesus, fountain of life and holiness, *have mercy on us.*
Heart of Jesus, propitiation for our sins, *have mercy on us.*
Heart of Jesus, loaded down with opprobrium, *have mercy on us.*
Heart of Jesus, bruised for our offenses, *have mercy on us.*
Heart of Jesus, obedient to death, *have mercy on us.*
Heart of Jesus, pierced with a lance, *have mercy on us.*
Heart of Jesus, source of all consolation, *have mercy on us.*
Heart of Jesus, our life and resurrection, *have mercy on us.*
Heart of Jesus, our peace and our reconciliation,
have mercy on us.
Heart of Jesus, Victim for our sins, *have mercy on us.*
Heart of Jesus, salvation of those who trust in Thee,
have mercy on us.
Heart of Jesus, hope of those who die in Thee, *have mercy on us.*
Heart of Jesus, delight of all the saints, *have mercy on us.*

Lamb of God, You take away the sins of the world,
spare us, O Lord.
Lamb of God, You take away the sins of the world,
graciously hear us, O Lord.
Lamb of God, You take away the sins of the world,
have mercy on us.

V. Jesus, meek and humble of heart.

R. Make our hearts like Your Heart.

Let us pray: Almighty and eternal God, look upon the Heart of Your most beloved Son and upon the praises and satisfaction which He offers You in the name of sinners, and to those who implore Your mercy, in Your great goodness, grant forgiveness in the name of the same Jesus Christ, Your Son, who lives and reigns with You forever and ever. Amen.

Litany of the Blessed Virgin Mary

V. Lord, have mercy on us.

R. Christ, have mercy on us.

V. Lord, have mercy on us; Christ, hear us.

R. Christ, graciously hear us.

God, the Father of Heaven, *have mercy on us.*
God, the Son, Redeemer of the world, *have mercy on us.*
God, the Holy Spirit, *have mercy on us.*
Holy Trinity, one God, *have mercy on us.*

Holy Mary, *pray for us.*
Holy Mother of God, *pray for us.*
Holy Virgin of virgins, *pray for us.*
Mother of Christ, *pray for us.*
Mother of the Church, *pray for us.*
Mother of mercy, *pray for us.*
Mother of divine grace, *pray for us.*
Mother of hope, *pray for us.*
Mother most pure, *pray for us.*
Mother most chaste, *pray for us.*
Mother inviolate, *pray for us.*
Mother undefiled, *pray for us.*
Mother most amiable, *pray for us.*

Mother most admirable, *pray for us.*
Mother of good counsel, *pray for us.*
Mother of our Creator, *pray for us.*
Mother of our Savior, *pray for us.*
Virgin most prudent, *pray for us.*
Virgin most venerable, *pray for us.*
Virgin most renowned, *pray for us.*
Virgin most powerful, *pray for us.*
Virgin most merciful, *pray for us.*
Virgin most faithful, *pray for us.*
Mirror of justice, *pray for us.*
Seat of wisdom, *pray for us.*
Cause of our joy, *pray for us.*
Spiritual vessel, *pray for us.*
Vessel of honor, *pray for us.*
Singular vessel of devotion, *pray for us.*
Mystical rose, *pray for us.*
Tower of David, *pray for us.*
Tower of ivory, *pray for us.*
House of gold, *pray for us.*
Ark of the covenant, *pray for us.*
Gate of Heaven, *pray for us.*
Morning star, *pray for us.*
Health of the sick, *pray for us.*
Refuge of sinners, *pray for us.*
Solace of migrants, *pray for us.*
Comforter of the afflicted, *pray for us.*
Help of Christians, *pray for us.*
Queen of angels, *pray for us.*
Queen of patriarchs, *pray for us.*
Queen of prophets, *pray for us.*
Queen of Apostles, *pray for us.*

Queen of martyrs, *pray for us.*
Queen of confessors, *pray for us.*
Queen of virgins, *pray for us.*
Queen of all saints, *pray for us.*
Queen conceived without original sin, *pray for us.*
Queen assumed into Heaven, *pray for us.*
Queen of the Most Holy Rosary, *pray for us.*
Queen of families, *pray for us.*
Queen of peace, *pray for us.*

Lamb of God, You take away the sins of the world,
   spare us, O Lord.
Lamb of God, You take away the sins of the world,
   graciously hear us, O Lord.
Lamb of God, You take away the sins of the world,
   have mercy on us.

V. Pray for us, O holy Mother of God.
R. That we may be made worthy of the promises of Christ.

Let us pray: Grant, O Lord God, we beseech You, that we Your servants may rejoice in continual health of mind and body; and, through the glorious intercession of Blessed Mary ever Virgin, may be freed from present sorrow, and enjoy eternal happiness. Through Christ our Lord. Amen.

Litany of St. Joseph

V. Lord, have mercy on us.
R. Christ, have mercy on us.
V. Lord, have mercy on us; Christ, hear us.
R. Christ, graciously hear us.

God, the Father of Heaven, *have mercy on us.*
God, the Son, Redeemer of the world, *have mercy on us.*

God, the Holy Spirit, *have mercy on us.*
Holy Trinity, one God, *have mercy on us.*

Holy Mary, *pray for us.*
Holy Joseph, *pray for us.*
Renowned offspring of David, *pray for us.*
Light of Patriarchs, *pray for us.*
Spouse of the Mother of God, *pray for us.*
Guardian of the Redeemer, *pray for us.*
Chaste guardian of the Virgin, *pray for us.*
Foster father of the Son of God, *pray for us.*
Diligent protector of Christ, *pray for us.*
Servant of Christ, *pray for us.*
Minister of salvation, *pray for us.*
Head of the Holy Family, *pray for us.*
Joseph most just, *pray for us.*
Joseph most chaste, *pray for us.*
Joseph most prudent, *pray for us.*
Joseph most strong, *pray for us.*
Joseph most obedient, *pray for us.*
Joseph most faithful, *pray for us.*
Mirror of patience, *pray for us.*
Lover of poverty, *pray for us.*
Model of artisans, *pray for us.*
Glory of home life, *pray for us.*
Guardian of virgins, *pray for us.*
Pillar of families, *pray for us.*
Support in difficulties, *pray for us.*
Solace of the wretched, *pray for us.*
Hope of the sick, *pray for us.*
Patron of exiles, *pray for us.*
Patron of the afflicted, *pray for us.*

Patron of the poor, *pray for us.*
Patron of the dying, *pray for us.*
Terror of demons, *pray for us.*
Protector of Holy Church, *pray for us.*

Lamb of God, You take away the sins of the world,
    spare us, O Lord.
Lamb of God, You take away the sins of the world,
    graciously hear us, O Lord.
Lamb of God, You take away the sins of the world,
    have mercy on us.

V. He made him the lord of his household.
R. And prince over all his possessions.

Let us pray: O God, in Your ineffable providence You were pleased to choose Blessed St. Joseph to be the spouse of Your most holy Mother; grant, we beg You, that we may be worthy to have him for our intercessor in Heaven whom on earth we venerate as our Protector, You who live and reign forever and ever. Amen.

Index of Topics

Numbers shown refer to page numbers.

About the Author

Fr. Wade L. J. Menezes, CPM, is a member of the Fathers of Mercy, a missionary preaching religious congregation based in Auburn, Kentucky. Ordained a priest during the Great Jubilee Year 2000, he received his bachelor of arts in Catholic thought from the Oratory of St. Philip Neri in Toronto, Canada, and his dual master of arts and master of divinity degrees in theology from Holy Apostles Seminary in Cromwell, Connecticut, where he also received an Honorary Doctorate in Moral Theology. His secular college degrees are in journalism and communications.

Fr. Wade has served as the Assistant General and as the Director of Vocations and Director of Seminarians for the Fathers of Mercy. He has also served as the chaplain in residence at the Shrine of the Most Blessed Sacrament of Our Lady of the Angels Monastery in Hanceville, Alabama (affiliated with Eternal Word Television Network). While at the Shrine, Fr. Wade was a daily Mass celebrant, homilist, and confessor; he gave spiritual conferences on specialized points of Catholic Christian doctrine to the many pilgrims who visit the Shrine. As an itinerant preacher for the Fathers of Mercy, he has preached throughout the United States, Canada, and Australia.

Fr. Wade has been a guest on various episodes of EWTN's *Mother Angelica Live* and *Life on the Rock*, during which he discussed such topics as the sanctification of marriage and family life, vocations, and the Sacred Liturgy. He has also hosted several televised and online series for EWTN, which have covered such topics as the necessity of the spiritual life, the Four Last Things, the Ten Commandments of Catholic Family Life, and the Gospel of Life versus the Culture of Death. He is host of the EWTN interstitial series *The Crux of the Matter*, *The Wonders of His Mercy*, and *In Defense of the Eucharist*. His many theological and doctrinal presentations have been featured on EWTN Global Catholic Radio, Ave Maria Radio, Guadalupe Radio Network, Covenant Network Radio, Catholic Broadcasting Northwest, and Voice of Virtue International. Fr. Wade is the host of EWTN Global Catholic Radio's *Open Line Tuesday*.

Fr. Wade has also been a contributing writer for the *National Catholic Register, Our Sunday Visitor, Catholic Twin Circle, Catholic Faith and Family*, the *Wanderer, Pastoral Life*, the *Catholic Faith, Lay Witness, Legatus*, and *Christian Ranchman*. Several homiletic series of his have appeared in *Homiletic and Pastoral Review*, an international journal for priests. Fr. Wade is the author of three books: *The Four Last Things: A Catechetical Guide to Death, Judgment, Heaven, and Hell; Overcoming the Evil Within: The Reality of Sin and the Transforming Power of God's Grace and Mercy*; and *Catholic Essentials: A Guide to Understanding Key Church Teachings* (from EWTN Publishing in conjunction with Sophia Institute Press).